GOD'S JOY IN MY HEART

P9-CAM-023

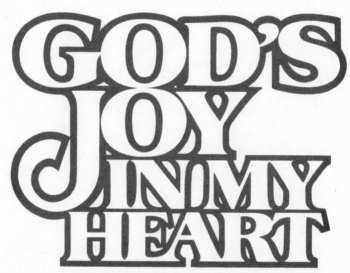

GOD'S JOY IN MY HEART

Ruth Youngdahl Nelson

Written with
Karen Matison Hess

AUGSBURG Publishing House
Minneapolis, Minnesota 55415

GOD'S JOY IN MY HEART

MANUFACTURED IN THE UNITED STATES OF AMERICA

This collage of life is dedicated to my family:
  To my parents, sisters, and brothers who loved me
    and helped me grow,
  To my husband and our children who not only put up
    with me but added new dimensions to my life,
  To my church family in many different places who
    provided a fellowship of faith,
  To the family of the world for whom Christ died.
Put these pieces together and you have life—
    abundant and rich!

CONTENTS

PREFACE

This book is multiauthored. My beloved partner, Clarence Nelson, is in every page, not only in the direct quotes from his memoirs "Bent Nails," which were written for and distributed to all our family members, but also in most of the content. And Karen Hess has been the patient and skilled engineer, the "put-ter-together" of the myriad sources.

God's Joy in My Heart has only one justification for being: to glorify the Lord and witness to the way he assembles the fragments of our lives, to witness to the wonder of how he takes ordinary human beings (the Apostle Paul uses the term "common earthenware jars") and uses them to bless and serve others. It is to acknowledge, also, that "we are a part of all that we have met." Countless people have contributed to the creation of this human collage.

AS FOR ME AND MY HOUSE

1

"It can't be real! It just can't be real!" That thought overwhelmed me as I sat in the waiting room of the King County Jail in Washington State. It was paradoxical, feeling panic simultaneously with numbness—no feeling at all. Was Jon, our firstborn son, really there behind a glass cage? Had his hands been manacled, and had he been ignominiously led into the paddy wagon to have his liberty denied him for what seemed endless days?

I thought about the day he was born in St. Paul's Bethesda Hospital. Words couldn't express the joy we knew at the wonder of this gift. He had been prayed for those months in my womb. How eagerly we awaited his arrival. Now here I was, waiting to visit this son, now a mature man, a father himself, waiting to visit him in jail. I recalled the letter to the editor he had written to the *Seattle Times*. Perhaps he had been preparing me for this day.

Editor:
I plan to be a part of the demonstration and civil disobedience at the Trident Base because of my commitment to Jesus Christ and the hope he offers the world.

The futile illusion of power the Trident nuclear submarine represents is no security at all. Nations have been escalating weapons and arms budgets, and yet human survival and national defense is more precarious than ever. The trust in destructive power as defense is an empty trust that threatens to bankrupt all the nations of the world, creates impossible inflationary pressures, and cancels many jobs in the constructive sector of the economy. It eats at the whole moral and political fabric of society whether American, Russian, or Chinese.

It is time the world's people help their leaders to see our survival will not be guaranteed with nuclear holocaust, but with a new international order superseding the nation states.

When I look at the children around my table, I know I must take every opportunity to declare the present course of human affairs as suicidal, and to witness to another order that knows reconciling love that is willing to suffer is the only future for the planet. Even if that is only a last testament in a world that is extinguished in fire, it is something worth living for.

Jonathan C. Nelson

I looked around at the others who were also waiting. A group of students was there to visit Bill Stalder, the young man who had been arrested with Jon. There was the wife of an inmate, nervously opening and closing her purse. There was a couple, obviously parents, whose sagging shoulders and blank stares witnessed to their discouragement and bewilderment. And there I was, Ruth Youngdahl Nelson.

After what seemed an eternity, a voice over the loudspeaker blared: "Mrs. Nelson, Mrs. Ruth Nelson." Numbly I made my way to the area indicated. Behind the thick wall of soundproof glass, garbed in a jail-blue jumpsuit, was Jon. Thin before he went in, he was 17 pounds thinner now. He took the phone in hand, motioning for me to take the one on my side. Through the earphones I heard his voice, "Hi, Mom! It's good you can't get any closer. You see, we get just one jumpsuit a week, and I smell. I still jog four miles each morning. I've measured the circumference of the cell and figured the number of times around it takes to make the four miles." He grinned broadly, awaiting my response.

My husband Clarence had been called upon many times to visit some parents' son incarcerated for breaking the law. I had spent time counseling women inmates. Now I was facing our son who had broken the law deliberately, not for personal gain, but because of his consuming concern for the world's people. As campus pastor at the University of Washington in Seattle, he felt it his duty to confront the students with the kind of world developing around them. Weekly visits to the state prison at Monroe to share in the prisoners' rehabilitation classes, awareness of the need to defend the Native American's fishing rights—such concerns were the muscles of the Spirit being exercised to fulfill the Word shared in Bible study and worship. The ideas Jesus taught in the Bible were given legs through such programs.

Now, like a huge cloud, the threat of nuclear annihilation hung over their very heads. At the naval base in Bangor, Washington, Trident submarines were being constructed, horrible monsters with the potential to destroy the world. In the early stages of this development, concerned people used every available legal means to protest, but their voices were ignored. Refusing to give up, some 5000 concerned people marched to the base. Prayer surrounded the preparations and the orientation was solid: no alcohol, no drugs, no violence. They carried trash bags and picked up litter along the way as they marched to the rhythm of songs of courage and hope. At the base fence, 300 climbed over the barbed wire, committing civil disobedience. They were herded into a bus and brought before the court where they pleaded guilty. David, our second son, flew from Chicago to Seattle to be at his brother's side during the trial. God had blessed us in that the relationship we had hoped for when we named our sons Jonathan and David had been established far beyond our expectations.

The verdict, 45 days suspended sentence and three years probation, hardly rippled the sea of public consciousness. How were people to be awakened to the threat of world destruction? How many were aware that each submarine carried 408 warheads, each one four or five times more powerful than the one dropped at Hiroshima? We had visited the memorial museum at Hiroshima, and the inhuman, inclusive mass destruction of people caused there by that *one* bomb had haunted me ever since. Nor did it help to learn that, after all these years, 2000 deaths still occurred annually from the fallout, and the growing incidence of leukemia in newborn babies indicated that the horrible results were continuing; there was no end to the destruction.

Jon and Bill Stalder decided they couldn't give up. The next Monday morning they climbed the fence again, breaking probation. They were handcuffed and put in jail in separate sections so they could not support each other.

Friends at home asked what was accomplished. Who knows? But there was an amazing response of supportive letters from all over the United States and Europe. What does it take to get public opinion informed and aroused? Because a situation looks so hopeless, do we just sit idly by?

It was one thing to get Jon's letters from behind bars, but quite another to sit face to face with him, unable to touch him or hear him except by the phone. For the moment he was silenced, this loving man, the father of eight children (three biological, five adopted), who wanted so desperately to shout to the world: "Hold it. Please. Let's save our children. We're well on the way to destroying them all!" That's what his civil disobedience was all about.

Never in my life did I think I'd visit my son in jail. Or, more especially, that I would be proud and thankful to God for why he was there. Had I been there at the time of protest, I would have gone over the fence with him. The words of Joshua (24:15) were so in evidence:

> And if you be unwilling to serve the Lord, choose this day whom you will serve, whether the gods your fathers served in the region beyond the River, or the gods of the Amorites in whose land you dwell; but as for me and my house, we will serve the Lord.

Not only Jon, but all the children in our house serve the Lord. I thought of the situation our son David stepped into in the 60s. Bethel Lutheran Church on the west side of Chicago was in a riot-torn section of that great city. A rapidly changing population had decimated the church membership, leaving only 36 adults. A thrown brick struck his VW his first week at Bethel. Our daughter Mary, seated beside him, ducked in time not to be hit. In one week he held three funerals: a three-month-old baby girl

14

burned in an apartment fire where arson was found, a sixteen-year-old boy stabbed to death for refusing to join a gang, and an old man beaten to death in a robbery. From such a start rose Bethel Christian School, an active program for children from preschool through sixth grade with a reputation for such successful education that truant officers bring their vagrants to this school.

Mary, giving herself in a multifaceted community project with Bethel as her base, had her purse stolen seven times and was beaten almost to death in an attempted rape, yet stood firm. She now heads a new housing program which gives hope to a deteriorating neighborhood. The operation called its first project Anathoth Place, after Jeremiah's symbol of hope.

Our daughter, Biz, who at age 12 spent a year in bed with rheumatic fever, recovered to spend 20 years as a missionary's wife in Indonesia. She joined with an international group of women in Jakarta to work with rehabilitation programs for lepers whose disease had been arrested but who could not return to their families or normal living because of superstition. These people sat idly, doing nothing. This little band of women provided equipment and tools so the lepers could use their skills and talents in earning their own living.

A favorite dress when I speak is my "leper dress," made from countless pieces of leftover batik, all sizes, shapes, and colors, each little scrap carefully sewn together by these people. To me it has many meanings. It represents what the Master Designer can do with the leftover, discarded fragments of our lives. He puts them together and makes a creation. It also represents God's amazing world made up of all tribes and nations with their variety of gifts.

Another favorite of mine is a batik wall hanging made by a young man whose index finger and thumb were missing due to accidents caused by the numbness produced by leprosy. Yet he cradled a brush in the identation between where the thumb and finger had been and created a thing of beauty which now hangs in our home. Hidden gifts uncovered by the miracle of caring love.

The night after I visited Jon I couldn't sleep. A million memories flashed across my mind's screen. I went back in time to my parents, my grandparents. How were our personalities formed? What part

15

did our inheritance play? Grandma and Grandpa Johnson back in Sweden; Grandma and Grandpa Youngdahl and all they stood for; the Nelson line from which Jon's father came. Putting together what Clarence had shared of the Nelsons with what I knew of my family created a collage of living!

A gathering of the Youngdahl clan

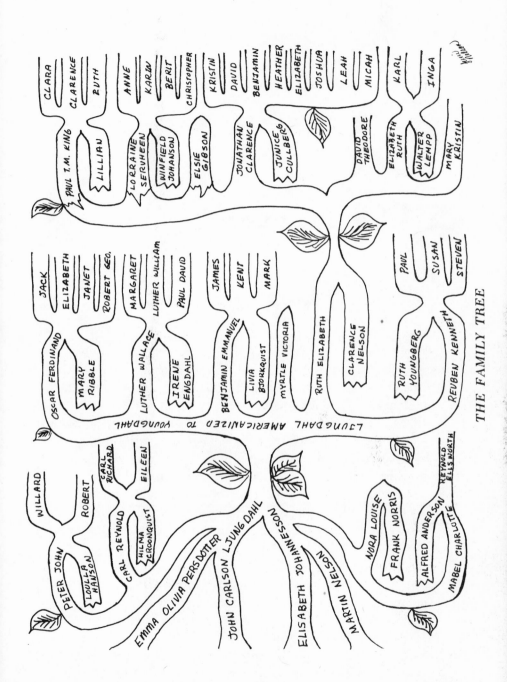

THE FAMILY TREE

17

A
FIRM
FOUNDATION

2

My heritage is a simple story, a tale of bread and butter, day and night, sin and grace, life and death. From it issues the fragrance of Christ's presence and the stench of the evil one's influence. It is the story of Christian parents battling in a materialistic world to implant in their children's hearts a longing for the things of God. It is the story of the Great Shepherd and his sheep.

It is also a story of America, with her arms open to immigrants from every land and with opportunities for their children to put back into this country something of what they have received. It is a story of the green pasture our country has been for millions of people from other shores. It's almost a Cinderella story, except at the stroke of midnight the chariot becomes golden and the gates open to everlasting life.

The story begins in 1817 on a beflowered hill in Dalsland, Sweden, where my maternal grandmother, Lisa Olsdotter, tended sheep. She was having a marvelous time with these woolly friends who so placidly nibbled the food the Lord had provided. It was good to be out on this early summer day with the air redolent with the fragrance of bursting buds and good earth. One little lamb, her favorite, had been so weak and wobbly in its beginning it needed special love and care. Lisa's warm, sympathetic heart prompted her to take it up in her arms and snuggle it close to make up in love what it lacked in vitality. She was utterly oblivious of the creature watching her until, with a startling suddenness, the huge brown animal emerged from the thicket. At first she thought it was a dog, but then to her consciousness came a name she had heard her elders speak—the horrid, frightening word *wolf*. Instinctively she hugged the little lamb closer, but the wolf lunged at the baby sheep in her arms, tearing it from her embrace. Horrified, she watched him devour her pet. Then, not one to stand by and do nothing, Lisa grabbed her shepherd's stick to hit the murderer with all the force she could gather. Angrily the wolf turned on her, only to discover his appetite already satisfied. She literally had been spared "out of the jaws of death."

This brave, loving little lady grew to young womanhood and hardly had a chance to gather a dowry when she was wooed by tall, upright Mathias Johnson (Johannesson), who also loved the out-of-doors. To have such a suitor was quite special, for Mathias was not only the adopted son of his uncle, Bishop Hederen, but was also an upcoming man with a partnership in the local bank and was much sought after because he was such good company. He loved to sing and made music wherever he went. His 6'8" frame towered above Lisa's 5', giving her a deep sense of protection.

Lisa and Mathias were married in the spring. Their home was filled with companionship, hospitality, and fun—all added to the spiritual oneness represented in their marriage. The blessing of one child after another, the oldest born in 1855, increased their joy. Sophie, Charlotte, Mina, Mathilda, Johan (the only boy), and Elisabeth (my mother) made the house ring with laughter and kept Lisa busy cooking, cleaning, and sewing, and Mathias challenged to provide the wherewithal.

One day, however, Mathias returned from work completely stunned. His partner had absconded with a huge sum of money from the bank, leaving Mathias to bear the responsibility. What a blow to one whose every fiber was honest and who had so little with which to cover the loss. The only honorable recourse was to sell everything they had, apply it on the deficit, and move to Norway for a fresh start.

Plucky Lisa, a true helpmate, shouldered this responsibility with Mathias. Tearing up roots from a place that had always been home wasn't easy, but neither was life. So, with a remnant of worldly belongings, Lisa, Mathias, and their family of five (little Johan had died; Elisabeth, my mother, was only three) moved into their neighboring country where Mathias became overseer on a huge farm. He was a jack-of-all-trades, mending farming apparatus, binding animals' wounds, sowing, and reaping.

A few years after this move, Mathias' father died, and Mathias inherited alike with Bishop Hederen's sons. The help that he had refused earlier was now at his disposal. Although in the eyes of his former neighbors Mathias was innocent and the bank episode closed, Mathias' conscience was so sensitive that he used his inheritance to wipe out the residue of the bank's debt. The money came and went, yet they were no richer. Or were they—in values not measured by coin?

Times weren't easy, nor was the work as overseer, but there was the honest satisfaction of earning a livelihood for one's family. To add to their difficulties, one day a metal splinter became embedded in Mathias' eye. No medical help was available, and the eye ached out. The hollow that remained symbolized the patience and ineffable calm of one who knew long, dark hours of agony. The faith that grew and flourished in this experience and was tested in the crucible of pain became part of the fabric of young Elisabeth's character and, in turn, was her heritage to her children.

Some of Mathias' and Lisa's daughters married Norwegians and accompanied their adventuresome husbands to the beckoning land of opportunity, America, from which they wrote enticing letters to the folks back home.

Meanwhile, Elisabeth came to confirmation age. She regularly walked the 15 long miles to church where she gave herself wholeheartedly to the teaching of the pastor. During these impressionable years she learned countless psalms, hymns, and beautiful poems, a rich spiritual background she later shared with her children.

Her love of the out-of-doors, too, found free expression in this land of pine and birch, of mountain and lake, of hillside studded with forget-me-nots and lilies of the valley. To enjoy God's creation was to know pleasure, a sensitivity she never lost.

Materialistically these early years were scant and difficult. "Give us this day our daily bread" was a literal prayer from Mathias' lips. This family lived simply and humbly, day by day, in faith that the heavenly Father who had created them would also care for them. Although poor by the yardstick of Wall Street, they were rich by the measurement of heaven.

Scant though their resources were, these were happy, home-sweet days with no poverty of love. Of an evening, hymns committed to memory were lifted in song as the family gathered for devotions. Sometimes the girls recited poems they had learned in school. Then Mathias would take down the big Bible and, with his huge, calloused hands, open the pages to share with his circle of loved ones the Bread and Water of Life. Such it really was to him, the very sustenance of his soul. Such it became to Elisabeth, the nurture that maintained her spiritual health.

No wonder there were no stomach ulcers. There was no rushing away to go somewhere and do something. Instead there was the happy relaxation of bodies that had worked hard out-of-doors, of lungs filled with clover-scented air, of muscles hardened by persistent, rugged toil; the peace of soul that comes from the forgiveness of sins and the awareness of God's care; the anticipation of the good feeling of a bed to a tired body; and a unity of spirit that permeated the simple dwelling like sweet incense.

But letters kept coming from America with urgent pleas for the rest of the family to come to this great country with so much room and so many opportunities. The prospects of better times in Scandinavia were bleak, and Mathias was worried about having to join the army, so after much prayer and planning they decided to join the rest of the Johnson family in America.

What were Grandfather's thoughts as he nailed together the crude trunk to hold their possessions? What dreams for his family, what hopes for his future did the hammer blows echo? What sort

21

of place did he visualize when he took the brush and, with the characteristic swirl of his handwriting, wrote on the front of the trunk: Gagen Forest County, Wis. Nort Amerika—the place that was to become home.

The trunk's contents tell their own story. First were the few pieces of linen they owned, covered with paper flanking the bottom. (I can still hear Mother say, "I've learned to take care of what I own.") Through the skill of her hands and her indefatigable energy, these linens had been produced from flax to the finished product. They were used only for very special company, like the preacher. On top of the linen was a meager store of woolen underwear for protection against the cold, penetrating winters they had been told characterized this Wisconsin to which they were going. They would carry shawls with them on the ship as armor against the invading chill of Atlantic evenings. Next were three sterling silver spoons Mathias' employer had given them on their wedding anniversary, perhaps the only real silver they would ever own, tucked safely into the corner. And three copper kettles with special items tucked inside: the tintypes Mathias thought could be left, but which to Lisa were the bread and butter of memory; the bottle of cardamom seed—such a luxury, but without which coffee bread just didn't taste right. Who could know if it was available in far-off America? Even Mathias agreed the coffee grinder must be packed, bulky though it was. No one questioned the place of the family Bible, regardless of the space it took and the pounds it weighed. To leave it behind would be to leave one's moorings and be set adrift in a wild, unknown sea. It was carefully wrapped in a cloth and placed in the heart of the crude trunk.

The value of the trunk's contents computed in dollars and cents was pitiable, but faith, hope, and love have no digits on an adding machine. These were the resources of Mathias' family in 1881 as they boarded the boat that carried them across the salted sea to the New World.

Mother never said much about the ocean journey, but she told many times of being a young immigrant girl on the streets of New York, not understanding a word anyone said, sensing that she looked different and that people were laughing at her. The heartaches experienced there were still vivid in her memory, as if they had been inscribed in indelible ink. From New York Mathias and his family boarded the train for Chippewa Falls, Wisconsin, and their family there, leaving behind the raw ache caused by the cruelty of a large city where it is too easy to forget that people are souls.

To begin anew in a strange land when you have passed the meridian of life and your skills are only crude, home-taught ones, is hard. But Mathias never indulged in self-pity, nor would he permit his family to do so. These were semipioneer days in this lumbering mill town on the swiftly flowing Chippewa River with its rapids gurgling with gold nuggets. Soon Mathias was a trusted employee of the Chippewa Lumber and Boom Company where he tread logs to get them into place in their river road. It was something to see this 6'8" man in his fifties skillfully stepping from log to log.

A devout man who lived his faith 24 hours a day, Mathias was often derided and poked fun at as he bent his head in prayer before opening his lunch pail. But his persistent patience and love, his willingness to help a fellow in trouble, the source of power he found in prayer, these fruits of the grace of God produced results. Soon men came to him for advice; soon other heads were bowed in grace.

Lisa quickly made the little dwelling at 1034 Warren Street into a home. The pungent aroma of freshly ground coffee permeated the rooms as she got out her little grinder and prepared the beans. As she ground, her eyes would wander to the windowsill where her red geraniums were abloom. Red geraniums against a windowsill, the fresh cardamom coffee bread under its snowy towel, her spinning wheel in the corner; this was now home, a good land.

Mina, Sophie, Mathilda, and Charlotte were farm wives raising families. Charlotte did not live long in this new land, and there was the sorrow of that fresh grave. But faith was to trust in the wisdom of an almighty God and to be a partner with him in bringing help. So Elisabeth, now 15, sewed for Charlotte's wee, motherless daughters and counted her blessings. The Good Shepherd watched over his sheep in this new land too.

Within Elisabeth's heart was a great upspringing of independence coupled with a large compassion compelling her to serve. Wanting to help her parents in their economic struggle, she obtained a position as a domestic for a wealthy family on "Catholic Hill." She arose at 4 A.M. to finish the washing and ironing before the family stirred. She always carried a dustcloth over her arm, prepared to rout "the great enemy, dust." She listened to the sincerity and observed the regularity of family devotions of these Catholics for whom she worked. Above the wall of church differences grew a unity of faith and devotion to Christ between this devout Catholic family and their Lutheran domestic. Elisabeth saw firsthand that faith in God through Christ transcended any barrier and that in God's sight, all people are one.

Elisabeth loved to sing, so she joined the church choir and added her rich alto to the harmonies lifted in praise to God. After her experience as a domestic, she became an apprentice to a dressmaker, learning to put the nimbleness of her fingers to good use.

The world, then, as now, was in an uncertain state. In America, that gay, young nation with its boundless, scarcely tapped resources, there was the new heartache of civil strife over the abolition of slavery and the seceding of the southern states. In Europe, times were hard and work scarce. In Sweden, dissatisfaction and restlessness smoldered like a peat bog among the young people. In 17-year-old John Youngdahl (my father, son of Carl Ljungdahl and Boel Nilsdotter), it erupted into an overwhelming desire to leave Skåne and launch out across the ocean to the great land of America. He secured a job on a ship and stoked his first journey across the great salt sea. In America he helped lay railroads in the Midwest and in Canada; he kept his sea legs in good fettle by cooking on the boats, the lifeline of the Great Lakes industry; and his culinary skill he put to work in a lumber camp where hungry men sat down to enjoy his cooking at the end of a long day of arduous, muscle-bending labor in the brisk out-of-doors. It was challenging, adventuresome, manly living in this great free country of America where it wasn't necessary to bow low to superiors, where a man's stature was measured by what he was within himself.

However, the way of a maid with a man had worked its devastating effect upon young John. The memory of a quiet slip of a girl back in Skåne had wound itself like tendrils about his heart. Life was good here, yes, but a man needed to be loved and needed someone to love. What did all the rest matter, lacking that?

So John found himself on an ocean boat again, heading eastward to the Swedish port of Malmö. Soon wedding bells rang as Emma became John's bride. They set up housekeeping on a modest farm John bought with his American savings.

Romance was also flourishing in America. The flowering out of Elisabeth Johnson's young womanhood did not escape the eyes of the men. Many accepted the challenge to captivate this woman of independent spirit who refused to cast sly glances in the path of the men she met. When a fellow became too "fresh" as they were walking along, she would shove him off the sidewalk with a sweep of her arm and laughingly say, "Serves him right for being so smart." In spite of such rough tactics, or perhaps because of them, the men persisted. She was such fun to be with and so completely lacking in the artifices employed by many young women. She was always playing a joke or starting a song and was game for anything that was wholesome and would include everyone.

Martin Nelson, observing her, thought what a wonderful wife and mother she would make. He envisioned her jolly yet sterling spirit presiding over his household. His persistence won and, at 19, Elisabeth Johnson became the bride of Martin Nelson in the Chippewa Falls Lutheran Church.

Martin, a contractor, had an opportunity to do some building in the little town of Bayfield on the shores of Lake Superior, so here the bride and groom set up their household. Elisabeth, a good cook and an immaculate housekeeper, loved nothing better than to share a hospitable table. Martin's building business was doing well—he had the contract for the large school that was being built in Bayfield. For diversion he had right at his door the sport he loved best of all, fishing. The great unsalted sea of Lake Superior was a rich field for luscious lake trout. It was an unpredictable sea, too, where a quick squall could whip up a wave that would test the mettle of the best sailor.

The Nelsons were blessed in many ways. A baby christened Nora

Louise born in 1889 enlarged the circle of family love and delighted her parents. Two years later a sister, Mabel Charlotte, kept Nora company. For keeping her household running smoothly and maintaining a sense of calm and joy amidst the pressure of all the physical demands, Elisabeth's deep faith and a wonderful sense of humor were invaluable. She taught and lived two Bible verses, her Siamese twins: "Sufficient unto the day is the evil thereof" and "As thy days, so shall thy strength be." No day went by but what God's Word was shared. No bread was broken without first giving thanks to the giver. The consciousness of God's presence in the simplest task made each day a new adventure and made life good. Laughter flowed easily.

Meanwhile, in Sweden, John Youngdahl dreamed of America. Farming had lost its appeal; his only thought was to return to America. He was so persuasive and enthusiastic that within three years he, Emma, their son Peter John, his brother and sister, and their parents were standing on the wharf, earthly belongings packed, with faces to the west. John's brother and sister, infected with their brother's enthusiasm, looked expectantly to the new land and the future. John's and Emma's parents, however, weren't quite so sure. They were leaving all that was familiar and dear. Yet what would it mean for them to live here with their loved ones so far away? No, it was better to cast their lot with the family and trust God to assuage the heartache and longing for the old home. They huddled a little closer, one to the other, finding comfort in their togetherness.

Chippewa Falls, Wisconsin, was the destination of this little band with their enthusiastic promoter. Here they set up their household; here John found work as a grocery clerk. As was their custom in the old country, they turned their steps on the Sabbath to the house of God. Since Chippewa had no Swedish church, they worshiped in the Norwegian church. Although it wasn't easy to understand everything, in the sanctuary was a holiness they remembered from back home, and it was comforting to know that God was everywhere the same.

Life was hard, and some days Emma wondered what glamour John saw in this new world. She worked as hard as ever, but her health was not robust. A daughter christened Selma Botilda

26

(from whom my third name came) entered life for a brief visit and departed. Carl Reynold made his appearance in 1887. John, in a quandary as to who should sponsor Carl in baptism, went to the pastor for help. He suggested Mathias Johnson's girls. Two were duly asked, and on Carl's baptismal certificate is Elisabeth Johnson, listed as the baby's godmother. This was the first meeting of John and Elisabeth.

Dissatisfied with the progress he was making in his job, John looked for more promising opportunities. North of Chippewa was lumber country with men in need of housing and food. John and his bachelor brother Peter decided to open a hotel in Tomahawk, Wisconsin, a frontier town where life was rugged and exciting. John was concerned with protecting his wife and sons from exposure to the roughness of the men as well as that of the wilderness. He received help in this in a strange way.

One day a huge animal, half wolf, half dog, came limping into camp. With a natural love and tenderness for all living things and a proffered hunk of beefsteak, John coaxed the dog to a place where he could examine the injured foot. He washed out the dirt, applied balm to the cut, and carefully bandaged it. From then on, John and his family had a source of protection that would defy anyone.

One evening as the family was sitting in their dining room eating their meal, sounds of raucous quarreling came from beyond the door where the lumbermen spent their leisure time in the dining room and bar. John left the table to see what the disturbance was, carefully closing the door behind him so his family might be spared any unpleasantness. He tried to separate two angry, fighting men, but in the unreasonableness of anger coupled with the recklessness of drink, one man lunged at John, grabbing him by the throat. The dog, sensing that all was not well with his master, dove through the paneling of the door, lunging at the throat of John's assailant. Imagine the heartache of the family a week later when this faithful canine friend was found—poisoned.

This incident, coupled with Emma's failing health, made John decide a lumber town was no place to rear a family. He moved to Minneapolis and secured a job driving a baker's wagon. The gaunt specter of sickness called on the Youngdahl home, adding to the inevitable ache of being strangers in a foreign land. Emma became ill with cancer and soon the boys lost their mother, a turning point in John Youngdahl's life. The heartache of losing his chosen life companion left him forsaken and helpless, his youthful confidence shaken.

Although reared in the church, he had not experienced a personal confrontation with God. Then the patient witness of his wife's faith, this young mother who, as she died, committed the care of her family into her heavenly Father's hands, and the deep need and longing of his own lonely heart resulted in a consecration, a dedication that marked the rest of his life. Never again would he have anything to do with alcohol and its concomitant evils. He became so strict and rigid in his stern discipline of both himself and his family that sometimes the hearts of his children inwardly rebelled. One day followed another as he provided for his little ones and his parents. With whatever leisure time he had he served the church; Christ was now his first love and the embodiment of all that he wanted for himself and his family.

Back in Bayfield, Elisabeth and Martin were relishing life. Each day was a new adventure. On this particular day Elisabeth had bathed and fed three-month-old Mabel and was listening to the prattle of two-year-old Nora as she worked. Martin had gone fishing, so she was preparing a tempting evening meal for the men who would come home ravenous. Suddenly there was a knock at the door. Little Nora toddled behind her as she went to answer it. She opened the door expecting her neighbor or some other friend, but instead found Olaf, one of Martin's friends. He was awkwardly twisting his cap in his red hands, looking for all the world as if he wished he could be any place but there. As he stuttered some unintelligible words, Elisabeth intuitively blurted out, "Olaf, is it Martin?" When Olaf nodded his head, grateful for her assistance, she pursued, "Is he drowned?" Again Olaf nodded, and his heavy frame convulsed with sobs. Elisabeth invited him in.

It was simply another story of the sea and its erratic toll. But to this household it was a tornado. Yet the center of calm was not missing. Uncle Andrew came up from Chippewa Falls to help the young widow make funeral preparations and meet the many friends who came with sympathy and food. Elisabeth, however, gave rather than sought comfort. The one who blessed her life in prosperity stood with her now. All her life this quality of strength in a crisis, of calm in the midst of confusion, of making order out of chaos, characterized this woman who to her family was as the Rock of Gibraltar.

Life went on, and with purpose. Finances were not of immediate concern because of Martin's building investments, so Elisabeth devoted herself to her two little girls and helping others. She put her dressmaking training to practical use and took in sewing. She couldn't understand what had happened, but she trusted her heavenly Father, turning often to his Word and to prayer for strength.

Meanwhile, John Youngdahl was finding the going in his household rough without his wife and the mother of his boys. His own mother was aging and ill, so rather than assisting, she was an added care. His father, too, was failing. John knew he needed help, but wanted the right kind for his household. He remembered the Johnson girls from Chippewa and thought maybe one of them might help. A man of action, he wrote the Chippewa pastor for the Johnson girls' address, explaining why he wanted it. The pastor replied that all the girls had married but that Elisabeth's husband had recently drowned, leaving her a widow with two little girls. Seeing a possible chance, John wrote to Elisabeth, stating his need and offering her a position in his home and a place for her two little ones.

When the letter arrived, Elisabeth, startled at the thought of moving to the big city of Minneapolis, wrote back that she wasn't ready to make a change; she thought it best to stay where things were familiar for now. So John found what help he could in Minneapolis. He was working from early morning until late at night clerking in a grocery store to provide for his family. His one outside interest was his church where he found fellowship and strength.

Elisabeth's little girls were growing and becoming more and more of a joy to their mother. One day Nora, the eldest, complained about a pain in her left wrist. At first Elisabeth thought it was just a childish hurt, but when the pain persisted day after day, she took Nora to the doctor in nearby Ashland. His manner was grave, his diagnosis given without cushioning: "I think your daughter has tuberculosis of the bone. I recommend you take her to Minneapolis to a specialist. There isn't much I can do for her." Elisabeth's eyes blurred as she looked at her daughter's arm. She thought of the skill possessed by the right hand—already she could draw beautifully. Thank God the infection wasn't in her right wrist. But it could spread. Minneapolis! A specialist! How could she ever make her way in that big, strange city? But if Nora needed such attention, make her way she would. She asked the doctor to write to the specialist about their coming and then went home to think about the other arrangements she needed to make.

Everything seemed in a whirl. First the knock at the door; now this. She couldn't think clearly. Taking down her much-used Bible, she opened it to the verse from which she so often extracted power: "As thy days, so shall thy strength be." Had the Lord failed her? Hadn't he promised special care for the widows and the fatherless? Weren't his eyes on even the sparrow? She fell to her knees in prayer and, as she was pouring out her heart to God, something rang a bell. Minneapolis—didn't she know someone there? Why, that was where John Youngdahl lived. She had sponsored his son in baptism. Maybe he would help her. Getting up from her knees, she sat down to compose her letter. She must come to Minneapolis to see a doctor for Nora's arm—could Mr. Youngdahl recommend a safe place for her to stay?

With a heavy load lifted from her heart, Elisabeth mailed the letter and went about her daily duties, awaiting a reply from John Youngdahl as well as word from the Minneapolis doctor. Both arrived the same day. From the specialist came word of his willingness to examine Nora and setting a time for an appointment. From John Youngdahl came word that if she would tell him when she'd be arriving, he'd meet them; they could stay at his home and he'd see that they got to the doctor's office.

Nora's sessions with the doctor were lengthy and numerous, ending in a decision to operate to remove the infected bone. Meanwhile, Elisabeth stepped into the Youngdahl household, organizing it to the point of such smoothness that it seemed it was meant to be. At times mischievous Mabel delighted in teasing John's serious son Carl, but, considering the household had four small children, two elderly people, and Elisabeth and John, things moved along with a smoothness that came from having someone who cared at the helm. Sugar cookies were made and consumed by the hundreds, and the cardamom aroma from the coffee bread sent its tempting spiciness into every nook and cranny of the house.

Elisabeth and her girls became a part of the table-time devotions. The unity of faith between the two families was undeniable. Elisabeth taught all the children the hymns she loved. John, too, loved music, and nothing pleased him more than when they all joined in a round of song. Sometimes when Nora did not sit as still as she should during a long scripture passage, John would pause and look at her sternly. Then she would snuggle closer to her mother.

So the days went along until the operation. With the calmness of one who has known the sufficient grace of God each day, Elisabeth brought Nora to the hospital, asking the Shepherd to guide the surgeon's knife. The bone was removed, and Nora quickly recuperated. For the rest of her life, however, she carried a scarred, shortened left arm.

When Nora was able to leave the hospital, Elisabeth made plans to return to Bayfield. As she thanked John, he wondered what would happen to his household when she left. She had brought a spark he had not known before, for despite her burdens, her sense of humor flashed out unexpectedly and added zest to humble living, a glint in a gray day. Her industry and organization had created a smooth-running household, and her companionship was a boon to a lonely heart. How empty the house would be without her.

As for Elisabeth, she knew she must go back to Bayfield, but Minneapolis was no longer frightening; it was now as if she were leaving home. As the farewells were said at the railroad station, each was aware the separation wouldn't be for long.

Nor was it. God's remarkable working in the lives of men was visible again. In the old Augustana Lutheran Church in Minneapolis, with Dr. C. J. Petri officiating, on August 25, 1892, Elisabeth Johnson Nelson became the bride of John Youngdahl. What this union would mean to the four little children witnessing the ceremony, whose lives were inseparably interwoven with theirs, only the Lord knew. They committed their lives into his good hands and faced the future unafraid.

John Youngdahl and Elisabeth Nelson were married on August 25, 1892

GOD
LIVES IN
A RED BRICK
HOUSE

3

When Elisabeth lost Martin and John lost Emma, each received a wound they thought would never heal. But for both this second union was a new beginning, a new challenge. Only vital Christian grace can make a stepmother or stepfather into a real parent. Nor was it always simple and easy. Little Mabel, bubbling over with fun and vitality, would irk sober, orderly Carl. And Nora, with her artistic temperament already refusing to be pigeonholed, often tested John's patience which could readily snap with a terrific outburst of temper. But again Christian grace was in evidence. John would return after such an outburst with a special offering of ice cream for the family—his way of saying, "I'm sorry."

To all situations Elisabeth brought love, understanding, an unquestionable sense of fairness, and her refreshing sense of humor. Little jokes, delightful little surprises, spiced every day and made home a delight.

John brought to the family the unwavering dependability that characterized his whole life. His word was as sure as the Federal Reserve Bank. His standards of discipline were known and not to be taken lightly. His devotion to God and love for his family were the breath of his every day. These same characteristics carried over into the business world where he was known as "Honest John," a man who wouldn't think of having a bill go over two weeks and whose name on credit was as good as gold.

There was lots of hard work in this home, but as Elisabeth always said, "Work never hurt anyone." John's parents were failing and required care. Washing and ironing with a scrub board and flatiron heated on a coal stove took countless hours. Cleaning, baking, and meal preparation absorbed any leftover time. Meals were rigidly on time, adding to the sense of stability. When Elisabeth said dinner would be at six, that's when the mashed potatoes, gravy, and meat were ready to go on the table, and she expected grace to be said on time. All were early risers, ready for bed after family devotions in the early evening.

Days were filled with labor mingled with laughter. Although it was hard to make John's grocery clerk wages stretch to feed eight mouths, these were days of togetherness.

Eight mouths? Not for long. On October 12, 1893, Oscar Ferdinand Mathias was born. Was there something prophetic in the lusty gusto of his voice which filled the house those early weeks? One day he would be named the number one orator in Minnesota colleges. Later his silver tongue would be heard on the floor of the United States Congress.

As they were anticipating the advent of their firstborn, Elisabeth and John conferred on names. "Our children should have a sense of destiny," said John, "a sense of their stewardship of life to God. Their names should be a constant reminder of their responsibility." They decided to include a historical name, a biblical name, and an ordinary name. Thus, Oscar Ferdinand Mathias.

As the family circle increased with the birth of Oscar, it soon decreased with the going home of John's parents. Within a year of one another, these two who had left their homeland to stay near their children slipped their moorings and set sail for eternity.

Soon, however, the family was back to eight—in 1896 Luther Wallace Augustinus was born. And it continued to grow. 1897 saw the birth of Benjamin Emmanual Lincoln, 1899 the birth of Myrtle Victoria Magdalene, and 1904 the birth of Ruth Elizabeth Botilda. All during my childhood I blushed if I had to divulge

34

my third name. Mother would scold me, reminding me I was named after father's mother. How the English of Boel could be Botilda I could never figure out. But there it was on my baptismal certificate: Ruth Elizabeth Botilda.

With such a large family, Dad had all he could do to keep food on the table. One evening he told Mother of an opportunity to rent a store. Both he and Mother agreed they wanted their children to have the educational opportunities they had never known. Both were avid readers and pursued a daily educational program, but they wanted college and its concomitant opportunities for their children. That this could be possible for families like theirs was part of America's greatness. They decided that Dad should go into business on his own.

So Dad launched into the competitive world of retail groceries. Already a United States citizen, he believed that the country from which he extracted his living should be the one to whom he gave his allegiance. English was the language he preferred to use at home. When the Swedish spelling of his name proved difficult in the business world, Ljungdahl (meaning "heather dale") was anglicized to Youngdahl.

Dad bicycled back and forth to work, which often provided an outing for me. When is pain pleasure? I loved riding the handlebars on Dad's bike, even though I felt them leaving a mighty imprint on my behind. In the late spring and summer he was at the market before dawn. The store was open from seven to seven except Saturday nights when it closed at eleven. Despite these long hours of work and the weariness of the body, these were good days, family days, church days.

Home-sweet memories. Carl would sit on Dad's lap on a Sunday afternoon and literally sing through the hymnbook. A fitting place for a music career to be born—at father's knee lifting up the songs of souls rejoicing in their Savior. It followed as naturally as breathing that music should become Carl's life—35 years as choir director at Augustana College, Sioux Falls, South Dakota.

As the grocery business flourished, the dream of owning our own home became a reality—a red brick house with five bedrooms and an alcove at 1600 Eleventh Avenue in Minneapolis. It had a wonderful big kitchen with an adjoining pantry; there was ample

Our red brick house in Minneapolis

room for the whole family to gather around the friendly round table. Aromas rising from the cheery coal stove mingled as they filled the house: bread fresh from the oven; pepparkakor thin as paper and crisp to a crunch; rolled sugar cookies coupled with a glass of cold milk; a steaming pot of split pea soup cooked with the ham hock and delicately flavored with grated onion; vegetable soup in which carrots, celery, potatoes, and onions all yielded their flavors to the soup bone, king of the kettle. The kitchen was a production center of vitamin-filled, flavorful food that built strong, sturdy bodies. No need for supplementary vitamins in Mother's kitchen. More than this, the sharing of the food was a time of happiness, fellowship, and togetherness.

The parlor, separated from the living room with sliding doors that disappeared into the walls, was used only for special company. It was a cold room with heavy, stiff mahogany furniture upholstered in red embossed leather. But the living room was another thing. A gas fireplace with an asbestos burner framed with shiny green tile was a beautiful screen for the flame's dancing shadows. A reading chair, whose back tilted, and its matching footstool were sheer comfort. What luxury to curl up in that chair with a cold, juicy apple in one hand and a good book in the other. The shelves were filled with books, almost all religious. It could well have been a preacher's library. The room, the fireplace, and the chair were veritably the gate of heaven. Also adjoining the living room and separated from it by sliding doors was the huge dining room, a gala place on Sundays and other festive occasions.

Upstairs, a long hall with four bedrooms extended from the front bedroom to the back. The upstairs bathroom, as large as a bedroom, had a spacious tub where I once was given a second lease on life. On that occasion, Father was at a deacon's meeting at Augustana Church, four blocks from our home. Mother sensed something was wrong with her year-old daughter and was rocking me when I had a convulsion. She sent Mabel to church to get Dad and one of the boys to get the doctor. Then she took me upstairs to the bathroom, turned on the hot water in the tub, and submerged me. When the doctor arrived, he told Mother her quick thinking had saved my life.

That was Mother, always up to any challenge. Her chief domain, the kitchen, was the heart of our home. Here we talked while she kneaded her limpa (Swedish rye bread) or mixed her meatballs. I can still see her with her eyes squinted almost shut, kneading in the flour or mixing the meat. Such occupations deterred neither her ears nor her tongue as she listened to our stories or shared in her own inimitable way some observation, advice, or joke. What a place for fellowship.

And what a place to come home to. Dashing in from school we'd have fresh-baked bread spread with butter and sprinkled with sugar, sometimes brown, sometimes white. The kitchen was the setting for other experiences too. On Saturday nights, when the second floor bathroom was filled to capacity, the younger members of the family took turns in the big washtub in front of the warm kitchen stove. Although soap in the eyes or the vigorous rubbing of strong hands sometimes made us cry out in protest, that Saturday night bath was wonderful. Clean and dried, we slipped into warm flannel gowns. After a snack of cold milk and sugar cookies around the kitchen table, we crawled into bed between fresh sheets. We felt literally enfolded by the Almighty as Mother, after hearing our prayers, gathered us all in her arms and presented us to her heavenly Father—surely a foretaste of heaven.

The red brick house's yard was also special. Two apple trees in the back provided delightful shady places for tea parties, and the hayloft in the big red barn behind the house was the setting for many a straw fight. In front of the house was one of my favorite spots, a concrete block on the boulevard inscribed with 1600 and Youngdahl. Here we sat at deepening twilight watching the lamp-lighter coming down the street. He made a crisscross pattern as his torch lit a gas lamp on one side of the avenue and then on the other. Before him was comparative darkness; behind him a path-way of light. When we went in after he had passed, Mother told us that was the way God wanted us to walk in life, leaving a path of light wherever we went.

Our neighbors were all Lutherans, except the Fryes who were Catholic. One day we children got into a terrific argument. We were sure Catholics weren't Christians, and the Frye children were just as sure they were. With self-righteous indignation we approached our mother: "Catholics aren't Christians, are they?" Mother gathered us all about her and told us to never judge others, that whoever loved Jesus Christ as their Savior and fol-lowed him was a Christian. Then she treated us to cookies warm from the oven and sent us on our way with our arms around each other's shoulders. The red brick house was a school of living for here and now, and for eternity.

What a hospitable place the red brick house was, for everyone from bishops to beggars. Any church convention saw the house overflowing with preachers. On any day the coffeepot might go on quickly to offer hospitality to a neighbor dropping in. Anyone, anytime was welcomed. Like Peg-Leg John. As sure as burgeon-ing spring, permeating the air with its delicate fragrances, was the visit of Peg-Leg, thumping down the avenue to turn in at our red brick house. Ensconced like a king in our kitchen, he did jus-tice to the spread tastefully laid out on the fresh white cloth in front of him. We learned early that every soul is as precious as any other, regardless of economic status, color, or pedigree.

Life in the red brick house had its trials too. A thousand fears sometimes struggled to possess me: What other people thought of me (didn't they laugh when I was awkward?), what the consequence of some childish sin would be (here I suffered the torments of a very vivid hell), or what evil those strange figures lurking in the dark corners of my bedroom at night might portend. I timidly shared these with Mother, one by one, and she took me in her strong arms and dispelled each of the bogies in turn. There was something of God in her love, in her arms, in her strong faith, that has never left me.

Basically the red brick house was a happy place, with its warm hospitality, its fragrances, its liveliness, its sense of security. Often Grandma and Grandpa spent the winter with us; often the cousins from Chippewa Falls added to the fun. And God was always there.

When I was almost four, I learned a song for the Sunday school program, a special occasion when everyone came to hear the children perform. Afterward we each received a box of Christmas candy and a book. Sometimes the handle of a candy box broke, scattering the contents and causing a flow of tears. But usually the programs were joyous. My song that year was very special to me:

> *I am Jesus' little lamb,*
> *Therefore glad at heart I am;*
> *Jesus loves me, Jesus knows me,*
> *All that's good and fair he shows me,*
> *Tends me every day the same,*
> *Even calls me by my name.*

I flavored the meaning: since I belong to Jesus, I am glad at heart; even though he knows me (yes, the time I ate the forbidden candy, the time I lied), he loves me. He is with me every day; he even knows my name. I walked around the house saying, "Ruth, Ruth" as if he were talking to me. The idea of that personal relationship remains with me still. When I have unworthy thoughts, mean ambitions, unloving judgments of others, I hear him say, "Ruth, do you want to be my follower?" And I quickly respond, "Forgive, Lord! Forgive! Help me!"

As we grew, Mom and Dad felt the long summer vacation on the city streets didn't challenge us enough. So they ventured again and bought two islands at Lake Independence, a fish-filled lake with a beautifully wooded shoreline 30 miles from Minneapolis. The large island had an apple orchard and fields of raspberries and strawberries, nearby out-of-doors work for us growing children. We picked crate upon crate of berries, hauled them across the bridge to the mainland, and on into Maple Plain where they were shipped to Minneapolis to be sold at Dad's grocery store. No middleman here. The family labor market was supervised by Ole, the hired man just come from Sweden. He was not only an industrious worker, but a versatile entertainer as well. Often in the evening he would play his guitar and sing for the family gathered about him.

The house on the large island was the scene of many family gatherings, a happy place for relatives to visit. The larder was always ample and bursting. Two jersey cows provided rich milk and cream. The two-gallon ice-cream freezer was cranked to its capacity more nights a week than not. Strawberries fresh from the patch, crushed and sweetened, topping a bowl of cream-yellow, homemade ice cream tasted delicious after working hard all day in the berry patch and just coming in from a fresh, invigorating swim.

What a lake for fish that was, and Mother—what a fisherman! We often arose before dawn, teeth chattering, to sleepily net minnows. We had to hold our end of the pole just right and keep the net close to the bottom, or our take would be nothing. When we gathered unsuspecting eels or turtles into our net, Mother recalled the incident of our Lord with the fishermen: "What father among you, if his son asks for a fish, will instead of a fish give him a serpent? . . . How much more will the heavenly Father give the Holy Spirit to those who ask him?" (Luke 11:11, 13). Minnows gathered, we shoved off for the crappie bed. Arriving at the spot marked by an object on the shoreline, down went the homemade anchor and the fun began. By then the sun was stretching its rosy arms in the eastern sky and the world was fresh and clean for a new day. Down went the cork with the jerk characteristic of crappies. What a sense of triumph in seeing the pail fill with those game, beautiful creatures.

One rare day when the fish didn't bite, before we made our way to the house, Mother filled the pail half-full of stones and then

40

labored up the hill. Those at home, seeing us return, came shouting: "Did you catch any fish?" Mother answered, "Come, help me." When they arrived and saw the stones, she shook with laughter. But she hadn't lied.

Dad came out late Saturday nights after closing the store, bringing huge crates of graham crackers, white crackers, and marshmallow cookies. We never had an empty cupboard in the Youngdahl home.

One day Oscar, 12, Luther, 10, and Ben, 9, were rowing across to the Maple Plain landing to meet a guest. Vigorous, active boys, they were trying to see how fast they could go. They hadn't learned to swim yet since we had just bought the islands. Lute and Occie were at the oars, each trying to outdo the other. One of Lute's too-vigorous efforts catapulted him overboard in the middle of the lake. His coat caught some air and for a time acted as a water wing, but he began sinking. Occie stood up in the boat and yelled, "Kick and swim! Kick and swim!"

Across the lake some fishermen heard the cry, speedily pulled anchor, and raced to the scene. One took off his coat and shoes and dived in to pull up Luther who had gone under for the third time. It was a sobered three who continued their way to the other side.

They excused Lute's wet condition by prevaricating that he had fallen in while shoving off from the landing, but their subdued attitude made Mother wonder. She was not too surprised the next morning when two men came up the hill to our home. The one who had rescued Lute said, "I don't imagine the boys told you what happened yesterday, but I believe you should know so you can warn them. Also, I want to share the experience with you because it's very special in my life. I was ready to go home the day before, but something held me. I couldn't explain it, but a voice within me said I must delay another day. Now I know that God was speaking so I could be his instrument to save your son. Surely God has a special purpose for his life."

That night as Mother knelt for prayers, she dedicated her family anew to the Lord. Did this experience contribute to the motivation that caused Occie to write his oration "Big Brother" or Ben to dedicate his life to social work? Was "God's special purpose for his life" being manifested when Lute, as governor, opposed the slot machines that were destroying young people and supported more humane and helpful treatment programs for the mentally ill and, as a United States district judge, made the decision for freedom in the Lattimore case at a significant time in our country's history? How wonderful are the ways of God with men!

Another afternoon Mother and Cousin Emma were out fishing when a tornado hit. Ole herded us children down into the storm cellar and ordered the hired girl to stay with us. Then he went out to seek Mother and Emma. After what seemed like hours but was really only about 15 minutes, the cellar door opened and there stood all three. When they caught their breath, they told of how their boat had overturned as they were trying to get to the little island. Fortunately the overturning place was no deeper than their shoulders, so they waded in. On the little island, as far removed from trees as possible, they stretched flat on the ground, where Ole found them. A real thanksgiving service was held in the cellar as Mother knelt to thank God for our safety. In any crisis Mother was a tower of strength and calm. She immediately thought of ways to remedy a situation rather than bemoaning it. When you walk knowing your times are in God's hands, what is there to fear? Coupled with our thanksgiving was our concern for others who might not have fared so well. As soon as possible, Ole made his way across the lake to see how we might help.

Those summers at Lake Independence were memorable, but so were the times we had back at the red brick house. While we lived there progress came to Minneapolis and to us. Peter and Carl were at college, both working their way through school. Peter spent a year at the seminary, then shifted to law. Carl's heart was rooted in music. Mabel took teacher's training and, with her happy, outgoing personality and her way with people, was well-equipped for this profession. Nora had private lessons to develop her talent for art.

Dad's grocery business was prospering too, and one proud day a Ford drew up in front of our house with Dad in the driver's seat. We had enviously watched rich ladies maneuver their electric cars up and down our avenue, but here was an auto all our own standing proudly high on its axles. This car didn't have curtains to snap on as later models did, but it was beautiful. Dad paid $1100 for it. (At the time bread was a nickel a loaf, eggs a dime a dozen.) The car made possible many wonderful outings, and imagine the difference it made in our transportation problem to the lake. Mother made us girls automobile bonnets with long, chiffon streamers that blew in the breeze. We wore them proudly as we rode in the car.

Of course, the boys still had to walk the cows over those 30 miles from the lake place to the red brick house in the fall—Oscar's, Luther's, and Ben's annual job. And sometimes those animals well earned the name Bossy. The boys persevered, however, and not once did they call for help—good preparation for handling their "bossy" constituents later in life.

Soon after he bought the Ford, Dad bought a secondhand launch. But regardless of these seemingly extravagant purchases, we were definitely *not* rich. Everyone worked hard to keep things going. The skills Mother had learned as a dressmaker's apprentice came into good use as she mended and remade old garments and skillfully fashioned new ones. Often after everyone had retired, she worked the treadle of her sewing machine so her family might be well clothed. As a little girl, I often felt the rough place on her left forefinger where the deft needle took its toll of her skin as she embroidered some little trim or sewed a hem. I lovingly caressed it—it was the price she had paid that I might have a lovely new dress of robin's egg wool. It was my favorite dress, made even more special by the care Mother took in making it.

Yes, we all learned in that red brick house. I'll never forget the day Mother made one of her luscious cakes with chocolate frosting, the gooey kind that dripped down. After coming home from school, I made my way to the pantry to see what the prospects were. (In our home the word *diet* was one that only doctors used.) There stood that cake—a culinary creation that made my mouth drool. Mother, intuitively sensing my temptation, said, "I have to see Mrs. Olson next door for a few minutes. Don't touch the cake. As soon as I get back, I'll cut you a piece." Then she left on her errand.

I couldn't pull myself away from that pantry. I stayed right there, in the place of temptation, and the battle was on. One little voice within me said, "You could run your finger around the bottom and get that frosting. It'll drip down again so your mother will never know the difference." Then another voice responded, "But she told you to wait until she came back." The first voice was overpowering, however, and before I knew it, I was climbing up on a stool to reach the cake. My elbow knocked down Mother's favorite blue cream pitcher and it shattered as it hit the floor.

I immediately forgot the tempting cake. Now what to do? The little voice lost no time. "Pick up the pieces fast and put them in the ash can. Your mother will never know the difference." With speed that came from the fear of being caught, I gathered the blue fragments, swept them into the dustpan, and flew into the alley behind the barn to dispose of the evidence in the ash can. The allurement of the cake was completely gone. How to quiet my beating heart? I took my jump rope and put it to such use as it had not had for some time.

When Mother came home, Mrs. Olson was with her, so the coffeepot went on. Soon Mother was at the door calling, "Ruth, have you seen my blue cream pitcher?" Before I knew it, I replied, "No, I haven't seen your blue pitcher." Mother must have found another one, for she pressed the point no more. But how miserable I was. With every jump of the rope a voice repeated, "You told a lie. You told your mother a lie." Finally I could stand it no longer. I abandoned the rope and ran up the front stairs to the deepest closet and pulled Dad's fur-lined winter coat over me. In the hot stillness the voice became even louder. In desperation, I flung the coat from me and almost fell down the steps into Mother's arms, sobbing, "I told a lie. I broke your blue cream pitcher when I was trying to reach the cake. I told a lie. Oh, please, forgive me."

As Mother's arms enfolded me, she told me that God sees everything and that he sealed his promise of forgiveness by sending his Son to be our Savior. "He forgives me, Ruth, and he will forgive you too. But please, love me enough to tell me right away when something happens." The little bebraided girl who snuggled into bed that night included in her prayers a thank you for God's wonderful forgiveness—and her mother's.

Not long after that at one of the Sunday evening services, the pastor preached on "Heaven Our Home." One phrase stuck with

Myrtle: "Eye hath not seen, nor ear heard . . . the things God hath prepared for them that love him" (1 Cor. 2:9 KJV). Myrtle plied Dad with questions all the way home. After we got home, as Mother was putting me to bed, Myrtle climbed up in Dad's lap and continued her questions: "What is heaven like, and how do you really know you'll get there?"

Dad, in his simple faith, told her heaven was paradise, a place of even more beauty than God's beautiful world. The key to getting there was to believe in God's only Son, Jesus, who came to earth, became a man, and died on a cross for all the evil men do. "Jesus is my friend," said Myrtle, snuggling closer into Dad's arms. Then the two of them sang again the hymn that was sung in church:

> There's a land that is fairer than day,
> And by faith we can see it afar;
> For the Father waits over the way
> To prepare us a dwelling place there.

On Monday Myrtle and I went blithely off to Adams School as usual, playing bean bag most of the way. I was 6, Myrtle was 11. When I came out at noon to go home with her, a neighbor met me saying, "You're to go home with me; Myrtle wasn't feeling well and has already gone home." When we arrived, Father was home from the store and a hush about the place made me feel deeply solemn. The doctor and a nurse were there, and a specialist had been called. Peeking into the bedroom I saw Myrtle, unconscious, her head encased in ice packs. Spinal meningitis was the diagnosis.

Wandering aimlessly about the house, I stumbled upon Mother kneeling in prayer in the dining room. Early the next day, before the sun gave any evidence of rising, a sorrowful father leaned over the bedside of his golden-haired daughter. She opened her eyes wide, looked him full in the face, and with her eyes gleaming said, "It's true, Dad; there's a paradise in heaven." With that the curtain of life was pulled, and Myrtle Victoria Magdalene went home. So quick were the ravages of the disease that had infected her body that by four o'clock she was gone. But her words hung as a star of hope in the dark night of grief. Both

Mother and Father, in spite of their grief, had an undergirding of faith and hope of an eternal reunion. Myrtle's body was laid to rest in Lakewood Cemetery, but her soul was waiting for us to join her in our heavenly Father's home.

Myrtle's death took all joy out of the launch, and because Lake Independence was so filled with memories of her, the folks had no desire to return there. They sold our property, launch and all, without ever having used the pretentious boat. Life continued on with the faith that God was watching over us all.

On May 17, 1911, I was jumping rope home from school at noon and found Dad sweeping the sidewalk. For Dad to be home at noon meant something unusual had happened. Grinning broadly, he took my hand and said, "Would you like to see your new brother?" We went upstairs to Mother's bedroom. Mother, in bed, smiling, reached out her arms to me and hugged me. Then our church's deaconess took me into the alcove. There in a lacy, pink bassinet lay my new live doll—Reuben Kenneth Nathaniel. (It

Reuben became
my special charge

46

seems strange today to think of that great big 6'2¼" hulk in a pink satin-lined bassinet.)

From that day, Reuben became my special charge. Unbeknown to my parents or anyone, I prayed, "Bless Reuben and help him to grow up and be a minister, and help me to be a missionary." One day this object of my affection *would* be the shepherd of the largest Lutheran church in America, Mount Olivet. And yet, unknowingly, how proudly I took him out for his first buggy ride. What fond memories I have of my childhood in our red brick house.

DAD'S NEW VENTURE AND WORLD WAR I

4

With a prophetic sense of how Minneapolis would grow, Dad again ventured and bought four corner lots at 40th and Lyndale. In 1912 these lots were at the edge of the city. Men on "commission row" said he was crazy to think there would ever be any business out there, but Dad rented the corner building for a drugstore and moved his business into the grocery store and meat market and his family above in two flats. At the time a contest was being held to name this new subdivision, formed from a huge farm. Some ingenious person translated the name of the owner of the lone store, Youngdahl, into its original meaning, so it became Heatherdale Addition.

We all pitched in to make the apartments home. Not much time passed before Mother had geraniums growing on the front boulevard, nor was it long after that the whole section beyond 40th and Lyndale was dotted with lovely homes. The pattern of long hours of work continued from the early market hours until the books were closed at night. Always, however, there was time for church. Dad and Mother joined Messiah Church, the English daughter of Mother Augustana, so we could get our religion in English.

Dad never neglected his responsibilities as deacon or his preparations for his well-loved Bible class. Though unschooled, he was a natural student who loved sharing the truths he found in Scripture.

Every month we had a Bible class party where I was introduced early to the game "Winkom." I also would watch with fascination as Nora wrote fortunes on slips of paper with gold paint that didn't show, neatly folded them, and put them inside empty walnut shells with a pretty piece of ribbon extending from them. She then glued them together so they looked like they had never been opened. At a set time, a candle was lit and each guest chose a walnut. Then they took turns holding the slips of paper retrieved from their enclosures over the flame, high enough not to burn but close enough so the heat brought out the writing. Magically, a fortune appeared on each one. Gales of laughter filled the house as each read what was in store. The evening ended with a singspiration, a finale of hymns, and a closing prayer.

All was not merriment and good times, however. Brother Reuben certainly had his share of catastrophes. We thought he'd never grow up whole. One day Lute was frolicking with him upstairs in the flat when Rube decided to make his escape down two flights of steps to the basement. In his getaway rush, six-year-old Reuben slipped through the wooden rail and fell the two stories to the cement floor below. Imagine Lute's distress as he came up carrying his brother's limp form. Rube recovered and received a beautiful toy automobile in sympathy which he loved to pedal madly down the sidewalk.

Another time Rube was riding on the back of the grocery wagon on Bryant Avenue. Father's young clerk was really making the horses prance when they hit a bump and Rube bounced off the wagon. He came home with the skin on the entire side of his face removed and gravel and dirt ground in, but again, he recovered.

Yet another time he and I went to visit my brother Carl's family across the street. Reuben, who loved to jump, was using their four-step porch as a platform and having a gay time when one jump landed him wrong. His cry of pain made me take him in my arms and carry him home. And was he heavy! The doctor was called and pronounced the leg broken. To entertain the little convalescent, the doctor brought over his guinea pig. Poor me. Cleaning up after that creature was much harder than taking care of the invalid.

The older brothers loved playing with the youngest one. One day Ben was swinging Rube around in a circle by his arm when he heard a funny snap. Rube's arm had gone out of joint, and again the doctor was called. Something of God's special providence rested with Rube.

In addition to Rube's seemingly unending scrapes, there were plenty of quarrelsome, troublous times, times of disturbing misunderstandings. Nora's artistic, independent personality often clashed with Dad's stern ideas of proper behavior. Mother's generous, overflowing heart was sometimes a great source of irritation to father's sense of economy, and her sprightly gameness could easily exceed what he thought were the boundaries of dignified decorum. One minute Mother would be joking around and the next minute she would be leading devotions; this was not in the least bit inconsistent to her. Christ was part of her total living. She didn't put on special airs in her communion with him. She taught us that religion can be fun, that you can't be truly happy or radiant without religious faith.

Despite their differences, Mother and Dad spoke with one voice when it came to the basics. It was truly God's grace that united this three-divisional family into a loyal, happy whole. Nothing else would have been sufficient. They were one in affirming, "As for me and my house, we will serve the Lord."

Every Saturday evening we shared at family devotions the Gospel text for the next day, good groundbreaking to precede the sowing of the Word from the pulpit. Then we prayed for our pastor. What practical lessons in religion we received in our home! If ever we were bold enough to venture a criticism of someone, Mother invariably retorted, "If you can do any better, go out and do it. Don't sit there criticizing." Or, "If you have anything good to say about someone, say it; otherwise, keep still." Her attitude reminds me of a mother whose children decided to gang up on her, each saying something derogatory about the devil. Surely, they reasoned, their mother could find no objection to this. She sat quietly listening to their harangue. After the last one finished, she said, "Are you through now?" Smugly, they nodded yes. Her response was, "If you were as busy as he is, you wouldn't have time to sit around and criticize him like this."

It wasn't that Mother and Dad curtailed our freedom of speech. We could criticize principles and procedures, but not people. And even our criticism of principles had to be constructive, to indicate a willingness to step in and help the situation rather than simply finding fault. Our parents strove to attain the spirit of Paul's word to the Philippians: "Whatsoever things are just, whatsoever things are pure, whatsoever things are lovely, whatsoever things are of good report; if there be any virtue, and if there be any praise, think on these things."

Not only were we prohibited from speaking ill of others, we were constantly challenged to help those in distress or need. As Christians we were to bear one another's burdens. Any distressing situation called to our attention became our responsibility. We were taught this most effectively by the example our parents set.

We learned and we grew. But living in flats was confining, especially during the heat of summer. Since Mother loved the outdoors, Dad purchased a lot at Deephaven, Lake Minnetonka, and built a little cottage on one corner. Here Mother and we younger children spent the summers for 16 years. Minnetonka was in its heyday for summer cottagers. Every hour streetcars from Minneapolis came to our bay, and, simultaneously, streetcar boats came from other sections of the lake. What great sport to slip on the back of the boat as it left the dock and dive into the swirling current it made.

Company came to our cottage in droves, and on Sundays the whole family converged. Even though we were 15 miles out, we never missed a Sabbath service in the home church. We drove in early Sunday morning and were back at the lake for dinner. Mother always went with us, yet dinner was on the table a half hour after we came home no matter how many guests we had— all a matter of planning and organizing. Saturday she baked the pies, set the salad, peeled the potatoes, prepared the vegetables, baked the biscuits, and set the table. She put the roast in the oven early Sunday morning, and when we returned from church it was only the length of time it took the potatoes to boil until dinner

51

was ready. Without any feeling of pressure, Mother sat down to enjoy dinner with us and our guests.

After dinner we'd swim, sing, play games, talk, and enjoy each other's company. Sunday night supper followed a pattern in terms of both food and fellowship. If we weren't at least 20 strong, we wondered what was wrong. We always had old-fashioned fruit salad made with whipping cream, cold sliced roast from noon, Mother's crab apple pickles, and hot baking powder biscuits followed by either cake or cookies.

These were college days for the boys, Oscar first, then Lute and Ben. Oscar spent two years at Hamline University and then transferred to Gustavus Adolphus College, our church school. Lute spent his first year at the University of Minnesota and then transferred to Gustavus. Ben registered at Gustavus as a freshman. All three boys met their life mates at this college—they heartily recommended Gustavus for this reason, among many others.

At home, Mother busily shuttled laundry cases back and forth to St. Peter. Always sandwiched in between the clean clothes was some delectable product of her kitchen. Dad and Mother ignored their own needs so the boys could have an education. Dad didn't buy a new suit in three years, and Mother wore her two-year-old dress as if it were straight from Paris.

The boys had a great time in forensics, both debate and oratory. Oscar won the state oratorical championship for Gustavus, Lute won a tri-college oratorical contest, and Ben was a star debater. One payoff came when Lute was chosen to represent his graduating class in directing the remarks to the juniors. Ben was chosen to represent the junior class. Somehow Lute obtained Ben's notes and, to Ben's obvious consternation, Lute told the audience everything Ben was going to say. Ben got in his inning, however, as the delighted audience witnessed the brothers fight it out with quick wits and even quicker tongues.

During this time I was in high school, attending our church's Christian academy. My favorite teacher was the woman I had for my Christianity course. Something about the glow behind her eyes first drew me to her. But the exclamation point of her influence on me was the day she sang at her mother's funeral. Without wavering, she witnessed in song, "My Faith Looks Up to Thee" —the way it should be at every Christian homegoing.

I was also taking confirmation during this time. Not only did Mother see that I knew my Catechism, she helped me understand what I was memorizing. Our confirmation pastor made it clear that we weren't "graduating" from Sunday school, but that we were promising to accept Christ as our Savior. Finally the big day arrived—Confirmation Sunday. My long hair was neatly braided and tied with a gay ribbon. Since it was warm, our car top was down. Not until we reached church did I discover my hair ribbon was gone. I wept! I would be different from all the other girls. The pastor put his hand on my shoulder and said, "Ruth, man looks to the outward appearance, but the Lord looks to the heart." My tears subsided, and I forgot about the ribbon. However, a friend remembered that the girl next door to her had been confirmed the previous Sunday in a neighboring church and she had worn a hair ribbon. So down the street she went to borrow the ribbon, and just before we processed in, she had it neatly tied on my braid.

What an experience—my first Communion! The Holy Spirit was truly in the believing heart of the 13-year-old who knelt at the altar and knew the joy of God's forgiving love.

By now the four older children had established their own homes, Mabel in Cambridge, and Peter, Carl, and Nora in Minneapolis. Soon after, the tense international times that broke out into World War I reverberated in our household. On one occasion Mother had prepared a delectable chicken dinner, but just before we began to eat, Nora started talking to the boys about enlisting. Dad and Mother both hated war and did not want their sons carrying guns. Dad became so aroused at Nora's prodding that angry words ensued. Nobody felt like eating—the chicken went untasted. Only Christian forbearance wiped out that misunderstanding. When the time came that the country needed them, the boys went; Oscar into the navy, Luther and Ben into the army.

Boxes of goodies went at regular intervals to wherever the boys were stationed. When Mother shopped, she bought every extra edition of the papers, hoping to find some word indicating the war's end. More than once she found herself at the end of the streetcar line, having obliviously ridden past her stop while engrossed in the news.

We were fortunate; the blue stars never turned to gold in our home. What a Christmas we had after the armistice! We were saddened that Occie hadn't been released yet, but there was the promise of his homecoming soon. Ben and Lute were back in their handsome officer's uniforms with their shiny leather puttees and spurs on their heels. A strange combination of melodies rang through the halls that Christmas. The swing of the old artillery song, "As Those Caissons Go Rolling Along," seemed odd when intermingled with the message of the Christmas carol, "Peace on earth, good will toward men." Before long, however, the carols predominated, and in humble thanksgiving we gathered to sing and thank God for letting us be together again.

Christmas was a loving, joyous, festive time. It began when the Advent wreath was centered on our dining table on the first Sunday in Advent. At the beginning of each week a new candle was lit to remind us the King was coming. During the lighting, Dad read the Isaiah prophecies. When the week began with four candles lit, we knew Christmas was near. We all participated in the preparations for remembering "the least of these." Forgotten old people, poor families Dad had come across, our missionaries— these were first on the list. We knew that exactly the same amount of money was spent for every child, whatever our age. No favoritism here. Each had his own place and was of the same value. We were taught the concept of God's family—no preferred race, class, or individual in our home.

We also observed many Swedish traditions on Christmas Eve Day such as "doppa i grytan." For this the juices from all the cooked meats used in the various delicacies were combined in a huge pot on the stove. We stood around this aromatic kettle, broke off chunks of bread, and dipped them into this protein liquid. What a combination of fellowship and gastronomical joy was this preliminary to the Christmas Eve midnight banquet! The banquet had to be midnight because Dad worked until 11 o'clock. This feast followed the Swedish pattern, with lutefisk and many varieties of meats, cheeses, breads, fish, and goodies spread out to choose from.

(In later years our Christmas board was a turkey feast with a meringue pie—our culinary bow to America.)

The meal over, we gathered about the tree, glowingly alive with the green and red paper chains we had connected link by link with flour and water paste, cranberry chains we had beaded, and popcorn that was such a temptation as we strung it—all encircling the branches with scallops. Then, most breathtaking of all, were the vari-colored candles attached by snapping holders to the ends of the branches. At the tree's base were piled packages of assorted sizes and shapes.

We were breathless at that first glimpse of the tree. Then followed the quiet adoration that belongs to Christmas. No package was disturbed until Dad, Bible in hand, shared the story of the first Christmas and bowed in prayer to invite the Christ child anew into our hearts. Then our voices joined in beautiful Christmas carols. After our family worship, the gifts were distributed and we were off to bed for only a few hours sleep. Early Christmas morning Dad came from door to door with a tray of steaming coffee. He bid us Merry Christmas and announced we must be on our way to the great climax, the Julotta Service at church. There we would join with the angels in triumphant adoration of the coming of the Prince of Peace.

Five o'clock Christmas morning found us crunching through the glistening white snow in the darkness with the thermometer well below zero, greeting other pilgrims with a "Merry Christmas" as we converged on the church. We heard the organ roll out its diapason as if its deepest tones were inadequate for the occasion. Then, as if the packed church were one person, the singing of "Var Hälsad Sjöna Morgonstund" began. We stood and added our voices to that queen of chorales:

> *All hail to thee, O blessed morn!*
> *To tidings long by prophets borne*
> *Hast thou fulfillment given.*
> *O sacred and immortal day,*
> *When unto earth, in glorious ray,*
> *Descends the grace of heaven!*
> *Singing,*

Ringing,
Sounds are blending,
Praises sending
Unto heaven
For the Savior to us given.

After church we visited friends and relatives and then returned home to greet the many visitors who always came to call on Christmas. We spread out the culmination of Mother's week of preparation: fattigman's bakelser, rosettes, spritz, pepparkakor, Jule bröd (Christmas coffee bread), sandbakelser, and many other scrumptuous delicacies. And always there was singing.

The postwar days were ukulele days. The brothers loved to harmonize: "I Met Her on the Beach at Waikiki," "I Want a Little Bungalow," "I Want a Girl Just Like the Girl that Married Dear Old Dad," "Down by the Old Mill Stream," and dozens of other melodies filled the evening air on their weekends at the lake.

Grandma would wait for them to come out on the 11 o'clock streetcar after the store closed. She kept checking on Mother to see if she had the coffee ready—as if she needed to. She was in her 90s, but would stay up as long as they kept singing and love it. They loved her too, and kidded her as if she were a young girl.

When the boys went back to school in the fall, they sometimes earned their train fare with their singing. They would strike up when the train was hardly out of the Minneapolis depot, someone would pass the hat, and most of the time they would collect the price of their tickets before they arrived in St. Peter.

These were also the days when the first radios were in use. Those crystal sets were miracles to us. To be able to put earphones on and hear music or voices speaking from some distant place was truly a wonder.

The boys graduated from college. Ben started his teaching career; Occie began teaching and then went into law; Lute headed right for law. Shortly after that Dad and Mother retired. Since Reuben was still in grade school, they became young all over again to pal with him. Dad wrestled with his athletic son and was interested in every phase of his school activities. Mother often took Rube out sliding on snowy winter evenings. Our cat, who behaved more like a dog than a feline, would race down the hill after the sled, then lead the way back up. Quite a picture: a white-haired mother, a robust young lad, and a black and white cat—all enjoying an evening of winter sport together.

Dad didn't retire just to sit in a chair. He sat only when he was catching up on his reading. He devoted many hours to his Bible class and to other church work, spending many afternoons calling on recalcitrant members or visiting new prospects. He made weekly visits to the homes of the bedridden, and some beautiful friendships ensued. The underprivileged and the needy were also his concern. He enjoyed chauffeuring Mother and as many other ladies as the car would hold to various circles and meetings. Our car become known as the Missionary Bus. Mother and Dad became a team in the house in a way that had never before been possible. He helped her with the clotheswashing, dishwashing, grocery shopping, and even vacuuming.

Two glorious long trips and many short ones fulfilled their dreams to see more of this great country that had offered such wonderful opportunities. A six-week automobile trip to the West Coast, going the southern route and returning the northern way, gave us all rich insight into the vastness of the United States and the majesty of her western mountains. Dad was alert to and aware of every changing scene and completely forgot his many health complaints. Many scenes reminded the folks of the Old Country. One sensed the blending of their homeland with their adopted country in a new way. It wasn't to love the former less; it was to bring all the richness of that heritage to this great land, so new in its culture and development, and so abounding in opportunities.

As we rode through the Big Horn Mountains of Wyoming, Mother, delighted with the forget-me-nots that blue-bordered the mountain streams, exclaimed, "Just like the hillsides of Dalsland."

Traveling through the bing cherry orchards of Oregon, we stopped to buy some of those red beauties for which our mouths had been watering for the last hour. A man, his wife, and their two children came running up to our car and greeted us. They had recognized our Minnesota license plates—their home state. For a half hour we chatted and exchanged experiences of familiar places and mutual acquaintances. Amazing America.

As we returned to southern Minnesota with its rich waving fields of grain, Dad sighed, "O how beautiful. It reminds me of the fields of southern Skåne." America had truly become a second home for the folks.

Our trip along the eastern seaboard through historic New England, down into New York and Pennsylvania, and on into the nation's capital gave us an entirely different background on our country. We became aware of the roots of democracy and the price that was paid to achieve and maintain it. Mother and Dad impressed on us that we must steward well our opportunities for education, then give back in good citizenship and loving service for the betterment of humanity what our country had blessed us with.

FROM GIRL TO WOMAN

5

At 16 I graduated from Minnesota College, our church academy. That I would go to Gustavus was a foregone conclusion. What fun living on a campus where the enrollment was small enough that I could know almost everybody. The professors' dedication, the sense of family, the friends I made, and, underlying all, the philosophy of faith and the parallel responsibility and concern for one's fellow man motivated and challenged me. Daily I received spiritual nourishment in chapel and in Christianity courses.

At Gustavus I heard a missionary doctor from India challenge us to give our lives in service in that distant place. My heart responded, and I prepared to go, vowing, "Lord, I'll serve you as a single person all my life if that's what you want." Although the decision came easily, I was very romantic and strongly desired a home and children. But, God's will be done.

On graduation day in 1924, my heart pounded as I sang with my classmates:

> *Thrice hail Alma Mater*   *We have thee forever;*
> *Thy children are true!*   *Our love we renew.*

We'll stand by thy standards   *Thy battle, our battle,*
Our phalanx is strong   *Gustavus live long!*

I played football on a
women's team at Gustavus
in the early 1920s

Since 20 was too young to become a missionary, I became a teacher. My first assignment, Miller, South Dakota, was out on the prairies which I loved. At night I could see lights almost 50 miles away, and the stars seemed to hang as close as chandeliers.

Ben had received his master's degree in social work from Columbia University and then returned to Gustavus to teach. Oscar left teaching to pursue law and later to become congressman from Minnesota's Fifth District. Lute worked in our brother Peter's law office as secretary during the day and went to law school at night. Without anyone's knowledge, he took the civil service examination for assistant city attorney and, topping the examinees, was awarded the job. Reuben was launching his basketball career at Gustavus.

After two years at Miller, I accepted a teaching position at Roosevelt High School in Minneapolis, another exciting challenge. Often, as a Christian, I was asked to witness to young people's groups and church forums. One fall I undertook a series of six Sunday evening presentations at First Lutheran Church in St. Paul, planning the series around the theme, "The Treasure Hunt." We explored Christ in literature, painting, sculpture, and music; in the office, the classroom, the factory, and on the street. Young folks from neighboring churches joined our group, and soon the sizeable social room was filled with eager, enthusiastic youth. Little did I realize that two of those in attendance would play a large part in my life; one would become our foster daughter.

During this time the family circle was again broken when, at 44, Nora died. This highly artistic soul with her sensitive, generous heart had had some tempestuous days. But she had a good many more years than the doctor predicted as he removed the bones from her left arm when she was six. During this time of sorrow, the family again witnessed faith in action and a complete trust in the one who does all things well.

Mother and Dad were enjoying retirement. In a very real way the lines of Browning's "Rabbi Ben Ezra" came alive:

> Grow old along with me!
> The best is yet to be,
> The last of life,
> For which the first was made.
>
> Our times are in his hand.
> Who said: "A whole I planned,
> Youth shared but half.
> Trust God; see all; nor be afraid."

New doors opened for Mother and Dad, and life was rich and full. Retirement was walking into the sunset, hand in hand, expectantly, and in faith.

No one was more elated than Dad and Mother when Reuben made the first-string basketball team in his freshman year at Gustavus and made headlines for being top scorer in a crucial game. That this now-16-year-old child of their old age should be so well coordinated and so accurate pleased them, and they entered completely into the spirit of the competition. They rarely missed a performance of the Gustavus team those four years, often traveling icy roads to be in the rooting section and cheer Rube as he swept up and down the court.

Mother's sense of humor was constantly a joy. After one game the relatives had gathered at home for the postmortem, almost as much fun as the game itself if we won. We were busy in the living room with our bleacher observations, thinking Mother was getting coffee and refreshments ready. Our discourse was interrupted by the doorbell's ring. One of the boys went to answer it and found, to his amazement and amusement, Mother standing there, shaking with laughter, garbed in Rube's ebony and gold sweat suit. This white-haired grandma had slipped quietly out the basement door into the frigid night to make her way to the front door and provide mirth for her family.

The last game of Rube's college career, he lacked 16 points to become high point-scorer in the state. Never had I known Dad to offer money for anything in which we were expected to do our best, but before the game this night, Dad promised Rube two dollars for every basket over the needed 16 points. Whether Rube needed that money to take his girl friend out, I can't say, but he went like a house afire. Each time he made a basket after he had garnered the 16 points, he would look significantly to the balcony where Dad and Mother sat. And he collected too. When Rube graduated, the seventh of our family to receive his sheepskin from Gustavus, he went directly into the seminary.

Meanwhile, my dream of becoming a missionary was renewed when I began corresponding with Dr. Mary Markley about a call to India, eagerly anticipating dedicating myself to God in that far-off land. I was also active in Luther League work, both locally and on the district level. One blustery, rainy evening I attended a district meeting at Ebenezer Church where the presiding pastor was the very eligible Clarence Nelson. Recently ordained, he was shepherding the young mission congregation of Mount Olivet. After the meeting my friend Bernice Larson and I were standing on the corner in the downpour, waiting for a streetcar, when who should drive past but Pastor Nelson, taking the speaker to his hotel. He must have seen us, yet not a glimmer of concern about our plight was evidenced. Contradictorily I commented to Bernice, "You know, I think I could like that guy."

That summer I signed up for the state Luther League convention at Lake Independence. Eight of us were asked to make up a double quartet. Again, by some providence, Clarence Nelson was one of the bass participants as we blended our voices in "Out of my bondage, sorrow and plight; Jesus, I come."

My plans to go to India were nearly complete when I attended a youth retreat at Lake Independence. Some of us decided to swim the three miles across the lake, with a rowboat accompanying us, of course. Our boat had to wait because one of the swimmers, the state president of the Luther League, had a committee meeting first. I chafed, but the youth manning the oars wouldn't budge. He had promised Pastor Nelson he'd wait. If we hadn't, I might never have known the joy of "swimming" through life with a wonderful partner. It was at that point I began to be persuaded the Lord could use me in home missions. Numerous other episodes during our courtship are vividly recounted by Clarence in his family memoirs, "Bent Nails." Although I blush at some of what he says, his rendition is so much better than I could ever tell that I include it here.

. . . Who was this Ruth Youngdahl, soon to become my wife? She was a grocerman's daughter and a Minneapolis high school teacher. Our meeting was so utterly uncontrived; Ruth and I were random partners in a three-mile swim across Lake Independence. The distance across was as nothing to Ruth who was as much at home in water as a seal. But for me it was quite an endurance test. I had to rest frequently, yet kept stubbornly at it, not wanting to be shown up by this self-confident schoolmarm. When I finally pulled up on the dock on the far shore, gasping for breath, I felt I'd really accomplished something. Ruth, to the contrary, leaped to the dock and with a flashing smile said, "Come on gang, let's swim back." My more cautious counsel prevailed, and we made it back in the bowboat, flaunting the camp rule that mixed youth in swimming togs must not be in a boat together.

For this bachelor the event proved to be one of life's hinge moments. My admiration for Ruth's staying power was tremendous, and I was determined there would be more times together.

Soon after I called Ruth, suggesting we take a Sunday afternoon ride into the Minnetonka fruit orchards to enjoy the autumn sun on rosy-cheeked apples. She was willing. How enjoyable it was to have a gal at my side who was so easy to talk to. How relaxed we were in each other's company—a good sign.

En route back I suggested a restaurant snack. Ruth knew just the place, right on the lake in Wayzata. High on this new dimension of female company, I gave no thought to checking my billfold, thinking I could always write a check. Our dinner was delightful, but what an embarrassment when the cashier informed me they did not accept personal checks. Ruth to the rescue. "Think nothing of it," she said. "I just cashed my teacher's check yesterday. Hand me that slip." Extracting a solemn promise that she'd let me reimburse her, I let her pay the bill and we drove home.

A follow-up date was a necessity. The very next Sunday I stood at her door on West 48th Street, ringing the bell. When she opened it, I explained, "Here's Shylock, come to return his pound of flesh."

Like a string of beads, other dates followed as our friendship thickened to love. There were late-evening skates on a nearby rink, late because of church meetings or home calls. We often arrived after the warming house was closed. I still recall the thrill I felt as I knelt before her to pull on her skates and lace them. Always our conversations led to spirited exchanges of ideas. The stinging of the winter cold helped to make chumminess almost a matter of survival.

Ruth had a consuming love for God's out-of-doors. Unashamedly she would scream at a ravishing sunset or the trill of a lark on a fence. In her lively imagination, trees became people forms. "See those two trees bending towards each other? They're in love." Then there was a tree on a hilltop that a lightning bolt had broken and torn. "Ah," she said, "the price of prominence."

We enjoyed also early-morning tennis matches played on the hillside courts overlooking Lake Harriet. These had to be early so Ruth could be off to teach. It wasn't easy for me to be awakened by the raucous, insistent alarm clock, especially after a late visit to Ruth's found me climbing into bed long after midnight. Ruth, however, was not only game, but utterly inexhaustible.

One winter a preacher friend of earlier years was visiting me,

64

so Ruth volunteered to plan a picnic. When I asked if this was the season for picnics, she brushed my objection aside, observing that the new-fallen snow would only make our special spot overlooking the Mississippi River all the more breathtaking. We had no contenders for a grill and had a rollicking good time.

Often on winter evenings I would drop by Ruth's house for a late visit following some church meeting. On one such occasion, I suggested we walk through the new-fallen snow on the hilltop close by. Along the way we admired the homes looking so inviting in the snow and the soft winter light, weaving dreams about the home we hoped to establish. At the top we stopped to scan the starlit heavens. I suspect that a bit of stardust sifted into our giddy hearts because the next thing I knew Ruth was challenging me to join her in making snow angels. We lay flat on our backs and made wide sweeping movements with our outspread arms to form the imaginary angel wings.

It was very late when we finally arrived home. In a trice Ruth had a cup of coffee in my hands. I teased, "Ruth, you must have tied a string to a coffee bean and then pulled it through the boiling water." She took this teasing in stride and egged me on to sing at the piano. When I protested that it might awaken her sleeping parents, she retorted, "What if it does? They'll simply adore listening." I gave in to her pleading and began playing the music already spread open on the piano, "Love Never Fails." Father Youngdahl later loved to tell Ruth's brothers and sisters that when he heard me singing this song that night, he knew my attentions to Ruth were serious.

That evening I finally took courage and sprang the question: "Ruth, would you share my life and be my helpmeet?" Can you imagine what she answered? "Clarence, why I can't even cook." My response was, "Think nothing of it. You'll soon learn. How can a daughter of Elisabeth Youngdahl help but be a good cook? I'll teach you." Then I trepidaciously went to Father Youngdahl to do the old-fashioned thing of asking for his daughter's hand in marriage.

And who was this Clarence Nelson soon to become my husband? He was the son of a minister, sixth in a family of eight boys and one girl. After three years at Augustana Seminary he was serving Mount Olivet, his first parish. To me, Clarence Nelson was the epitome of what any girl could ever want. If I could have chosen a man for his profession, he would have been a pastor. Here, in addition to a pastor, was this handsome, gifted, lovable, much-sought-after eligible bachelor, knocking at my door. Both of us loved music, the out-of-doors, people, and the Lord. My heart overflowed with gratitude to God for his goodness.

Many little things began to disturb my schoolmarm calmness. When Clarence called me "dearest," something in me melted and warmly coursed through my every fiber. When unexpectedly our fingers met, or when sitting at a concert I felt his pulse beat through the somber cloth of his suit as arm to arm we listened to the music and heart to heart heard one sweet harmony, I sometimes wondered how this wonderful man could have fallen in love with *me*. Many evenings found me seeking to express these strange new feelings by setting pen to paper while searching my heart. One night I wrote:

Oh, often have I wished that I were beautiful
That God had made me fair and pleasing to behold.
It is not vanity, for I would that I were lovely just for you.
That I was small and dainty, that you might be proud of how I
  looked.
I've longed, and yearned, and wished—
And then I wonder God does not punish me.
Ungrateful wretch I am who knows his wisdom and his grace.
Am I a pauper when he has given me so much of richness from
  his heart of love?
I have two eyes to see the world's great beauty,
To see the love that lights my mother's eyes;
I have two ears that hear sweet tuneful music,
That are not deaf to sounds of trees and wind;
I have two nostrils that inhale the morning,
The freshness and the dewy smell of earth;
I have a body, vital, clean, that serves me,
A body quite untouched by grim disease;
I have a mind that knows of God's great wisdom,
That seeks to know more of the world he made;
And then I have a heart where he has made his dwelling,
A king has deigned to house himself in me;
A heart that loves, knows friends, feels joy and sadness—
Oh, God, forgive me for my great presumption!

I thank thee for all these—and, Lord, I thank thee, too,
For knowing what was best for me!

I wanted to share with Clarence the great joy he'd given me, the new glow I was experiencing. And once again, I set pen to paper:

I've tried to find a new way to say it. I have poured over voluminous dictionaries and encyclopedias; they just leave my tongue dry. I have pursued the emotional records of countless poets and have drunk from their oasis; this experience has but whetted my thirst. Hungrily have I studied faces for inspiration; momentarily I have had glimpses of footprints of what I sought. But before I could make them mine, they were gone.

I have delved into all the cupboards of my mind; I have opened long-closed doors and searched through shelves whose use has been but for myself alone. I have dusted away cobwebs and let light in corners where light has never before shown. I have hunted in the forests of my heart and listened to the wood-folk singing there and have returned even yet empty-handed.

And then . . .

I looked into your eyes and felt your pulse beat and knew the lovely fragrance that is you! And it came in the words that are as old as living (skeptics laugh them scornfully away); it came in an overwhelming of riotous peace and flooded my mind, heart, and body—all! I'm sure I do not have to tell you: you feel it in my fingertips and see it in my eyes and read it in my joy when you are near. But I do want to write it for then I shall be author of it. Plagiarism, you say? No! No! It's mine! All mine! So here goes:

I love you!

This newfound love permeated every facet of my life. I tried to concentrate on my teaching, sometimes not too successfully. "Good morning, Ann Marie." *(He loves me.)* "Is your cold any better today?" *(Why does the time go so fast when I'm with him?)* "Let's see, class, who is absent this morning?" *(Is it really true that this has happened to me?)* "For tomorrow we'll read Pope's *Essay on Man.*" *(Next year at this time, I won't be doing this.)* "Write a synopsis of each paragraph, selecting the theme." *(I wonder if they can see there is something different about me?)*

"Mary, will you copy this poem on the board?" *(I love the way his upper lip curls.)* "Before we go to our other work, we'll read the portions of 'The Universal Prayer' written on the board."

Teach me to feel another's woe *(He loves me)*
To hide the fault I see *(I love you)*
That mercy I to others show *(I love you)*
That mercy shown to me. *(How can he love me?)*

That same question was reiterated in the little piece I wrote to Clarence:

A plain and stiff and gawky-looking sunflower
Yet there's reflected in its upturned face
The golden smile and radiant, glowing sunlight
The adoration for its Master's grace.
It follows him across the path of heaven
It gathers all the glow that he will give.
It is not praised for form or grace or color
Yet its heart, too, can laugh, and love, and live.
A plain and stiff and gawky-looking sunflower—
Why didn't you pick a blushing, wind-kissed rose?
A rose would make your garden beauteous fair.
Beloved,
Are you sure you want the plain old sunflower there?

As with any romance, there were tense moments too. Having been brought up with a family of boys, Clarence was unaware of some of the things that please a woman. When he proposed and I suggested postponing our marriage until I could earn a little more money, his unromantic comment was, "We'd better not wait too long; you're no spring chicken."

Another time he promised to call, but didn't, and then made no attempt to explain his thoughtlessness. A verse which resulted from that trifling incident bears witness to the depth of the emotions I was experiencing:

A promised telephone call that wasn't made
Nothing more.
Of just such little things
Arise life's tragedies.

I wouldn't ask why
And he wouldn't explain.
We were as strangers
Who had never stood
Atop the hill and thrilled at lights below,
Who had not buffeted the burning blasts of hard, clean snow,
Who had not sat before the open fire
And dreamed, and planned, and hoped—together.
He did not call
I wouldn't ask why;
He wouldn't explain
And we were strangers.
The lovely night
Became as ashes.
It had given promise of a mellow spring—
Pussy willows and growing things in the air.
I didn't sleep that night
And as the minutes heavily dragged along,
Pulling their balls and chains through my mind
And leaving torn flesh and open wounds,
I heard the weather change—
The wind impelled by the cold Canadian mountains
Tore down upon the city and howled its way around houses.
Snow—driving, wet snow—chased it.
Spring?
It would seem
That even spring has its off moments.

We both had strong wills and could be extremely stubborn, yet I firmly believed love could conquer as I wrote the following in March 1932:

MY THOUGHTS ARE HORSES

Some days they are bucking broncos
   Throwing over everything that tries to ride them;
Some days they are gentle ponies
   Drawing happy children in bamboo carts;
Some days they are worn-out nags
   Barely trudging along over the cobblestones;

Again they are prancing stallions
    Afire with the verve of living.
Some days they are plow horses
    Tediously making straight runs in the field of my mind.
And then, at times, they are racers,
    Their life is in running;
Again they're attached to a wagon
    Whose chief load is bread.
Some days they're broncos, ponies, stallions, racers;
    They're all kinds together
Each trying to be what he is.
So, my dear, if you can't understand
    My moods and vagaries, remember . . .
It takes time to tame wild horses
    And create order out of pandemonium,
But take courage—
For love has been known to subdue
    Even the friskiest steed.

Our love prevailed, our special kind of love. I had known love
all my life, the love of parents, brothers, sisters, friends, and God.
Now I was to know that special love between a man and a woman; soon this dreamy-eyed schoolteacher would be floating down
the aisle in Messiah Church to say "I do!"

Sometimes it seemed as if the wedding day would never arrive.
Clarence was out of town frequently that summer, but was ever
so faithful about writing. In June he wrote from Fargo, North
Dakota:

Ruth, my darling,

I have to admit it; you're on my mind constantly. Love is all it's
cracked up to be and more. As far as I am concerned, it hasn't
been too extravagantly depicted. I'm just "softish" enough to believe that this day would be lacking its crowning touches without
a chat with you. . . . [After recounting his activities in Fargo, he
signed off.]

You're my Ruth, until the cow jumps over the moon!

On a Thursday afternoon in August, less than three weeks before
our wedding, I received, from Sarona, Wisconsin, the following
letter:

70

To my old-fashioned sweetheart,

Yesterday you made miles seem inches. We were on our overnight hike and the road stretched on endlessly because of the heat. Bud Serley drove up with the mail *and your letter.* From there on it was easy. It thrills me beyond power of description to think that this is the way hard places in the road of life will be changed by your companionship. Pal-o'-my-heart, you'd make a road through a desert seem like a walk through the garden of the gods. I could miss a train and not worry; I could miss a meal and not know it; I could miss an eye and somehow get by; but I couldn't miss you and not show it. . . . Last night through the long watches, my thoughts often turned to you. The stars twinkled through the leafy ceiling overhead so steadily luring forth in my mind thoughts that really did shine and drift, such light and flying things that my soul was gleaming with the gold dust left by their brushing wings. When you enter the chambers of my thoughts, you come with trailing clouds of lovely and glorious thoughts, my love! . . .

I'm beginning to despair of making these lines legible any more. If the bees that hum and busy themselves about just a step from where I am writing these lines knew how sweet you were, they'd make a beeline to Minneapolis and you. Just know my thoughts are like honeybees and they are making that beeline with an exchange load of sweet thoughts, kisses, and love.

from Clarence

Clarence. I loved the sound of his name. Clarence Nelson. *Mrs.* Clarence Nelson. Soon that would be *me*—Ruth Youngdahl Nelson. God's joy sang in my heart.

I, RUTH, TAKE THEE, CLARENCE

6

On August 25, 1932, I awoke to the melodious sounds of "Tis Thy Wedding Morning." The Messiah choir was following its custom of serenading a bride from its number early on her wedding day. Clarence arrived to have a cup of coffee with the well-wishers.

Later in the day a special letter arrived, an official call to the Arlington Hills congregation in St. Paul. The excitement of our wedding day, however, pushed this decision to the back of our minds. The thought of disassociating himself from Mount Olivet was too jolting for Clarence to even consider on this day.

Our wedding was a double celebration. Not only did Clarence and I exchange our wedding vows at the Messiah altar, but the ensuing reception was a salute to Mother and Dad's fortieth wedding anniversary. They were utterly unselfish in forgetting this to make it especially our day. The August night was unbearably hot, as if building for a storm. Not a breeze stirred. As head usher, Reuben was determined to look his best, so he changed his starched collar at least three times, but each wilted in succession. The church was packed beyond capacity with an overflow crowd pressing in to watch the procession form. They opened ranks when Luther, then a Minnesota Supreme Court justice, arrived with his wife, Irene, at his side.

As we waited for the ceremony to begin, Bernice Larson, my maid of honor, laughingly reminded me of my comment the night we were drenched in the downpour: "You know, I could like that guy." My first impression was certainly right that night!

I was a proud daughter walking down the aisle of my beloved home church on the arm of my dad who squared his shoulders and "processed" as if he were a king. (Was he that eager to be rid of me?) Clarence's brother, Carl, then pastor of Luther Memorial in north Minneapolis, assisted Dr. Leonard Kendahl at the altar. Clarence was so flustered he put my wedding ring on the wrong hand and spent several embarrassing moments trying to covertly switch the ring to the left hand. He commented later that anybody who suggests having a sermon in a wedding ceremony should know that the excited couple remember very little of what is said.

No couple could have a greater sense of being blessed than we were as we committed ourselves to "love in prosperity and in adversity." The Messiah choir sang with my brother Carl presiding at the organ. Florence Johnson sang the benediction:

May the grace of Christ our Savior,
And the Father's boundless love,
With the Holy Spirit's favor,
Rest upon us from above.
Thus may we abide in union
With each other and the Lord;
And possess, in sweet communion,
Joys which earth cannot afford.

The ceremony over, we embraced, kissed, and lightheartedly led the recession down the aisle. Just as we were about to leave, Clarence's mother put $50 in our hands saying, "Now when you get to Canada, buy a set of dishes with this."

My brother Reuben engineered our getaway. He had to muster all his driving skill to elude the hot pursuit of Clarence's brother

Clarence and I were married at Messiah Church on August 25, 1932

Arthur who was clearly bent on mischief. By dodging down alleys and side streets, we made it to a teacher friend's home. In the excitement, Clarence left a suitcase behind. Unfortunately it was the one with his money orders so carefully saved for the honeymoon.

We spent our first night together at a cozy little hotel in the hills above Marine on St. Croix. The August evening had turned cool by the time we arrived, so we cozied up at the fire burning on the hearth just outside our bedroom. There on the settee we flavored again the excitement of the wedding, recalling the people who attended and their gifts. We took time to amplify the sparse vows we made at the altar, setting them down in a keepsake book. The next morning we called Carl who was planning to visit his wife's relatives in Stillwater. We arranged a rendezvous there to obtain the missing suitcase.

Some of our beautiful honeymoon days were spent just south of Grand Marais in a fisherman's cabin perched on the rocks of Lake Superior's shore. We thrilled to the deep bass when a huge wave hit some cavelike hollow worn by the storm-tossed waters. Early mornings we were up with the sun to accompany Mr. Pederson, the herring fisherman, as he gathered his day's catch from his nets. Generations of fishermen's blood flowed in the veins of this hardy, blue-eyed Dane. No delicacy could outrank the herring fillets his deft knife readied for our breakfast. Fried in butter, the herring made a breakfast fit for a monarch.

On one of those honeymoon days I offered to prepare a chicken dinner, saying, "I know just how my mother fixes it." We drove back along the highway to where we had seen a sign: "Eggs and Dressed Chickens for Sale." Soon we were back with one we assumed to be a fryer, and I readied it for the pan. I boiled and boiled this blue-veined hen, testing it with a fork from time to time just the way Mother did. While waiting for the potatoes to boil and the chicken to get tender, I picked up a favorite edition of poetry and read aloud to Clarence Elizabeth Barrett Browning's "How Do I Love Thee?" At the climactic line, "I love thee to the level of everyday's most quiet need," Clarence interrupted with, "Ruth, I smell something burning." It was the potatoes. I tested the chicken, but it was still rubbery, so I put on a second pot of potatoes, and finished the poem in silence. When these potatoes were cooked, I again tried the chicken. It was still too tough, but I decided to flour it and put it into the fry pan anyway. It browned just fine, but when we tried to eat it, Clarence commented, "Ruth, this bird needed a bit more time, don't you agree?"

Sobbing, I retorted, "Clarence, you're so insensitive it hurts. That hen you bought must have been the Mrs. Methuselah of the flock." Shamefacedly, Clarence admitted he had not specified we wanted a spring chicken; we had gotten an old soup hen instead.

Another day we set out to follow a rushing stream, climbing up the rocky palisades to take in its pristine, tangled beauty, enjoying the gorge, quiet pools, and roaring cascades. By chance Clarence dislodged a boulder directly above me. Summoning every ounce of strength, he held it in place, shouting for me to jump clear. By the time I was out of the way and he could finally release it, he had a badly crushed finger that stubbornly refused to heal, becoming infected and rock-hard. We made an emergency visit to an old doctor in the village who lanced and dressed it as best he could. Of course, I gave my hero no end of sympathy and concern; hadn't he gallantly spared his young bride?

Also during our honeymoon we overnighted in a little cabin north of Two Harbors. At 11:30 P.M. we decided to take a dip in the icy liquid of Lake Superior. Down the rocks we climbed, and screamed with delight at the burning sensation of the cold water.

We concluded our honeymoon on the North Shore with a three-day stay at Port Arthur, Canada, reveling in the luxury of the Prince Edward Hotel. From habit, I signed myself in as Ruth Youngdahl while Clarence was parking the car. He shamefacedly corrected my error when he arrived at the desk a few minutes later.

In Port Arthur we came upon a real buy in dishes. A local fuel merchant had a stock of dishes he was selling at a discount. The wedding gift from Clarence's mother sufficed for an eight-piece set of English Wedgwood bone china, usually affordable by only the very wealthy.

All too soon the modest purse Clarence had hoarded for the honeymoon was nearly exhausted. We had enough left on the drive back to stop for an excellent five-course dinner at Hart's Inn in Moose Lake for just under two dollars each. As Archie Bunker puts it, "Those were the days."

Still facing us was the unanswered call to Arlington Hills. We were guided in the decision as events occurred which put a move to Arlington in a more favorable light. Mount Olivet's plans to build a church collapsed. The bank where the building funds were deposited had closed and the lot payments were defaulted on. We were in the trough of the Great Depression. We said to each other, "Won't it take a new pastor starting from scratch to reinspire the now thoroughly demoralized congregation?" Also, here was a chance for us to begin, on an even keel, to get to know a new flock. Arlington Hills was certainly a big challenge. For 11 years this congregation had worshiped in an ugly tar paper-roofed basement and it was now deep in debt. By the time we returned from our honeymoon, pulling up at my parents' house with only a bit of change left, we had decided to accept the call.

We wrote Arlington Hills accepting the call, and made plans to move to St. Paul by the first of December. My parents insisted we stay with them those months in the interim while Clarence served Mount Olivet. My reception by that congregation was all I could have hoped for, as described by Clarence in "Bent Nails":

> Ruth was warmly received by the Mount Olivet congregation. I can remember to this day how proud I was to have her sitting in the choir just a few steps from where I liturgized at the tiny white altar in that little shoebox of a church building. The temporary church stood spare and unadorned. Even that early our Sunday attendance strained the seating capacity. Proceeding with our beautifully completed plans for a new church was out of the question for now. When the time was right, a new pastor could launch a fresh drive for funds.
>
> What a shock my resignation proved to be, coming as it did on the heels of our marriage. The congregation had loved the idea of a young bride as their pastor's wife and had anticipated the shot in the arm her fresh energies would bring to the work. I recall so well one of the exuberant choir girls saying, "Pastor, we could tell the difference she made in that first sermon you preached on your return from the honeymoon." The choir, too, knew the strength and beauty of her alto. She was always ready to volunteer her time and talent.
>
> What a wonderful helper I had taken to my side when I married Ruth Youngdahl. Already as a single woman she was an experienced and much-sought-after platform speaker. At every turn she made a powerful witness to her love for Christ. She taught the youth Bible class at Sunday school. Always she was right at my side when the several organizations met, charming and encouraging both members and strangers. Ours was a team ministry from the beginning.
>
> The packed congregation that gathered hoped to persuade us to reconsider my resignation. A motion for the congregation to build a new parsonage was thunderously passed. But I stubborn-

ly stood by our decision, quashing in my mind the overwhelming urge to notify Arlington Hills that I had changed my mind. However, the three months we stayed on at Mount Olivet helped bind the wounds. But it really hurt when one member suggested that Ruth was to blame for our leaving.

No, she was like the Ruth in the Bible: "Thy people shall be my people." This was also her attitude in the subsequent moves we made. "The decision is yours, Clarence. I wouldn't for the world interpose my will. Let us in simple faith and prayers ask God to guide and then believe that he will make his will clearly known to you as you weigh the options." This we did, and looking back now from the vantage of retirement, we were never misled.

Mount Olivet today has become the spiritual home of tens of thousands. When my successor, Dr. Edgar Carlson, left it to become president of Gustavus, a Mount Olivet board member asked me to suggest another pastor. Aware of the strong leadership this flock would need after the doldrums of recession, I suggested my brother-in-law, Reuben Youngdahl, who was then having a remarkable ministry at Marshalltown, Iowa. This suggestion was acted upon at once.

Clarence and I had all sorts of great times together: hamburger fries in the snow, late night skates on Lake of the Isles, quiet hours of conversation, joyous hours of singing. When we both had been out calling or attending a meeting, we'd work together in the kitchen to get dinner. He took charge of the meat; I the accompaniments and table setting. Even when we were alone, I'd light candles for dinner, using them until they were down to stubs.

Times were difficult, too, however. Married during the depression, we faced economic as well as emotional problems and conflicts. Clarence had a stubborn streak as strong as mine, so when one stubborn Swede met another stubborn Swede head-on, there was quite a crash. Often the irritations were over little things, like me having to ask him for every nickel and to account for it—a little hard on a former teacher accustomed to an independent income. But we both loved sharing with God and others, so basically we agreed on what had priority in our budget.

We never let our angers fester. Always there was God, the

great bringer-together, and the "I'm sorry," with its ensuing, "Forgive me, beloved." More and more we grew to be a team whose goal was to serve the Christ we so deeply loved.

In September I penned the following:

A month—you're my husband—
I love you!
The sun is lifting its head;
'Twill be noon, then sunset, then evening. . . .
When our last "Now I lay me" we've said,
May we look back and see all the journey
And know in the depths of our heart
That we've lived and we've loved on together
And even death will not keep us apart.

ST. PAUL DAYS AND THE GREAT DEPRESSION

7

Will we ever forget the reception of the Arlington Hills congregation when we took up work there? Coming just a few months after our wedding, it seemed right that Clarence should lead me down that aisle too, dressed in my bridal gown. It put a flair in the occasion and was appreciated by the members since only a handful had actually been at the wedding.

The Arlington Hills Church Council asked Clarence to take over the instruction of their confirmation class before we actually moved which meant a weekly trip to St. Paul each Saturday. We agreed to memorize a new hymn en route each week, giving us a ready store of treasures to draw on at bedsides, hymn sings, and on trips.

Clarence plunged into the work of fanning the fires of faith in a congregation largely made up of skilled workers who were very hard hit by the depression. I taught Bible to the previous years' confirmation class. Here I met Lorraine and Arlene, two girls who had come to my treasure hunt series at First Lutheran Church in St. Paul. After one of the first Sundays with this class I said to Clarence, "Something about Lorraine Servheen deeply moves me.

If ever the opportunity came, I'd love to take her into our home as a daughter." I learned later that after one of those earlier treasure hunt Sunday meetings Lorraine had confided to Arlene, "I have a feeling that woman is going to mean something in my life." (This was before I had even met my husband.)

At Arlington Hills Clarence and I began the practice of taking birthday cakes to those in the parish over 65. (I chuckle now because from the vantage of my years today, 65 is young.) Baked from scratch, the cakes came out high and golden. I'd add just a touch of frosting and decorate each with the person's name applied by toothpick and frosting. They were joyfully received as we delivered each with a round of the traditional birthday song. Clarence searched out a special memory verse to share from Scripture, and we'd sing such much-loved hymns as "What a Friend We Have in Jesus" and "Children of the Heavenly Father."

The Arlington Hills call presented a sizeable challenge. The congregation was in low spirits. Under Pastor Albert Loreen's leadership, they had planned to build a small cathedral. But now money was hard to come by; 40% of the members were unemployed. The first step in resurrecting the building plans was to eliminate one imposing front tower and reduce the sanctuary seating by half. (Attendance at the time indicated that the planned sanctuary would be filled only at Christmas and Easter.) In the meantime the tar paper-roofed basement kept saying to every passerby, "The plans of this church were just too big for its resources." In addition, the congregation's mission pledge was several years in arrears. As Clarence said, "Like mountain sheep caught in a blizzard, they were eating their own wool and slowly dying." To him fell the responsibility of restoring their spirits.

Preaching never came easy for Clarence. He dared step into the pulpit only after long hours of study and searching. He spent hours literally burying his nose in his studies. Regularly on Saturday night I was the sounding board for the sermon he had planned for the morrow.

He also kept very busy at pastoral calling, remembering the admonition of his seminary teacher, "A house-calling pastor makes a church-going people." And didn't our Lord say, "The fields are white unto harvest"? His goal was to average five calls a day.

Hardly ever was a home visit wasted. Sometimes months afterwards, nudged by some trying experience, these folks would appear at worship and take Clarence's hand at the door saying, "You were really talking right to me today."

The calls were mainly to run-down rented homes whose vestibules were rank with the smell of boiled turnips and cabbage. Yet Clarence and I, bursting with great hopes and with Christ in our hearts, set out to initiate new programs. We made a personal call to every home and blew lustily on what coals remained in the ashes of their despair. The response was immediate. Offerings mounted. With a gambler's blind faith, Clarence declared himself unwilling to accept his monthly salary unless the synod's share for benevolence was also taken care of. Soon the albatross of debt to the Minnesota Conference was being lifted.

An important part of our work at Arlington Hills was our vacation Bible schools. Too short of funds to buy printed courses, we wrote our own, spending long hours cranking the mimeograph. Our school was usually well attended, and we managed to rent a nearby public school for the three-week sessions. Clarence and I joined other volunteers and taught classes, prizing this chance to personally get to know the children and thus share our witness to Christ early in their lives.

One Saturday night, on the very eve of confirmation, our doorbell rang and a class member stood there wide-eyed and disheveled. "Pastor, my dad's roaring drunk and has been chasing me around the house with a butcher knife." We drew her into the house to talk it out, wanting to quiet her jangled nerves. Afterwards Clarence went with her to find the father as meek as a lamb by that time. Imagine how thrilled we were when years afterward, at Arlington Hill's 65th anniversary Sunday (November 1974), this girl, now mature and lovely, sought us out to acknowledge tearfully what her confirmation had meant to her.

That our marriage had its share of stardust is witnessed to by the following lines penned by Clarence on Easter Eve, 1933, after preparing and rehearsing his sermon:

It's Easter Eve.
Sweet Afton lingers.
Above the clouds hang dark and heavy

82

but the west is hopeful. Through drifting
clouds is seen the glow of setting sun,
a harbinger of another dawn.
And so again heaven sketches the story of Easter.

The Master's words are ringing thru mind and soul:
"Go quickly and tell." A pastor's heart
thrills with the privilege of heeding him and
expectantly awaits the worship hour. All unworthy
he feels of joining the worthy line of those
who in every age have been the Master's voice
and deepening dusk finds him on his knees
asking of his Master's spirit and presence.

His prayers are spoken. "For Jesus' sake," he
adds. And heaven's echoing spirit sends the
assurance of another's presence for the morrow's
joyous task. And yet he lingers bowed in prayer.
Another surge of prayer arises deep within. Mind
and soul seem flushed with the enervating power
of a magnificent obsession. Words are flung aside.
They lime the winging prayer and only seem to tie
to earth a thankful spirit. He is thanking God
for a great love.

God gave him a love so great that it has shaped
and molded his whole life. It is the love for
Christ his Savior. Life turned a corner and now
passes down a glorious road since this love
brought to his side a boon companion that truly
makes the heart burn.

God has given him yet another love. It is the
love for another life companion. To have found
her has riven the clouds, has gilded the west,
has brought added resurrection experiences.
Her name is Ruth. It stands for one who is staunch
and true, like Ruth of old whose loyalty and love
not even life's darkest experience could ruffle.

We relished nesting in our first home, a small, two-story house
we rented on Forest Street across from the Children's Hospital
and near Phalen Park. We bought our furniture at a summer sale.

Altogether the dining room, living room, and bedroom pieces plus a carpet came to only $850. We cashed my teacher's insurance to pay for our first electric refrigerator. I hemmed hand-me-down curtains by hand and added touches of color here and there to create a livable home. The handcrafted pieces we both had collected caused visitors to exclaim, "It's all so homey and inviting." Clarence made me feel so good when he'd recite the Swedish proverb saluting a clever homemaker:

Med sin husliga flit	(With her homemaking skill)
Och sin ordnande nit	(And her sense of order)
Gor hon trevnad ock ro	(She brings beauty and peace)
I det ringaste so.	(To the humblest cottage.)

To our first dinner party we invited some Roosevelt teacher friends. We planned that menu with utmost care as Clarence's salary was minimal. (He never made a move during his pastoral career that promised a higher salary.) A downtown grocery was offering picnic hams already baked in a bread-dough blanket for 87 cents. Although unhappily they were tough, the other dishes were delectable. The teachers, loyal friends, "oohed" and "aahed," vowing the dinner the best ever.

About this time Reuben was ordained a Lutheran minister. His decision to enter the ministry was one of those amazing answers to prayer too rarely acknowledged in our materialistic, scientific age. From the time Rube was first presented to me I never missed a day but what I prayed, "Please, God, help Rube to be a minister when he grows up." I wasn't the only one. The folks felt if such a thing came to pass it would be the crowning joy of their lives, and they brought it to God in their own prayers. But one thing was certain as far as they were concerned: God's will is always best, and his judgment, with the long look of eternity, far superior to ours. So they committed this decision into his hands. Rube spoke many times of how he fought the compulsion out of sheer stubbornness. "It wasn't because I knew Mother and Dad wanted me to go into the ministry that I decided to become a pastor. In fact, that caused me to fight constantly against the idea. I am more convinced than ever that one should not go into the ministry if they can possibly stay out of it, and I couldn't." This inner com-

◀ *A portrait taken shortly after our marriage*

pulsion was the answer to prayer, and the answers kept coming in a rich ministry, with the "cup runneth over" kind of blessings that makes us wonder at God's loving mercies.

On Reuben's ordination day, Mother and Dad's theme song was praise to God for all his blessings and gratitude that they had been permitted to see this day.

After a year on Forest Street we moved to 492 Magnolia. An Arlington Hills member who was retiring and moving out of town offered the congregation his home on the corner of Magnolia and Burr for only $4800. We loved its site, crowning a hilltop, and the view of the city at night from the sun parlor was beautiful. Our dream of having a home with a fireplace had to be deferred. In this home we spent eight years.

On October 27, 1933, we were blessed with our first child. I awakened early, sat up in bed, and began darning socks, timing the contractions. When Clarence awoke, he helped me time the pain spasms. As the intervals grew shorter, we knew it was time to grab the suitcase that had been standing ready for days and be off to Bethesda Hospital.

After I was tucked into the hospital bed, the signals slowed. Clarence had been holding my hand, and I could tell by the pressure he exerted on it that he was nervous, so I persuaded him to take a walk into the autumn sunshine. When he returned, the hard pains had started. I bit my lips, refusing the comfort and release of a good cry. All the while the woman in the next room was rending the air with her wails. Within minutes I was being wheeled down the corridor, Clarence running alongside.

It was Dr. Sohlberg's idea that every new father should watch the miracle of his firstborn's arrival, so Clarence donned a mask and gown and stood by to witness the birth. He had to slip out into the corridor for air when the doctor used his surgeon's knife to ease the entry; the spurting blood was too much for him and he nearly fainted. The pain became unbearable. Dr. Sohlberg urged, "Now push hard once more, Ruth." Making a supreme effort, drawing on my last ounce of strength, I sighed, "I can't any more." At that moment son Jon burst into his strange new world.

I had experienced to the full the deep-down joy a new mother knows in being used of God to bring an eternal soul into being. Clarence reentered the room just in time to see the nurse holding the little guy by his feet. Then she slapped his back and, as the infant let out his first cry, Clarence said, "Who asks for proof of God's existence after watching the marvel of a tiny human coming into the world with all life's appurtenances intact? Yes, and with his soul stamped not alone with God's image but with mind and body bearing the unmistakable imprint of his parents."

Clarence rushed off to the phone to relay the good news to members of the family and then to fetch Mother. As I waited for their return, Jon was brought to me. When that little life was placed in my arms, I felt a new sense of my own helplessness and of the value of life from an eternal view. I wanted one thing above all: that the soul contained in those six pounds nine ounces of mortal flesh might open its wings and find its way home to God, and that in its flight it might bless all those whose lives it touched and lead the way for others to follow.

Clarence and Mother returned and visited only briefly, sensing my bone-weariness. As they headed home, Clarence was in emotional high gear repeating to himself, "By God's grace, I'm a father!" when he foolishly tried to beat out a big trailer truck while making a turn onto busy Seventh Street. The resulting crash didn't even dent the truck, but our Chevy needed some body work, and there on the street was Grandma Youngdahl tangling verbally with the trucker, insisting it was all his fault. No mother-in-law could be more loyal. And how proud Grandpa Youngdahl was that our firstborn was named Jonathan Clarence so his initials were J. C. like his granddad's.

Life was good and full, but financially we were struggling desperately. One day when our optimism was very low and our bank balance even lower, Clarence was as discouraged as I had ever known him. In the mail that day was an amazing enclosure. No written word, only a page torn from a hymnal bearing the words "Hold the Fort, Brother!" and two dollar bills. We never found out who sent it, but it wondrously performed the errand it was meant to accomplish. Our spirits were uplifted. What matter that we had no money and payday was two weeks away—God was with us.

Shortly after that Clarence received a call from a woman asking if we would stop by General Hospital and call on a little Swiss gentleman who was ill. He had no family and few friends, this Emil Welti. The next day Clarence paid him a call. When he returned, he shared with me what happened: "When I stepped into the ward, I found this little wizened old man at the far end with eyes sharp and penetrating like headlights and a large beak-like nose. He was a snuff user, and a trickle of brown oozed from the corner of his mouth, staining the white sheet. He seemed glad when I introduced myself. When I learned he came from the German-speaking part of Switzerland, I tried a few phrases from my school German. That really got through. He immediately pulled back the covers to show me the scars and lacings of his 14 operations. Then I shared some Bible verses and prayed with him. His eyes were moist and he gripped my hand when I left, promising to come back soon."

When Emil was released from the hospital, he returned to his drab little room in a section of the city where the rent was cheap and, as a bonus, he had the companionship of cockroaches.

His release from the hospital came shortly before Christmas, a very special time for us—our first Christmas alone together as husband and wife. We had shared the previous Christmas festivities with both sides of the family. Our firstborn, Jon, would be two months old, and we were sure his bright eyes would love the lights on our tree and his ears would tune in to the singing of the carols. It was to be just us, our little family, establishing our own tradition of blue lights on a simply decorated tree, of worshiping the manger child through scripture, song, and prayers before giving any thought to packages gathered under pine branches—beautiful anticipation.

Yet we were haunted by the kind of Christmas Emil would have. In ignoring his need, were we turning away the Christ child? After we prayed about it, Clarence went to hunt up Emil in his rooming house and invite him to spend Christmas Eve with us and stay overnight so he could be along at the early morning Christmas worship. When Clarence arrived at the three-story boarding house, a veritable firetrap with dingy, ill-lit halls, he knocked on the door and was greeted by Emil, attired in his winter underwear. He had gone to bed early; what else was there to do? Emil asked, "So you did get my letter?" Clarence hadn't the faintest notion of what Emil meant, but he invited him to join us for Christmas.

That evening Emil joined our family around the Christmas tree as we sang carols and listened as Clarence read the Christmas story from Luke. Following this were prayers, and then the opening of the gifts began. Emil's bony finger pointed excitedly to a small gift-wrapped box he had put under the tree, begging, "Open it first, Mrs. Nelson." He had learned of my love of candles and had bought me a pair of F. W. Woolworth crystal candleholders. Since he was on welfare and received only $25 a month, this was indeed a rich gift for him to give. We had made certain Emil had plenty of presents, and it was a truly blessed Christmas, the beginning of an entirely unanticipated tradition. The next morning Emil's letter arrived:

Rev. Clarence T. Nelson,

Will you be so kind and answer my question if I could join your house of God in about three months from December 30, 1934. I belong to the Lutheran Church in Switzerland. Since I came in connection with you I find Jesus Christ and I wish I could stay with him until my time has come. Will you kindly see the members if they would accept me? I know Jesus Christ will and therefore I like to join your house of God. It is not too far for me to come because I love your sermon. I don't think I'm too much of a sinner. God Bless you and your family as long as you live.

I will close my letter and hope you have a better Christmas than I have but I know God won't let me suffer.

The best thanks to you,
Emil Welti

P.S.   If I can make the morning service I will gladly be there to enjoy a good service. Please excuse my mistakes that I made in some of the words.

Emil became a member of our church and of our family. As soon as he could find a room nearby, he moved closer to Arlington Hills Church. Emil was adopted as a sort of mascot by the local businessmen's bowling team—they even had a jacket with the club's emblem that just fit his diminutive size. The first Sunday after Emil moved, the usual reception of new members before Communion took place, and Emil's name led all the rest.

Not long after this the telephone rang. It was Dr. Burton who had been named guardian of Lorraine and Walter Servheen after their parents' tragic deaths. "Can you help me?" Dr. Burton asked Clarence. "I must find a home for the Servheen children. The place they have been staying no longer has room." Putting his hand over the phone's mouthpiece, Clarence relayed the message to me. "Tell him we'll take them. I'd love the chance to mother them," was my immediate response. As quickly as that a decision was made that brought untold blessings to our lives. Lorraine and Wally came to live with us. A bit of rearranging of bedroom space and we had them settled in.

Emil, who always had Sunday dinner with us, took an immediate liking to Lorraine and Wally. Drawing on recollections from his boyhood in Switzerland, he made sparkling conversation at many a Sunday dinner. One Sunday, when the prospect of completing the church sanctuary still seemed off in limbo, Emil pushed back his chair, rose to his feet, and drew from his worn wallet a ten-spot that he put on the table. Then he said with a flourish, "Pastor, it isn't right for God's people to worship in a basement. I want this ten-spot to start the upper structure building fund."

Clarence winced, knowing that the remaining $15 of Emil's meager relief check would have to cover his necessities for the rest of the month. Nonetheless, he also remembered how Jesus singled out the two coppers of a widow, declaring that since they were her "all," her offering topped all the other gifts in that day's collection. He mused over the contribution all week, and by Sunday he knew exactly what to do. In making his announcements, he waved the ten-spot before the congregation, and, without naming Emil, tried to tell of the sacrifice involved. Emil, however, wasn't the least squeamish about it. Arising with great dignity right in front, he made it very clear whose ten it was.

Within a year those church walls were abuilding. Like the widow of the gospel with her two mites, our people subscribed from their very needs to make that sanctuary a reality. And today, with the more recently constructed chapel and educational structure, the Arlington Hills complex covers a third of a city block and surely is one of the most vigorous congregations in our synod.

Then came the day when Emil became very sick. He was so frail that Clarence carried him in his arms into the hospital, sure that the trip would mean his passing. But Emil was tough and recovered twice. The third time, however, took him. The merry twinkle of his eyes and his helpfulness had made him known and loved up and down the Payne Avenue business district. At his funeral the mortuary was filled to the last seat. His friends contributed generously to his burial, and that final salute measured not only their esteem for this diminutive, jolly gentleman, but also the bigness of their own hearts.

On November 8, 1934, our family again grew with the arrival of son David. His was a difficult birth as he was breach and we almost lost him. We were thrilled to have a brother for Jon and created a special birth announcement to herald his arrival into our hearts and home:

THE PARSONAGE KID

When people heard I was coming
    They almost blew their lid;
They said: "Poor Mrs. Nelson!
    There'll be another parsonage kid."

But Mommy and Daddy just chuckled;
    They were as pleased as punch instead.
They rejoiced that the Lord had given them
    Another parsonage lad.

My name is David Theodore,
    Jonathan is my brother's name.
We hope that we will be friends like
    The boys of biblical fame!

No matter what others are saying,
    The welcome I've had is not hid;
And I am very grateful
    To be another parsonage kid.

91

With Dave's arrival we had to reevaluate our house space. It became clear that we needed the upstairs room for our growing boys. So Clarence arranged for the Rolig family, who lived only a block away, to take Wally into their home. Mrs. Rolig, a motherly, loving person, had successfully raised a family of her own and had a beautiful way with this high school boy who was missing his own folks and was a little rebellious at living in a preacher's home. She had a son Wally's age, so he had a companion, and she soon made Wally feel accepted and loved.

But Wally always took his Sunday dinner with us. We wanted the ties with his sister to be nurtured. At one Sunday dinner, Wally said, "If anybody would have told me a year ago that I could be so at home in a parsonage, I'd really have hooted at them. But I want you all to know I feel at home, and I like it."

Wally served in World War II, becoming a lieutenant in the medical corps. Upon his return, he obtained an excellent job with an airline. Soon he married and set up his home. In the intervening years we followed his family closely, keeping them in our prayers. We were saddened when cancer took Wally to an early grave.

We were also often visited weekends by my sister Mabel and her husband Al Anderson. They were in charge of a cottage for the mentally disturbed in Hastings, Minnesota, bringing to the job all the love and personal sensitivity to another's needs at their command and giving themselves freely to make their wards happy. But they surely needed that weekly break. We saw to it that a warm welcome always awaited them at 492 E. Magnolia. Mabel adored our children and became their favorite aunt. Moreover she proved herself a wonderful helper in a crisis. One unfortunate day I suffered a miscarriage and fainted in the living room. Mabel frantically set to leafing through the phone book to call for an ambulance, but her eyes were so filled with tears she couldn't read. Clarence wasn't much better off, but somehow they succeeded and soon I was gently being carried on a stretcher to the waiting ambulance and then to Bethesda Hospital. Two other such tragedies were ahead for us in our years together, but for now we had Jon, David, and Lorraine.

One morning at breakfast Clarence prayed, "God, please break in on my day and order my steps." That evening we had arranged for a baby-sitter and were on our way to visit my parents in Minneapolis when Clarence remembered that he had neglected to respond to a call. The Bloomquist's daughter, who was a confirmand, was seriously ill. He immediately turned the car around, saying, "I'll not feel happy all evening unless I call on Betty Bloomquist. Her mother called me earlier." Mr. Bloomquist was stunned when he opened the door to find us standing there. "Would you believe it?" he asked. "At this very moment Betty has been calling for you." Ought we marvel at that kind of providential guidance? I agree with Clarence's statement: "We should expect it as the norm." Instead of being like one mother who, when her prayer found answer, exclaimed, "Isn't God wonderful?" we should think like her daughter who replied, "No, Mom, it's just like him." After leaving the Bloomquists, the time together with my parents later was all the happier.

Shortly after this we were again spending the evening with my parents. As I was playing the piano, Dad said, "Please play this one." The hymn he requested began, "O precious thought! Some day the mist shall vanish." After we had sung all eight verses, Dad said, "That is the hymn I want sung at my funeral, that one and 'Softly and Tenderly, Jesus Is Calling.' Please remember, Ruth."

For years Dad's health had been anything but robust. His delicate stomach needed constant coddling. Often we felt that if he thought of it less, it would be less troublesome. Yet who is to judge how another person feels? That he should have lived to see all of his children established both in their professions and in their homes was more than he ever dared hope for. His cup had run over.

At 74 he developed prostate trouble and was bedridden at home for a week. Sunday afternoon we drove over to see him. At his bedside sat a 15-year-old girl, a member of his Bible class. What a beautiful picture it made—this golden-haired adolescent and this white-haired grandfather in spiritual fellowship. Before she left, she asked, "May I pray for you?" Kneeling at his bedside, she asked her heavenly Father to bless this beloved teacher. After she had gone, Dad said, "Let me tell you about her. Her parents have done everything they can to discourage her from attending church and Bible class. They won't let her set an alarm for Sunday morning because it might wake them. Yet she never misses. And today she took her Sunday afternoon to come way across town to see me. That is pay enough for any time I have ever given to my classes. What more could I ever ask than the joy of her prayer for me?"

After being ill for a week, he went to the hospital for an examination. It was the last day in the church year that Saturday evening when he called for the pastor to bring him Holy Communion. Those of us gathered around his bedside shared the sacrament with him and witnessed the faith and anticipation crowned by a Savior's love as he prayed, "Come, Lord Jesus." His faith that he would meet his God was sure. The room became a place of light, hope, and joy, and peace was evident as he lay back on the pillow. The next morning he had his "advent" as the first day of the church year dawned and he began it in his eternal home. We could but rejoice; the best is yet to be.

At his victory service the messages in song he had requested filled the air, the message of eternal victory for the soul that makes its flight in faith. It was something to see 35 young people, 15 and 16 years old, form an honorary guard before the casket of their Bible teacher. Many a tear was brushed away from those youthful faces, for they knew that John Youngdahl had loved them and was a real friend. Engraved on his marker in Lakewood Cemetery are the victorious words: "For to me to live is Christ, and to die is gain!" The best *is* yet to be.

Now Mother was left to make the difficult adjustment to living alone. Because they had had those last 15 wonderful years together, the loss seemed even greater. It had never been like her to mope in self-pity or bewail her lot, nor was it now. She established herself in an apartment close to the church she loved and made this new home a mecca for family and friends. Her sense of humor was still much in evidence. She had four or five jokes she would try on each friend who had not heard them. Being such a good actress, she would get by with them. With such a sober mien that the listener would be all sympathy, she would say, "Did you know that our son Carl can't play with these two fingers?" indicating the index and middle finger of her hand. Carl was the

94

pianist, so the incapacity of his fingers would be tragic. When the unsuspecting friend replied, "That's too bad. Why can't he use them?" she would laughingly respond, "Because they're mine."

This wonderful heart that could so quickly create laughter, that had a warm compassion which responded to needs anywhere in the world, never spared herself. It is no wonder then that, just a little over a year after Dad had taken the great voyage, Mother suffered a heart attack. The doctor reported that her heart had so enlarged as to lose resiliency. Constantly she struggled for breath as though climbing a steep hill. For several weeks she lay in Swedish Hospital, in and out of an oxygen tent. This became the family gathering place.

One day we were sitting in the waiting room of the hospital while she was being given some tests. Into the room came one of the girls with whom we had grown up. "How is your mother?" she asked. "I haven't wanted to disturb her."

"She isn't very well," we responded.

"Well, will you tell her from me that us kids from the neighborhood will never forget how she mothered us all? She wasn't just your mother. We were all her family. If we hurt ourselves, she was ready to bind our wounds. If we had troubles, she'd listen to them. She mothered the whole neighborhood."

Since our boys were only one and two while Mother was in the hospital, planning and hard work were needed at home so I could be at her side daily. One day the news had been unfavorable and I was especially tired. I was driving along, alone, wondering how I could step into Mother's room calmly. The thought of losing her was overwhelming. Then, as though God were physically in the car with me, he spoke to me through words Mother had taught me, "I know whom I have believed, and I am sure that he is able to guard until that Day what has been entrusted to me." With calmness, even joy, I greeted Mother and visited with her that day.

After six weeks in the hospital, Mother came to our parsonage, bringing her nurse with her. The nurse would come laughing into the living room saying, "She's just like a young girl, so full of fun and jokes."

Oscar, then a United States congressman, stopped by almost

daily, as did Luther. During this time Luther was running for district judge and often talked with Mother about his situation. With his legal training he had been a great help in getting her finances organized after Dad died, and the repartee between them was always lively. Today, however, he was burdened with the gambling interests that were spending a great deal of money to defeat him. He was worried about the votes. Mother turned to him from her bed and said, "You will win the election, Luther, but that isn't the most important thing. The most important thing is how much you'll permit the Lord to use you to win souls for Jesus Christ."

At one of the first prayer breakfasts he attended in Washington, Judge Luther shared this experience as one of the important motivations behind his efforts on behalf of the mentally ill in Minnesota, his fight against slot machines, and his concern for youth. Displayed in the most conspicuous place available in the homes he has lived in has been one of Mother's last gifts to him—a large, somber picture of Munkacsy's *Christ before Pilate*, a constant reminder of Mother's compelling words.

One Sunday evening while Mother lay ill at our home, a call came from Marshalltown, Iowa, where Reuben was serving in his first pastorate. Dad and Mother had had the joy of seeing him installed as the shepherd of that flock. But Reuben's news today was not good. In giving birth to a nine-pound baby boy his wife Ruth had suffered convulsions. Both mother and child were almost lost, but now the doctor felt Ruth would recover. The baby, however, had died and was to be buried Wednesday. Since Mother's bedroom door was open, she heard our end of the conversation. She got out of bed and came to the phone. After speaking words of comfort to Reuben, she turned to us and said, "Always I have been able to go when my children have needed me. This time you will have to go for me."

As we talked it over, Clarence explained his situation to Mother. Our church had been in a basement for 11 years. Although these were depression days, the Lord had definitely directed us to go ahead with building the upper structure. Wednesday was the kickoff dinner, the key to the daring adventure. How could he leave at a time like this? Mother responded, "Clarence, do you think God is dependent on your being at that dinner to work his will? This unexpected need he knows about. I am very sure that if you will go to bring comfort, your faith in God's power to direct will be rewarded. I need you to go for me."

So we went, Clarence and I, Irene (Luther's wife), and Livia (Ben's wife), taking in the car the floral covering Mother had personally ordered for the little coffin.

The Arlington Hills congregation stood the test of faith. The members conducted their meeting without their pastor, praying for him as he did the errand which Mother had requested. Despite the depression, they went over their goal. Today the church stands as a monument to the faith of people who wanted to worship God in a place of beauty.

On our return from the simple, beautiful commitment of this newborn baby into his heavenly Father's hands, Mother had to hear every detail. We shared with her the undergirding of faith this young mother and father had borne witness to, and her heart was glad.

From then on, Mother failed rapidly. There were many nights that we thought would be her last with us on earth. The family came and went with a devotion the nurses constantly commented on. Jonathan and David often slipped into her bedroom and stood by her side, lisping their Sunday school songs for her: "Jesus loves me! This I know, for the Bible tells me so," or "Jesus bids us shine with a clear, pure light." When I came to take them away, Mother said, "Don't. I love them, and they're singing for me. They are so close to their heavenly Father."

Often at midnight, when Clarence and I quietly made our way to her bedside for devotions, she would say, "Sing." We sang one hymn after another, sometimes for as long as an hour at a time: "Jesus, Savior, Pilot Me," "Come Ye Disconsolate," and "O Safe to the Rock That Is Higher Than I." Always the faith of these songs' message eased her breathing, and we then tiptoed out to get some rest. Once when we were all together around her bed, the eight of her ten children still living, she looked at each of us and said, "You aren't all my children. You can't be. I'm not that old." Nor was her heart, only her body.

The last weeks of Mother's illness came during a record-breaking heat wave. The thermometer hit 100 every day for a month.

On one of those insufferable nights, Clarence and I took a drive along the river bluff in hope of catching a bit of a breeze. Observing the park boulevards literally covered with sleeping forms, Clarence commented, "It is almost as if Calcutta, with its street poor bedded down on sidewalk and boulevard, has taken over Minnesota's proud capital city."

The crowning experience of Mother's valedictory days was ours as a complete family circle. We were called to her bedside from near and far and gathered around, watching her trying to get her breath with the aid of an oxygen tent. She indicated to the nurse to remove the apparatus, and we witnessed a miracle. She sat up in bed—her beautiful white hair crowning that strong face with the wrinkles etched by her quick sense of humor; those blue, blue eyes, reminiscent of the lakes and oceans she loved so well and capable of looking right through you—and we heard her voice, clear, strong, and unwavering, singing as she looked at each of us in turn, "God Be With You Till We Meet Again." Even now I can hear her crescendo on the chorus. "Till we meet, till we meet at Jesus' feet. God be with you till we meet again." She could sing with such confidence at this reunion because she knew the way of salvation which she had taught to us:

> *Just as I am, without one plea*
> *But that thy blood was shed for me,*
> *And that thou bidd'st me come to thee,*
> *O Lamb of God, I come, I come.*

This had been her favorite hymn.

As real as the oxygen tent pulled aside from her bed was the glimpse we had that day of a "land that is fairer than day." It shone with radiance on Mother's face; it drew us as we saw the look in her eyes; we heard it in the confident ring of her voice. The window of heaven opened to fill the room with a golden glow, and we could but wish our beloved, fun-loving, generous, big-hearted mother the prospect of a grand reunion where there would be no more partings. With the words, "Just as I am, without one plea, but that thy blood was shed for me," she put her hand in Christ's hand and, bidding us do the same, looked forward to the time when we would all be together again. Not long after the

98

thin veil parted, and she knew the complete joy of having accepted the Savior's invitation to come. The best is yet to be.

Not always is it given to those left behind to see a glimpse of the glory ahead for our loved ones. Sometimes we can only stand helplessly by through agonizing days and weeks as the soul releases itself from the body's shell. How grateful we were to God for sparing us this, and for drawing the veil of heaven apart for a moment that we might glimpse the glory beyond.

When my parents' estate was distributed, Mabel took her small share, and she and Al bought out a dime store in the village of Moose Lake. They rented a log cabin on Sand Lake as a temporary home and invited us to come and spend a week. At the idyllic beauty of the place Clarence exclaimed, "Oh, how I wish we could own a place just like this, a perfect vacation retreat for a growing family like ours!"

"Why not?" Mabel responded. "What would you be willing to offer the owner?"

As a joke and with no money to back it up, Clarence said, "Oh, $650, but that's a silly, unrealistic figure." But Mabel was dead serious and said she'd talk to the farmer that week and be in touch with us. A postcard in the next day's mail said, "It's yours at the price you name." Clarence visited Mr. Bloomquist at the bank, saying, "Is my face good for money like that?"

"Indeed it is," replied Mr. Bloomquist. "It's an honest one." In no time at all, Clarence had a check in hand.

What a new dimension this opened for us. A property all our own, a log cabin. Clarence could putter around and improve it, and it was a healthy vacation spot for our children to enjoy. Clarence choose the name *Koja*, a Swedish word signifying a humble cabin in the woods. Today, thinking of the 40 years of great experiences and memories clustered about this cottage, $650 was a tiny price to pay!

Our hearts were also gladdened and our lives enriched by the birth of a daughter on May 14, 1937. I wanted this lass to carry Mother's name, but Clarence thought it would be better that she carry mine. We compromised with Elizabeth Ruth. Imagine my astonishment at the baptismal font in hearing Clarence as the officiating pastor say, "I now baptize you Ruth Elizabeth. . . ." He claims it was a mere slip of the tongue!

Her brothers couldn't quite manage "Elizabeth," so it came out "Bizabeth," and then just "Biz." As she grew, she became a constant tagalong behind Jon and Dave. One day a neighbor across the street was burning leaves when a gust of wind blew sparks onto two-year-old Biz's coveralls and they started to burn. Six-year-old Jon put out the fire in the burning cloth with his bare hands and ran home with her. Her knee was burned, but she might have been consumed. Taking her in my arms, I rocked her and sang, "We Went to the Animal Fair," over and over until the doctor came and administered medication to ease the pain. We didn't know the value of the application of ice water in those days. The burn scar on Biz's knee is only one of many she acquired before she grew up.

At an early age the children also had an experience with deliberate human cruelty. We had bought them Easter rabbits, and their dad made a hutch for them on the empty lot behind our house. The boys lovingly fed these little creatures and watched them grow. One day, however, they came running home sobbing. "They killed our bunnies; they killed our bunnies." Some older schoolboys passing the lot thought it was sport to put the rabbits to death. Jon sobbed, "The bunnies weren't hurting anybody! Why did they kill them?" What can a mother answer?

At Arlington Hills we encountered many hurdles in constructing the church's superstructure. First there was a lath and plasterers' strike, then a sash and door workers' strike. For weeks there was no progress. However, once the workers were back on the job, the superstructure rapidly took form. Clarence kept a constant vigil. The day the mammoth steel girders for the vaulted roof were put in place, Clarence stopped by late in the evening to check the progress. He climbed high into the steel girders and stood silhouetted by a full moon, praising God. A passing police car stopped and the officers emerged, demanding to know what this prowler was up to. Clarence did some fast talking that night.

Finally the superstructure was completed. The morning of Dedication Sunday, the day Clarence had worked so hard for, we were at breakfast as a family. After reading the scripture lessons, Clarence began the usual family prayer. Then his voice broke, and he wept uncontrollably from sheer joy. This emotional high persisted through all those festal days.

Another daughter, a wee lass, was born May 20, 1940, and spent her first few days in an incubator. We named her Mary, thinking just as the biblical relationship between Jonathan and David was beautiful, so was the relationship between Elizabeth and Mary. So quickly did she make up for her slow start that when she was only two weeks old she attended Lorraine's graduation from Gustavus Adolphus in a basket.

Lorraine had experienced some great years at Gustavus. Each summer she sought out jobs to cover her tuition. Sometimes this meant scrubbing floors and acting as governess to overpampered children, which tested her mettle, but she never gave up. A crisis arose late in her college years when she began experiencing puzzling blackouts. The school doctor raised the possibility of epilepsy—a horrid word to a young woman. I, however, scoffed at this and drove with Lorraine to Rochester for exhaustive examinations at the Mayo Clinic. They felt the problem was not epilepsy but was an emotional problem rooted somewhere in Lorraine's psyche from the trauma of losing her parents, a stretched-out hysteria from unresolved fears and deep anxieties. Their prescription: plenty of rest and, above all, knowledge that she had security and love.

On Lorraine's graduation day the whole family drove down to enjoy the festivities that go with getting a college diploma. Home afterwards to pack her things in preparation for taking her first job as a college graduate, Lorraine looked at the pile of boxed belongings, then suddenly turned to me and asked, perplexed, "But where will I store all this stuff?"

"Why, right here with us," I answered. "Lorraine, this is your home for as long as you and we live." Suddenly tears flowed and Lorraine buried herself in my arms to weep away the last vestige of that tight knot of inner fear.

After college she became Reuben's first parish worker at Mount Olivet, making calls on her bicycle. Later she received a call to go into student work on the Iowa State campus and later still at Iowa University.

During those years at Arlington Hills we had to watch our pennies, but we never really lacked. Our children were well clothed, even though some of their best garments were hand-me-downs from cousins and friends. So usual was this that on the rare occasions when we purchased new outfits for them, they would merrily chant, "Brand new, brand new."

We did many things as a family. Whenever we entertained guests, the children kept their places at the table and enjoyed the visitors along with us. Often as not the guests would be missionaries, and we saw to it that the children got drawn into the conversation, eliciting stories of interest, making them an integral part of the event. Folks from such far-off places as Africa, India, Japan, and Australia had the choicest stories to tell, delighting our little ones.

It was from the Magnolia Street parsonage that the boys started school. How blessed they were with their first teachers. Angelo Patri, that great educator, once said, "If I were a millionaire, I would endow every kindergarten and first-grade teacher, for the start children get in school can well set the tone for the rest of their education." One teacher especially stood out—Miss Lamb (she was aptly named). In her classroom at Halloween there were pumpkin-face cookies, and at Christmas pretty little frosted Christmas tree cookies.

Our children also were taught at home. Clarence and I wanted them to learn that Christmas was a time for giving, for remembering people because we were remembering Christ's birthday. So we made a list of the old people in our church and baked Christmas cookies for them. Clarence got metal cans used for film reels, never considering how many cookies it took to fill each, and he enlisted the children's help to paint them—some blue, some green. They painted a star, candle, pine tree, or angel on each cover. I provided the filling—lots of cookies. Clarence and I commandeered every container in the house to protect them from the little human mice who found them so tempting. Finally, with paper-lace doilies lining them, the cans were filled and ready, and we had our list in hand. We waited for the children to return from school so together we could sing carols for the folks as we presented our

102

gifts. The old folks appreciated our visit, especially the children's singing. And our children learned the true meaning of Christmas.

We never asked the children, "What do you want Santa to bring you for Christmas?" No commercialism in our home. Yet one day I weakened and took them to the train department of a toy shop to see their Christmas display. They loved watching those trains. That night little Jon prayed, "And please, God, if I get two trains for Christmas, help me to give one to the poor."

Some of our best times together were family prayer times, particularly after the evening meal when each child added his own prayer. In the quiet of one such prayer time, a dog was heard barking in the distance. Jon prayed, "Bless all the dogs who haven't got a home," and then added, with true missionary fervor, "and all the folks who speak Swedish."

Their bedtime prayers often included some pastoral concerns Clarence and I must have shared in their hearing (little missed their keen ears). One night Mary prayed, "And bless, please God, Grandma Anderson. I kinda think you ought to take her to your home in heaven. But you know best. For whether she stays here with us or goes to heaven, she's with you." Another night when Mary had been bathed and tucked into her crib, together Clarence and I bent over her crib to hear her prayers. There were the usual petitions covering family and friends, but on this night she added, "Bless Daddy when he preaches and Momma when she stays home."

Clarence's description of our Arlington Hills days helps explain Mary's prayer and also clearly shows that it was not always smooth sailing.

Ruth was widely known for her ability as a speaker to lift the sights and challenge her listeners and so was eagerly sought after. When it was mother and daughter banquet time, this meant many evenings out for her, but never at the price of family neglect. Story time and prayers were simply moved to an earlier hour. At one mother-daughter banquet at a neighboring church, our Biz was deemed big enough to sit beside her mother at the speaker's table. She behaved beautifully during the meal and the usual preliminaries, but when Ruth, responding to her introduction, rose to speak, Biz vocally objected to the well-meaning gesture of a motherly soul on Ruth's other side who reached to take Biz in her arms. Ruth had no way out other than to take Biz in her arms for the whole talk. Biz blossomed under the attention this meant. Nor was the Madonna picture the two made at the front lost on the audience.

I hope I haven't given you the idea that our marriage adjustments came easy. There were some ugly times, times that admittedly the mist of years has softened. Ruth was generous beyond most women, but I would sometimes fault her for impulse buying when it came to groceries. I felt we ought to live more simply. Yet we never had steaks. We had to be content with hamburger. We had to keep close to our budget. An unexpected car repair bill or clothing purchase could shoot the works.

Accordingly, if there were "words," it would most often come from my pressing too hard. I remember with bitter regret that time driving toward downtown when Ruth demanded that I stop the car right there and let her get out and walk. She'd make her own way home. Moments like this were horrid, and more than we could endure. We both were endowed with strong wills. There were explosions and bitter exchanges of words. Oh, how good it felt when afterwards we fell into each other's arms, contritely asking the other for forgiveness. Then there would well up a prayer for God's forgiveness that restored the beautiful relationship that otherwise marked our home.

Another time I recall with regret is our visit to the Minnesota State Fair those St. Paul years. All the children were with us, loving the day. But I was grumping about Ruth insisting on a treat which, multiplied by six, took a deep bite out of my pocket. I was walking clammed up and sullen when a candid cameraman snapped several shots, offering to send us the finished pictures for a mere quarter. I took him up. That picture I claimed afterwards was valuable beyond the gold of India since it tellingly brought home what someone put so well when he said, "We're not responsible for our physical frame or features, but we are responsible for our faces." A frown so easily freezes on our faces. And doesn't it take twice as much muscle power to frown as to smile? Some favorite lines we both love go like this:

> God give me sympathy and sense,
> and help me keep my courage high!
> God give me calm and confidence,
> and, please, a twinkle in my eye (Anon.).

104

Now I look back with bitter regret that those ugly chapters ever had to be. No doubt they left scars on our children, unwilling witnesses to these ugly scenes.

I'm ashamed to put in words some of the defense mechanisms I contrived when there was an argument. "But Ruth, you make your points sound so convincing because you had all that training in public debate at Gustavus . . . I'm at a disadvantage." Then again I would just clam up and this would drive Ruth to distraction, these long, self-pitying spells of my silences. How hard it is for a male to say those little words, "I'm sorry. I'm in the wrong. Please forgive me." To my shame, it was mostly Ruth who came up with them first.

God invaded our home again and again with the freshness of joy through his Holy Spirit, and the ugly moments came to be fewer and farther between, for which we gave him praise. I give God all the credit for saving our marriage and making the bonds of love stronger than tempered steel. We have often asked each other, "How do people who have left God entirely out of their lives make it at all?"

An old Swedish proverb beautifully describes Ruth's and my love: "Gamal karlek rostar aldrig men den rostar ihop," which, translated, means "true love never rusts except to rust together."

Then came the Sunday when three fine-looking strangers were ushered into Arlington Hill's worship, a Duluth delegation come to look over a possible candidate for their pastorless church. Soon an intensive campaign began to keep us in St. Paul. But we felt a strange pull to the colorful port city on the shores of Lake Superior. Both of us loved water. Hadn't we spent our honeymoon on the North Shore? And we usually managed a week's vacation each year there. While she was alive, Mother would go with us—she loved to bathe in those cold waters. The rockbound coast and wooded shores reminded her so much of the Old Country.

Soon we were facing a call to Holy Trinity Church in Duluth. Hard as it was to leave the joy of worshiping in Arlington Hills' new superstructure and the many deep-rooted friendships, the adventure of a new beginning was impossible to resist. Although the salary offered no inducement, Holy Trinity presented a real challenge. The church structure was beautiful Tudor-Gothic architecture, but was heavily mortgaged, and the congregation had

105

stopped growing, competing with two other well-established Lutheran churches in the near vicinity. Clarence had high hopes for an inner renewal.

Our Arlington people, recovering from their initial disappointment at our leaving, gave us a farewell reception that overflowed with people and flowery encomiums. Each organization had a party. Although tearing up those deep roots was painful, we eagerly anticipated our new challenge. Before school started on the day we moved, Miss Lamb appeared at our home with a boxful of goodies for the children to have on the trip. The thoughtfulness of this action was characteristic of the great teachers who gave our boys such a good start.

Soon the moving van was at our St. Paul door, and we were packed up and on our way to Duluth.

DULUTH AND THE WAR YEARS

8

We loved our Duluth parsonage built by a lumber baron and standing high up from the sidewalk. The large bay window in the dining room was topped by a beveled glass panel so when the sun shown through, a rainbow of dancing colors reflected on the carpet. One of those very first mornings Biz was up early when suddenly she shouted, "Mom, Dad, look! Fairies are dancing all over!" Of course, we came running to see the dancing lights formed by the glass prisms.

Just off our master bedroom was a little alcove dressing room that connected with another bedroom. Here we installed baby Mary's crib. This gave her a sense of security since we were close by, yet it also permitted us privacy. We could have our window open even in winter without chilling her. At bedtime the children gathered about Mary's crib and we sang together, "Jesus, Tender Shepherd, Hear Me."

The house's third-floor apartment had a large central room with cushioned benches built against each wall and built-in bookshelves. The gabled windows afforded a generous view of Duluth's west side and the St. Louis River just beyond. Clarence immediately settled on this as his study. Board members questioned its practicality, feeling two flights of stairs could prove too much, but running those stairs afforded good exercise. Since our one phone was in the front entryway on the first floor, it did mean a lot of running, but our strained budget simply didn't allow for a second phone.

The third floor also had a bedroom with gabled windows off to the side. The boys begged for this room. Their bunk beds fit nicely into its abbreviated space.

We loved the location at the edge of Lincoln Park with its stream and wooded ravine. In the winter a skating rink was flooded to provide many fun family times on the ice. The children's public school was just the other side of the ravine. They could hear the burbling creek as they skipped across the bridge and made their way through the wooded park. Although the children keenly sensed the loss of their St. Paul playmates and the disruption from the familiar school, the hurts soon healed as they plunged into activities and met new friends.

Clarence and I became deeply involved with Holy Trinity's youth and its large confirmation classes. He continuously visited current members, prospective members, and the sick and shut-in. Often I went along, thoroughly enjoying visiting with young and old alike.

Although I realized the importance of such calls, I refused to let Clarence become a stranger to his children. "Clarence," I'd say, "we're going for a picnic supper tonight. You can pick up your calls afterwards when I'm putting the children to bed." Armed with loaded food baskets and blankets, we'd be off to our favorite cove on Superior's rocky shore or up to the heights of Enger Park where we roasted wieners, skipped stones, and played ball.

One lovely spring morning I was up with the sun and announced as the children came bouncing down for breakfast, "Today is so nice we're going to make it a holiday and drive to the cabin for a day at the lake. I suspect your teachers would think you've got a crazy mother to let you skip school for such a reason." As we hurried out to the car, chubby-cheeked Davy grinned and said, "I love you crazy, Mom!"

108

We continued our practice of taking birthday cakes to senior citizens in our church. Many mornings found me in our kitchen putting the finishing touches on a cake, the children happily licking the frosting bowl. More often than not one would ask, "Mommy, which Grandma's birthday is it today?"

Saturday was cleaning day, and all the children had an appointed job. Sometimes I would ask one to do an extra job. This particular day when I asked Jon, "Son, would you like to empty the wastepaper basket?" he answered, "Mother, don't ask me, 'Would you like to.' Just say, 'Empty the wastebasket.'"

"No, Jon," I replied. "If you wouldn't like to be that helpful, I don't want you to do it."

Saturday night when the house was scrubbed clean and so was I, I got into clean nightclothes and slipped between clean sheets, experiencing physically the sensation my soul has when all the dirt of sin has been removed by the forgiveness of God and I sense the fresh fragrance of the indwelling of his Holy Spirit. Spiritually we need not wait for Saturday night; the feeling is ours daily for the asking.

The Nelson family in 1944

A good part of our Duluth years were invested in the wider circle of the city. Clarence did a stint as officer of every citywide church organization, including the Lutheran Ministerial Association. We also did our share of services at Lake Shore and Afton Ro homes for the aged. The beautiful reed organ that graces our Sand Lake cabin came as the result of services we gave at the Afton Ro Home. After one of the services an elderly couple asked if we might want their reed organ. It had been ordered removed from the home's dayroom as the space was needed. We loved them for this gift which has sparked so many family and neighborhood sings.

Holy Trinity grew by leaps and bounds. The Sunday school took on new life under the leadership of hard working, idea-hatching John Morris. We hired a bus to bring in Sunday school children, scouring the Heights as well as Minnesota Point with its deteriorating waterfront housing. The bus rolled up to the church each Sunday crowded to the doors.

About this time Aunt Ruth, Reuben's wife, was found to have tuberculosis and was placed in a sanatorium. We prayed for her every night. One night, however, her name was omitted from the prayer and Biz came to me after our "Amen" almost in tears, pleading, "Mother, we haven't helped Aunt Ruth yet." To her, praying was synonymous with helping. Her faith was rewarded, for in a year's time Aunt Ruth was restored to her family, able to live a rich, full life.

Both Clarence and I kept a fast pace. I helped him with his calls, my speaking commitments continued to increase, and I was responsible for maintaining our big house plus providing for the needs of our growing family. Sometimes the obstacles seemed almost insurmountable. However, whenever I appeared downcast, one of the children would inevitably come to me and say, "We've prayed about it, haven't we? Why are you worried then?"

I was also invited to do the Children's Bible Story Hour on the radio each week. Believing that children have universal appeal, I drew our children into the program. They asked the questions that drew out the story, then I made applications to fit everyday life. This required the discipline of daily rehearsals, usually at bedtime. Yet the efforts were well worth it, for the response from people across the board—Protestant, Catholic, and Jew—was unbelievable. The musical signature was a violin setting of the much-loved hymn, "Children of the Heavenly Father," composed by Carl Youngdahl.

We all worked hard, yet never were the worse for it. One evening when Clarence and I had returned home from a church function, we found a note from Jon, who had been left in charge, on the stairs. It read: "Folks, wake me up as soon as you get home. I've an urgent message!" Shaking him awake from a deep sleep, we received the message: "I love you."

Another evening when we returned home, Jon greeted us with, "We're so sorry. It was all an accident. Dave and I were wrestling around for fun and the vase fell off the stand. But, Mom, you always say, 'No soul was lost.'" Although it was our heirloom vase, we didn't scold. Clarence simply took the pieces to mend. We believed our home was to be lived in. No room, including the parlor, was ever "off limits."

Our Duluth years coincided with the tragic years of World War II. The choicest of Trinity's youth went off to camps, each departure bringing pain and heartbreak to parents, brothers, and sisters. Determined to keep regular contact with these youth, now scattered over the United States, Europe, and the Pacific, Clarence personally answered each of their letters and also sent a monthly church newsletter. We invited every lad or lass home on furlough to a lunch of waffles, not ordinary fare in the armed services. We served a wide variety of waffles—a special favorite was apple-cinnamon. Because we were close to blueberry country, we had our own blueberry jam and syrup. Thoughtful friends gave us unused meat coupons that we squirreled away so we could buy a sizable portion of bacon or sausage links for these lunches.

Our delighted guests ate zestfully, but the food was the least important aspect of the occasion as they related their experiences and we shared our faith in God and our hopes for peace. There was Bob who was stationed in the Aleutians; Chuck, the marine from Okinawa who had eaten raw crow while awaiting rescue and who never returned from his next assignment; and Harold, in the air force, who loved flying: "It was as if we could reach out our hands and touch God's face as we soared above the clouds.

111

How inconsequential earthly concerns seemed up there," he said. Harold didn't come back either, but we could comfort his widowed mother by sharing the statement Harold made at our table: "Whether I live, or whether I die, I am the Lord's." When his personal effects reached his mother's home, among them was his well-marked Bible. Two verses of Psalm 139 were heavily underlined: "If I take the wings of the morning, and dwell in the uttermost parts of the sea; even there thy hand shall lead me, and thy right hand shall hold me." Clearly written in the margin was the date of Harold's last flight.

Forty-six of these fine boys never came home. The memorial services came one upon another as blue star after blue star turned to gold on our church service flag. As Clarence put it, "War is certainly a form of international madness, a throwback to barbarism, creating in its aftermath ever so many more grievous problems than those it set out to resolve."

During the war, the national church sought experienced pastors to minister to new communities that had mushroomed up at shipbuilding and naval installations on the West Coast. Reuben responded and urged Clarence to do likewise. Both took three-month sabbaticals and took to the rails, Rube to a San Diego suburb, Clarence to the north of Vallejo. Many of the people he ministered to were "Okies," people uprooted by the dust bowl that drought had made of their farms in Oklahoma and adjoining western lands. Reuben's work was largely with the families of United States Navy personnel. He was immediately master of the situation, hiring a sound truck to go up and down the street, personally inviting people to the school auditorium where he held worship services. Clarence took a crowded bus to visit him on location and thrilled to what he had been able to accomplish in so short a time. He surely had mastered the techniques of reaching people with the gospel.

During those three months, I "kept store" for Clarence at Holy Trinity, arranging for guest preachers at the church and responding to calls for help and counseling. The children and I kept up the weekly radio program, and the time sped past. One weekend Dr. Emil Swenson, president of our synod, was to preach and be our houseguest. I asked four-year-old Mary to show him to his

112

room so I could get dinner ready. When he came down, he was full of chuckles. After Mary had gone out to play, he told me that she had climbed on the bed and, jumping up and down, said to him, "I like to snuggle, do you?" We all missed Clarence. It was a great day when he returned.

That Christmas the ground was beautiful with its white covering of snow. We often joined our young people on crisp December evenings to carol for shut-ins. We piled out of the cars at each stop and somebody would begin the song, "Winds Through the Olive Trees." Other voices would join in sweet, simple harmony as the story of that first Christmas came from our lips in song. We could see our breath in the cold air, but our hearts were warm under our mackinaws as we saw candles lit in others' hearts in response to the message of the Light of the world.

Christmas during the war years afforded ample opportunity to share with others. We were angered by the injustices endured by our Japanese-American citizens after Pearl Harbor when they were herded into concentration camps and dispossessed of homes and property. Through the Duluth Council of Churches we learned of some young men in this predicament who could be released to fill jobs if these were available and if sponsors could be obtained. Fortunately a bean sprout industry was being launched in Duluth, so jobs were available, and we readily agreed to sponsor the young men. They came to us at Christmas and became part of the family. We had great fun shopping for their Christmas gifts: warm scarves and fur-lined gloves to shield them from Duluth's cold.

At "tree time" that Christmas Eve we read the incomparable Christmas story, each member of the family taking a portion. Our guests were completely attentive and joined us in singing the carols as best they could. In the prayers that followed, our children prayed on behalf of these new friends, for their families from whom they were separated, for their work and their housing, and thanked God that they had come to us.

Next came the distribution of the gifts. Jon, Dave, Biz, and Mary pointed eagerly to the gifts for the new friends as the ones to be opened first. The truth of the scripture, "It is more blessed to give than receive," was clearly demonstrated by the joy shining

113

on their faces as they watched their new friends open the gifts. These new brothers also went Christmas caroling with us to the shut-ins.

They soon found work and rooms of their own, but they often joined us for Sunday dinners and for happy family times. In the spring we picnicked on the rocky shores of Gitche Gumee, and the children shared some of America's origin as they told of the beautiful Indian people to whom our land first belonged. As we watched the sun set, we sat in quiet meditation, worshiping. Our friends reveled in the bountiful beauty of the north country. After the war ended, we rejoiced with them that they could return to their homes, but we hated to see them leave.

Living through the war years with our growing family was sometimes difficult due to gas rationing, sugar and meat stamps, and the curtailment of the free-flowing life-style we had known. We quickly learned, however, that ours were but minor inconveniences compared to the problems of thousands of homeless, beleaguered people left in the war's devastating wake.

Ben was assigned under the United Nations Relief and Rehabilitation Agency (UNRRA) to Europe for a year to assess the people's needs and recommend what help should be extended. Clarence's brother Cliff was on a similar assignment for the Lutheran church. The letters each wrote told of indescribable suffering and need. The question arose around our family table, "Isn't there something *we* can do to help?" The boys, even at their young years, had paper routes and immediately proposed that they tithe their income. The rest was to go into their educational fund. We wrote to Uncle Cliff asking him to recommend a family we could contact.

Cliff sent us the name of Pfarrer Polster, a minister who had been forced to flee from his beautiful home in Dresden with his wife and eight children because they would not go along with the Hitler regime. When Pfarrer Polster refused to nail to the door of his church the government decree denouncing the Jews, he became a marked man. Fearing for their lives, he and his family moved out in the dark of night, carrying what essentials they could gather, and headed west. The story of their trek through unknown terrain, entirely dependent on the help they could get from others nearly as troubled as they for food, witnesses to the reality of God's everlasting love and protection.

Finally they settled in Rohracker, the refugee section of Stuttgart. This city, too, bore the scars of bombing. Rubble and destruction were everywhere. Theirs was a cramped upstairs apartment of an old stone dwelling, but faith, love, and trust made the quarters beautiful. It was reminiscent of the story told by the director of relief for the World Council of Churches about an American tourist who exclaimed to a little girl in a refugee camp, "Oh, you poor thing! Isn't it too bad you don't have a home!" To which the lass quickly replied, "Oh, but we do. We have a beautiful home. We just don't have a house to put it in." Polsters' was such a home. It was at this home that our first packages arrived, just in time for Christmas. Their response was heartwarming:

Dear friends,

How wretched are my words! If I could tell you in the German language how my heart feels! You have presented us with food and clothes and with your love. A love that is crossing the ocean, from person to person, joined by Jesus Christus. Humbly we clasp hands and pray 1. Mose 32, 11 [Gen. 32:10]. It is an amazement in our eyes that the Lord presented us such faithful friends by Christus. Those who really do not leave us, and again and again spend money and goods, time and work for us, and make us such a joy, and help us bear hunger and coldness.

You don't believe how much force and hope this joy gives us. Those fine, warm clothes! What great help in winter. Our children will thank you themselves after Christmas, for now, we don't show them anything. Oh, they will be astonished when there is a Christmas table with coffee, cocoa, cake, raisins, chicken and rice. Your love makes us a rich present-table. My husband is happy over the cloth. It fits quite well. I am so glad over the sewing bag with its precious contents of needles, elastic, and thread. The knitted jacket is wandering property. The one who is cold may wear it.

Oh, you dear Christians, how shall we parents thank you for your presenting joy to our children at Christmas! I had been a little afraid for the festival of love, as it had been so cold and sad for us, since the Russians wasted our country.

A blessed Christmas and a very happy new year, we all wish upon you.

Yours very grateful,
Johannes Polster
Annelies Polster

Then, after Christmas came letters such as this one from the children:

Dear friends,

Since we left our home, we had not thought of getting anything to Christmas. When our little sister asked in church, "Is not the Christ-child at home?" we answered, "No, it doesn't come to fugitives." But to our great surprise, Mother said, "Yes, it is at home now." We wouldn't understand what this mean. And at home there had been a Christ-child, a real one sent by your love. If we looked at each other's eyes, they sparkled always. It was a wonderful delight. Of the white flour, of Jonathan's Care Package we baked a white bread and spred gelee on it. This looked quite as those of the American soldiers.

I've got the black dress, which enjoys me so much, as I shall be confirmed in three months. . . . A giant joy you made us with the rice and chicken. You can't imagine how well this tastes.

In gratitude,
Irmtrand Polster

Each of the children's letters echoed love and gratitude.

Through this international experience, our growing children learned the awful ignominy of war, the ashes, devastation, and blighted lives it leaves, and became sensitive to the needs of unfortunates close around them as well.

Other lessons were also learned during those all-important growing-up years. One day the children received a beautiful white-and-tan mottled cocker spaniel with feathered paws, shipped to them as a gift from Lorraine. Lorraine had moved to Iowa City to be director of the Lutheran Student Center at the University of Iowa. The children, beside themselves with joy, named the little puppy Spreckles. We tried to keep her in the house when she was in heat because male dogs surrounded our house. Clarence counted

116

17 at one time, all shapes and sizes. So we took Spreckles to the veterinarian to be spayed. Either from the operation or from eating some chicken bones, one day Spreckles began to bleed internally. We took her to a nearby animal hospital, and a heavy pall settled over our home. A few days later while I was working with the boys in my Scout den, the phone rang. Jon ran to answer it. The word was that Spreckles had died. Childish tears and trauma followed, but Spreckles had taught the children the dark fact of death.

Although I hadn't been too enthusiastic about having a dog to begin with, now I melted, and we looked for a replacement for Spreckles. We found another cocker (not a purebred), a male we named Puffer. He would run alongside the boys on their bikes and had a great time on the Duluth hills. One winter afternoon we had been out calling and didn't get home until after five. Evening came early this time of year, and it was dusk. As we turned on to our street, we could hardly believe our eyes. In the snow at the side of the street was little Dave, sobbing, his arms around the dead body of his beloved dog. A neighbor had not seen the dog in the dusk and, as Puffer dashed out, had run over him. Another tragedy, and again the tears.

Again I melted when the boys read in the paper about cocker pups for sale. They wanted to buy one out of their paper route money. They picked a roly-poly bundle of brown fur with his eyes hardly opened, and they named him Ole. That night we attended a "long-dress" wedding at the church, leaving the children to make their new pet at home. When we returned, the children were very disturbed. The little puppy had whimpered the whole time we were gone. Their dad sensed that the pup missed his mother, so we heated an old-fashioned iron, wrapped a piece of woolly blanket around it, and held it next to the pup. It worked like magic. Soon he was sleeping as soundly as if in his mother's embrace.

Ole turned out to be a Heinz 57 variety, part cocker, part golden retriever, with an orange plume on his head and a real personality. One day a neighbor discarded a deer's head in the alley garbage can. Another neighbor thought she had lost her mind when she looked out her window and saw a dog's body attached to a deer's

117

head. Ole had tried to get some meat left inside the head and then couldn't extricate himself.

The Duluth days were growing-up days for our children, but sometimes we wondered if they'd ever make it. Biz had more than her share of escapes. One day she was riding handlebar on her brother's bike and her foot got caught in the front wheel, cutting it down to the bone. Another time she was riding in the backseat as her Sunday school teacher was driving along the skyline drive. The car swung around a corner, throwing Biz against the door handle. The door flew open, and Biz flew out, scraping along the gravel road. She was a bloody-looking gal after that mishap. The doctor had to use a brush to clean out the gravel, and her forehead still bears the telltale marks.

Childhood accidents occurred at Koja too. One day when we were at the lake, I was brushing my hair when I heard Biz cry out. Rushing outside, I saw blood flowing from her mouth. She had been getting into the car, slipped, and caught her lip on the corner of the door. We rushed into town to the doctor who took two stitches to close the wound.

Dave had his scrapes too. Our neighbors had a pump a block away from which we got our drinking water. Somehow or other he got his thumb caught in the mechanics of it and tore off the fingernail. Another day they were playing King of the Raft. Dave was going to be smart, go under the raft, and pop up on the other side. But something sharp under the raft cut his head open, and it took 12 stitches to close it. It's good we have our children when we're young ourselves.

One day I was having some women friends in for coffee at Koja and sent the boys across the bay to fetch Florence Cassel to come along. The boys made no protest; it meant using the boat with the new motor they'd purchased with their hard-earned paper route money. As they neared the other shore, a sudden surge of power unhooked the motor, and with a slurp and some bubbling, it sank to the bottom. Jon took a quick sighting of the approximate location and then, each grabbing an oar, they headed for home.

Jon sought out his father to break the bad news. Unmindful of the self-castigation he and David had already endured, Clarence ripped into him, "What carelessness! Why didn't you fasten the chain before starting out?" Jon turned from the fusillade, broke into sobs, and ran to embrace Ole. However badly he'd messed things up, he still had one friend who would not abandon him. Later Clarence commented, "If only we could have a trial run in raising kids and could crunch up and throw away that first crude attempt to begin all afresh."

Clarence recovered enough to go with the boys to identify the spot. Then they hurried to town to have the blacksmith fashion a long-handled iron rake, but this was too heavy. Next they had him make a set of grappling hooks, but weeds made it impossible to pull the hooks through. On each day that followed they set aside some time to probe for the motor using a simple wooden pole with an iron point at its end. They found an assorted collection of old bedsteads and rubber tires, but no motor. On our last Sunday at the lake, after coming home from church, they decided to have a final try while I cooked dinner. This time they felt metal. Dropping anchor, Clarence went down hand-over-hand along the pole to check it out. Success!—it was the propeller. Upon surfacing, he motioned for the coils of rope. Going down again, he tied the end with a firm knot around the propeller. When he got back into the boat, they hauled up the motor. The victory shout the two boys sent out would be hard to match. All around the bay folks hearing it said, "Those Nelson kids must have found their motor."

Koja offered a variety of fun: the crude diving tower we constructed from poles, that first float a neighbor gave us, forays into the deep woods for blueberries—healthy activities for our family. There also was the added joy of having family close by.

Mabel and Al owned the dime store in the nearby village. They were the ones who actually were responsible for so many of us driving down our tent stakes on these shores. Their spacious home in Moose Lake had room for us all to gather. Mabel was an inimitable hostess, jolly and loving. Her spreads were legendary, and her rippling laughter would pull the rip cords for all of us to be merry.

Reuben acquired a cabin just across the bay from us, close to the golf course. We spent a lot of time together those early years before he moved north and drove deep roots at Lutsen on Lake

Superior. There he developed the phenomenal Cathedral of the Pines youth camp. Often Rube drafted Clarence to preach or me to give an evening chapel talk there. I loved hearing the prayers of those youth as we sat quiet and bowed, closing our eyes on the incomparable view of the sun setting behind the pine-covered hills that rose abruptly from the shore. Probably Rube's greatest work was in raising up a whole generation of youth who learned to talk and walk intimately with their Lord on these hallowed grounds.

Ben and Livia also acquired a log cabin across the bay from us. We called theirs the beefsteak side and ours the hamburger side because we lacked a golf course. Electricity on our side was brought in by the Rural Electrification Administration, Ben's by Northern States Power. Our lights came on first, and we gave a party to celebrate. Then, at long last, came the day when the inside plumbing was installed. Luther, then Minnesota's governor, was driven down the narrow sylvan road to Koja in a sleek, black, chauffeur-driven limousine. The dedication of our inside plumbing included a clever speech by our neighbor, the Reverend Eric Gustafson, clever limericks by Ethel Lundgren, and a procession from the dilapidated "tooky" to the indoor facility. Governor Luther cut the ribbon, a lovely creation fashioned from a roll of toilet tissue. What a fun-loaded evening.

During his term of office Luther was satirically dubbed "The Sunday School Governor" because he refused to conform to the patterns and habits society expected of him. He refused to stand by and let organized gambling in the form of slot machines wind its enslaving tentacles around Minnesota youth. Because he stood up to these powerful, sinister interests in the name of humanity, he was for a time spurned by his own party. But Luther, like his grandfather, had an inner commitment to a higher power that made him know righteousness would win. Not, however, without a fight and a price.

One evening Reuben chided Lorraine that she ought to be thinking about getting married. When she asked, "Who will it be?" Rube named several very eligible young bachelor preachers. She declined, saying, "But Rube, there's no stardust." Rube's advice was, "Forget that stardust business!" We all laughed, but

120

I knew exactly what Lorraine meant and gave thanks to God that I had found mine.

All sorts of family fun exploded during our weeks at Koja, and it was always difficult to leave. But it was good to get back to our Duluth friends and Holy Trinity's many challenges. So much remained to be done there. However, one day, six years after our arrival in Duluth, Dr. Sig Engstrom, a neighbor at Sand Lake, sounded Clarence out about a call to Augustana in Washington, D.C. Clarence was disinterested, and he discouraged a visit to Washington feeling it would be a waste of their time and money. Still, at Dr. Engstrom's insistence, he presented the "feeler" to the board. He decided to make the trip to Washington only as a courtesy to give the Augustana congregation a chance to lay its proposition before him.

When his plane landed in Washington, Clarence was met at the airport by an interesting, intelligent young man who was extremely eager for Clarence to become the pastor of their church —"Washington's Little Cathedral." The caliber of the men serving on the board and their conviction that Augustana was greatly needed there in the capital, plus their deep concern lest a long vacancy tear that congregation apart, captured his heart. When he called me from Minneapolis, I said, "Clarence, I already know your decision. I can hear it in your voice. We better begin packing for D.C."

Since our first days in D.C. would be spent at the Roosevelt Hotel, we knew that taking Ole in the car with us was impossible. We talked about giving him to some kindly folks in Duluth, but the children became terribly upset. Mrs. Setterholm, my helper, interceded for Ole, saying, "You'll make a terrible mistake. The kids are going to be lost at first there in Washington, having to make new friends, adjusting to their schools, and learning their way around in a strange new city. At best it won't be easy. Pastor, you're handy with hammer and saw. Why not build a cage and ship Ole by express? It can't cost that much." We took her sound advice.

Our farewell party was literally drenched by parting tears. We realized in those hours what deep roots we were tearing loose. To see strong, poised men shed tears as we shook hands caused a deep-down pain that only the challenges ahead would ease. It was hardest to part with "Ma" Lufholm. She had met us with a welcome and hot food at Trinity's parsonage the day we moved in and had shared with me out of her gathered experience as mother and homemaker. Also present were ever so many of the poor and lesser endowed we had reached out to in our ministry. Others were there with whom we had shared one of life's four great days: birth, confirmation, marriage, and death.

In late fall of 1946 we headed our heavy-laden Plymouth east, leaving behind beautiful Lake Superior, the ore docks of Duluth, and a large band of friends and well-wishers. The children's first feelings were the excitement and adventure of the unknown, little aware of the heartache and loneliness that changing schools and friends would bring. Both Clarence and I, however, felt drained to the core. We drove out of Duluth with raw, heavy hearts.

A farewell gift that came too late to be included in the moving van, Edith Circle's seascape of Lake Superior tossed by a storm, had been put on the back shelf of the car. With every quick stop the painting dug into the necks of the children, the luckless back-seat passengers. Someone commented, "This is really a pain in the neck," and we all began to laugh. We helped ourselves to spirit and began singing our many familiar hymns. Singing on our trips was a family custom. One person suggested a hymn, and we'd sing just the first verse. The next person had to think of another hymn suggested by it. We could easily cover half the United States by such a chain of songs. Another traveling pastime was to divide the passengers in the car into two teams, one assigned to the left roadside, the other to the right. We would then shout out the consecutive letters of the alphabet as we saw them on a sign board, postbox, or what-have-you, racing to see which side made it to Z first.

Mary's teacher and a close neighbor, anticipating the strain the long cross-country trip would be to little children, gave us a bagful of surprises to be opened along the way. Dealt out at intervals, they broke the monotony. How many thoughtful people there are in our world.

THE WASHINGTON YEARS: BREAKING DOWN BARRIERS

9

We were warmly welcomed on our arrival in Washington. The congregation had reserved a suite of rooms at the Roosevelt Hotel right next to Augustana Church. For the children that hotel experience was a lark, but after only two days in our capital, they experienced the harsher side of big-city life. They had put some special coins in their wallets and then put the wallets in the car's glove compartment. While parked in front of the church, the car was rifled and their wallets stolen.

We were all happy when our household goods arrived at the recently purchased parsonage on the wooded edge of Rock Creek Park. After everything was unloaded, we surveyed the stacked mess. In the light from the uncurtained windows every scratch and worn place was fully exposed. "I wouldn't give 10¢ for the whole caboodle," said Clarence. There was the Jacobean dining room table on which Biz as a very little girl had scratched her name deep into the gloss, proud to be able to spell it. Worse, she became worried about how we'd react, so she tried to scratch it out. The same glaring light showed every crack in the mended heirloom vase Jon and Dave had broken. However, as if touched by a fairy's wand, order and beauty soon appeared. Clarence and I worked the next few days until we were bone tired, determined that our first need was for an inviting base our children could come home to after school. We, too, needed to know peace and orderliness at the end of a day's work.

Finally the express van delivered Ole, and we quickly opened the crate. After sniffing each of us, Ole sailed off down the street, running in wild circles as if to prove he still had legs—a dog's way of telling us how glad he was to be back with his family. The affection our children bestowed on Ole proved that Mrs. Setterholm's advice was ever so right.

At first our children's loneliness made them dig all the deeper into family togetherness. Early they made the hard choices a Christian must make in our unfriendly world. Most of the time we were not even aware they were making them. One night I awakened to hear a muffled sob coming from Biz's room. When I asked what was wrong, Biz, putting her arms around me, said, "Everything is OK, Mom. Really, it's all behind. Don't you worry." Years afterward she confided to me that many nights she quietly wept herself to sleep, missing Duluth and all her friends.

They soon found, however, that the church, especially the choir, afforded them opportunity for friends and well-rounded social lives. Soon our home overflowed with youth. On Sunday nights there'd be a blazing fire on the hearth and hearty sandwiches and cake to please those gathered before it. Many internationals also frequently joined in our gatherings.

The challenge of Augustana Church was overwhelming because the people were scattered across the whole metropolitan area. Distances made home-to-home visitation seem hopeless. Furthermore, many who attended our worship were single government workers, difficult to seek out. Those who came to church came on wheels. Worship over, they went their separate directions. Our beautiful church stood dark and empty most of the week. During those first weeks, even the ring of the telephone in the church study was a welcome sound.

Soon the boys took on paper routes. Ole delightedly followed along, sniffing at shrubs and posts and running ahead to scavenge

Worship at Augustana in Washington, D.C.

in garbage cans. Wherever there was a backyard pool, Ole's cocker blood asserted itself. He never missed a chance for a swim.

It wasn't long before Biz agitated to have a paper route too. So in time a third was added. She enlisted tagalong Mary to help. Since the Sunday paper was extra heavy and the church school hour demanded an early delivery, Clarence and I were up at early dawn to help. A big bonus were the spring mornings when the blooming shrubs and yard flowers drenched the air with sweet perfume and birds sang their cheery concerts.

One spring day as I was hanging out clothes, a brilliant cardinal made his momentary resting place in the climbing yellow rosebush which was covered with voluptuous bursts of gold. The glory of the view was too much to contain: "Oh, God, how beautiful. Thank you." Spring in Washington!

The people of Washington were marvelous too. When Biz was confined to bed for a full year due to rheumatic fever, the D.C. school system provided her with a tutor who stopped regularly at her bedside so she didn't fall behind her class. It was a proud day for us when she took a high prize in a citywide speech contest. In fact, all four of our children brought home reports that were a joy to read and sign.

Finally the church began to grow, the result of many calls Clarence and I made as a team. After Clarence got home from sick visitations and other parochial duties, we spread out a city map on the floor and staked out prospect call cards, clustering them by areas. As soon as the children came home, ravenously hungry from school and their paper routes, we had a piping hot dinner while we shared what had gone on during the day. The boys told of the fun they had with their pals at the backyard basketball ring, and the girls were full of talk of their teachers and school friends. Then followed our evening Bible readings and prayers. Each made his own link in that golden chain. The dishes were hurriedly put out of the way, the children settled with their homework, and Clarence and I were off.

Many of the calls were on youth, recent graduates from high schools across the Midwest who found quarters in the cheap rooming houses that abounded close in to downtown D.C. While Clarence made the calls, I'd circle the block, taking advantage of any chance to park. I didn't need much room to squeeze in our little VW bug. I often teased Clarence with regard to the confidence the calls required of me, waiting outside while he visited all those pretty young girls. Whenever I could park below a street light, I made good use of my time: reading, preparing for an upcoming speech, or knitting. Sometimes when my schedule was especially crowded, Clarence enlisted Gus Tornquist, one of the church bachelors, to drive.

One night when Gus was driving for him, Clarence called on a young woman just out of high school, away from the restraints of her Christian home and friends, who was literally drinking herself to death. Her last dollars went for three quarts of bourbon. Her words to Clarence from out of her alcoholic haze were, "Pastor, so you've come in response to my call." Clarence was unaware of the telephone call she had made which I received at home while I was preparing my next speech; he was calling to follow up the registration card she signed at last Sunday's worship. Minutes later I arrived, responding to the phone call. Clarence and I literally carried her to our car. Reaching home, I undressed her and put her to bed. We tenderly nursed her through the painful days of withdrawal. As soon as she felt well, she wanted to go home. We augmented her dollars with church funds and bought her a bus ticket. Then we called her parents to let them know her arrival time and that she had been ill and needed to rest at home. Their response was warm and concerned. We left up to the girl what she wanted to tell them of her problems. At Christmas we received a beautiful letter of gratitude saying she had renewed her confirmation commitment to Christ.

In spite of the long hours of work, we also had many fun times. Washington had ever so many places of interest to explore, and we dedicated each Saturday afternoon to checking them out one by one as a family: the FBI building, Mount Vernon, Fort Washington, the arboretum, the Museum of Natural History, the Smithsonian Institute, the Washington Art Gallery, General Lee's home on the hills above the Potomac. We developed a deep pride in being able to say, "Washington, D.C., is our home." Returning from these Saturday excursions we often stopped at a frozen custard shop for cones. We also kept a close check on movies, watching for those that could be taken in by the whole family. Since Washington was also a cultural capital, we availed ourselves as a family of opportunities for great stage plays. On summer Sunday evenings we went to free concerts at the art gallery, to the Watergate concerts under the open skies, and to Carter Baron's Amphitheater.

Lorraine returned home to live with us in Washington and led a busy, dedicated life. Besides holding down a job in a national youth temperance organization, she plunged into the youth program at Augustana Church and strengthened our work in every direction.

Since Washington had six army, navy, and marine bases in and around it, lonely service folk away from home filled many pews at Augustana on Sundays. Knowing what a touch of home could mean, every Saturday I sent Clarence to the grocer's saying, "Now, Dad, when it comes to the pot roast, buy a big one. You never can tell how many might join us tomorrow for dinner." It was always needed. Often as many as 20 shared our meal. Card tables were set up in the living room on short notice many Sundays.

One Saturday the children pleaded, "Please, Mom, let's make it just us tomorrow." I promised and instructed Clarence to buy only enough chops for the family. The next morning in church Mary and Biz made a bet that I wouldn't be able to keep my promise. And sure enough, in the narthex that morning stood a youthful sailor, fingering his cap. An usher, learning that he was from Minnesota, brought him to meet me. Unaware that Mary was close by, I asked the inevitable, "Do you have any special plans for dinner?" When Mary heard his "No, Ma'am," she was off with her braids standing straight out as she ran to tell Biz she'd lost the bet: "What did I tell you? Mom's invited a sailor to dinner." The girls and I had a hastily opened can of tuna in the kitchen while the men had the pork chops seated around the dining room table. I vowed I'd never again allow myself to be caught that short.

Then one Sunday a timid, frail, elderly black lady appeared at Advent vespers, the first black person to attend an Augustana worship. She drank in every word. Wanting to be unnoticed, she tried to slip out before all the rest. Clarence ran down the aisle, took her hand, and invited her to return another Sunday. She asked, "Is a black person welcome to worship here?" What had we done that she should ask that question?

One Sunday in Lent another black couple, the Lewis Greenes, appeared at morning worship. Clarence asked Mr. Rothrock to hurry out and speak to them after the service. He had to run across the street; they were already in their car. He extended a welcome and learned their address. That same week Clarence was at their door. Mr. Greene, a postal employee, and his wife, a district schoolteacher, were unhappy with their present church and gladly accepted Clarence's invitation to our membership class. They attended the series faithfully. When the class ended, however, they asked Clarence to call at their home—something was troubling them. In the security of their parlor, Mr. Greene confided, "Caroline and I have taken a great liking to you. The fact that we would become the first black members could make serious trouble for you. So we have decided not to go through with our membership application. It was wonderful to sit in your class, and we thank you for all you have given. We'll shake hands and part as friends."

Then it was Clarence who was disturbed as he replied, "Lewis, you don't know how long and earnestly I've prayed that God send Augustana its first black family. I believe you and Caroline are his answer, and I intend to fight to keep it that way. You are concerned about the trouble this might stir up for me? My concern is entirely for you. Leave me out of the picture. Are you tough enough to take the slights, snubs, and discouragements that will come your way from Augustana members with deep racial prejudices? I'll do everything in my power to make you first-class members, but I can't be sure of the others. I see this integration operation as a two-way street, each of us working at pulling down the Jericho walls of racism."

Deeply moved, Lewis put out his hand to Clarence and said solemnly, "Pastor, we accept your challenge. Count us in."

Augustana became the first church to promote an open-door policy toward the city's growing black population, months before the Supreme Court decision made integration "popular." We organized as a congregation and went from door to door, personally inviting blacks to share in our worship and work. This really stirred up dissension.

One day a woman called me and said, "You have been reported as saying you would be happy if your daughters married blacks. Is that true?" I answered, "What I've said is, it is ever so much more important to me that they marry committed Christians. Skin color is merely an outward thing. The Bible you and I believe in knows of no such distinction. Recall St. Paul's words, 'In Christ

Jesus you are all sons of God. . . . There is neither Jew nor Greek, there is neither slave nor free, there is neither male nor female; for you are all one in Christ Jesus.' I stand with that."

Another angry parishioner from the suburbs, upset that we were receiving blacks into the church, called Clarence to demand his letter of transfer. In his Swedish brogue he snapped, "Ve had a nice Swedish churtz with everybody happy till you came, Pastor. I know who's done it. It's dat communist brother-in-law of yours, Judge Luther Youngdahl. He done it!" Clarence suggested they talk it over face-to-face, but he would have none of it. We learned from the young pastor of the church that received him that on the very Sunday he was accepted into membership, the sermon had dealt entirely with the need for Christians to rid themselves of racial intolerance.

This shameful hejira from one church to another because of racial differences concerned the Lutheran Pastoral Association. It designated a committee to seek some solutions and asked Clarence to be one of the members. The committee decided to call together councils from all the Lutheran churches to see if an across-the-board open-door policy could be agreed on. But the selectmen got involved in such a heated debate they had to adjourn, hoping for a second, more favorable attempt. But this, too, failed to achieve a consensus. We had put forth an idea whose "time had not yet come." Yet even broaching the subject accomplished some good. As Clarence said, "The Rip van Winkles of the church are on notice that we cannot expect to sleep through a revolution."

Clarence realized that Augustana must hack its own way through the thorny wilderness of racism as he received letters such as, "Last Sunday, sir, your ushers seated a black male next to me. This is to serve notice that I refuse to let my worship of God be disturbed by having a sex-hungry buck nigger seated next to me." Another letter read, "Dear Pastor: Strike my name from the roll. I came to church for a word of comfort and strength. As a pregnant woman soon to assume the role of motherhood, I needed it. Instead I became so agitated I had to leave church early. My doctor believes this definitely contributed to my subsequent miscarriage."

By and large such members were from among the Christmas and Easter churchgoers, so their absence was hardly felt. On the other side of the ledger, others in the city took note of Augustana's determination, cost what it may, and joined us.

Unfortunately, however, not even all our own church council approved of the integration. There were frequent grumblings. We were shocked when at a heated council meeting one of our most loyal councilmen said, "But, Pastor, we have an investment to safeguard. Opening our doors could mean that eventually the blacks will take over."

An equally dedicated lay leader answered, "That'll happen only if we whites run up the white flag and rat out!" What bitter irony when it is more comfortable to send white missionaries thousands of miles away to evangelize Africa than to seek out the black neighbor next door.

Ironically, little Herman Davis was Augustana's best missionary. Soon three-fourths of our Sunday school was made up of little black children. We counted 35 children Herman personally brought in. It was a great day when the Davis family stood at the font to receive the Sacrament of Baptism. When he came to Herman, Clarence added to the traditional formula, "I baptize you, Herman Davis, in the name of the Father, Son, and Holy Spirit," the words, "hopefully to be Christ's minister of the gospel."

That Herman held a like thought became evident when, not long after, Africa missionary Oscar Rohlander was with us. The Sunday school children were seated in a ring at his feet as Oscar directed this special word to them: "The day is soon at hand when we white missionaries won't be welcome in Africa. My hope is that folks from your ranks will then be ready to go for Christ." Seeing Herman's hand raised, Oscar asked, "What is your question?" Herman answered, "I was trying to decide whether to go by plane or by ship." In his mind, Herman was already en route to Africa.

At about the same time we began our open-door policy, we launched "Operation One Mile." Volunteer house-to-house callers were enlisted and met monthly for training. After a common meal they were given area assignments and instructed to knock on doors, introduce themselves and Augustana, give the people a folder picturing Augustana and its program, make their personal witness to Christ, and invite them to come worship with us. They were to report back after completing their calls. Our goal was to get to know everyone living within a mile of our church, anything but an easy project. Women on our teams were apprehensive of the dark apartment hallways, as well they should be. Mary, then in her early teens, had a drunk try to put his arm around her. But at her simple word that she was from the nearby church where he could find help for his alcoholism, he abandoned his dark thoughts.

One Sunday the callers had hardly left the church when one of them, a marine colonel, returned, clearly irked, and said with some gravel in his voice to Clarence, "Pastor, just what are we up to? I found two shiny Black Marias pulled up at the door of my first call. Several police were making a raid. Don't you think we're biting off something we can't handle?" Clarence responded, "Colonel, don't you really think we got there just a little late?" He got the idea and went on to finish his assignment.

We enlisted a promising young man, Bruce Laingen, to help us form our first Boy Scout unit comprised of black youth from our immediate neighborhood. Some of these boys had police records, and most were tough and difficult. He stuck with them, applying discipline as needed. One evening after he had sent some troublemakers home, locking the door behind them, the youths set up a rumble, throwing rocks at the church windows and creating a general disturbance. A church council committee was meeting in our study, and a member asked, "Why should we make the church available to such disturbed youth?"

"Aren't these the very lads who need scouting?" answered Clarence. Under Bruce's firm but loving leadership the troop thrived. Bruce later became charge d'affaires for the United States government in Teheran, Iran, a post he held during the 1979-1980 hostage crisis. Not long after the Boy Scout troop began, a gifted, mature black woman school principal from our congregation organized a Brownie group.

Another exciting program was enlisting our youth in regular Sunday visitation of shut-ins and the sick. After having dinner at the parsonage, they fanned out in groups of three and four, each

132

with a driver, and called on those needing companionship, singing, reading Scripture, and praying with them.

Our Washington Thanksgivings were high points. Knowing this was a time when youth away from home could be homesick, we set about to give them a happy day. A lovely friend baked biscuits and pies. Two of the three turkeys were roasted at church since our oven accommodated only one. The aroma wafting up into the sanctuary was surely a proper incense for a Thanksgiving worship. Ready hands at the close of service helped load them into the car's backseat to be toted home. As many as 65 shared these Thanksgiving dinners at the parsonage.

After the festal dinner, our guests teamed up for shut-in visitation. Later that afternoon they returned to the house aglow, eager to share their experiences. Toward evening the turkey carcasses were put on the table to be picked over. Big turkey sandwiches were served, together with tantalizing chocolate brownies. Then we sat around the blazing hearth singing our first Christmas carols as we watched the light and shadows of the fire.

One December the men served a lutefisk dinner. Luther's jolly humor as MC was infectious. He admonished that we all "eat up" because when we got to heaven lutefisk would certainly not be served. He could prove it, he said, reading from Revelation, "Nothing that makes a lie shall enter here." Then he added, "you know, of course, that important to preparing lutefisk is the lye bath it gets before it can be cooked." Almost always the ambassador from Sweden would be our guest and speaker.

When King Gustav V died, Clarence was called to the embassy to plan his memorial service. He was to preach and Gosta Bjorling, the famous Swedish tenor, to sing. All foreign diplomats in Washington were asked to attend. Clarence was escorted by the cathedral beadle to the heavily carved pulpit. It was an awe-inspiring crowd, all diplomats in full dress: gold-braided lapels, long rows of decorations on their chests, and swords at their sides.

One day we received a call from Win Johanson, a bachelor pastor whose parish was in Chicago. He had met Lorraine at a student ashram some time before and was coming to Washington. He wanted to have lunch with her. Lorraine and Win began to see more and more of each other. One night Lorraine phoned Rube and opened the conversation with "Rube, there is too stardust!" In response to his bewildered, "Lorraine, what on earth are you talking about?" she announced her engagement. We all grew excited about the upcoming wedding. Lorraine's young brothers, eager to plumb the depths of her love to her betrothed, asked, "Are you willing to share your toothbrush with him?" Her only answer was a giggle.

It was a lovely June wedding in Augustana's cathedrallike church with Biz and Mary as junior bridesmaids. Somehow, amidst the busyness of it all, I sensed her mother's presence and the beautiful answer to her faith-filled prayers.

Biz and Mary
were attendants
at Lorraine's wedding

Soon after, Agneta, a winsome Swedish lass with golden hair, sky-blue eyes, and a rosy outdoor complexion, came to Augustana seeking fellowship with youth her own age. Her parents had allowed this 17-year-old girl to travel to America to perfect her

134

English and to gather experience from a year of living abroad. She had found employment as a maid and nursemaid in a suburban home, but was desperately isolated and lonely. She immediately became involved in the activities of the Young Adults, going out to visit the shut-ins or the hospitalized and returning afterwards to the parsonage for sandwiches and cake. A crackling fire on the hearth made the perfect setting to draw out their experiences of the day or their probing questions. Talk, singing, prayers, and laughter mingled.

Agneta loved these gatherings and quickly became a regular in the group. She became so involved in church life that she quit her job and became a volunteer to Augustana's program, often accompanying Clarence on his hospital and shut-in calls and attending the various group meetings to get a well-rounded picture of an American pastor's role. During these months she made her home with us. When her year was over, a large group of her friends gave a farewell party. How we all would miss her. She was weeping unrestrainedly; she would miss us and America.

I was forcefully reminded of just how wonderful our country is as we bid Agneta farewell. This same reminder frequently occurred as I conducted sight-seeing tours for friends from other countries. One day I was taking Pastor Stefano Moshi, a bishop from Tanzania, East Africa, on a tour of Washington. That night at dinner he commented, "Now I understand America better. In Europe the monuments are raised to men who go out and conquer other lands. Not so here in America. You raise yours to the men who fight for liberty and freedom for every individual person." I cringed as I realized how often we had not lived up to these ideals.

One day I received a call from the Lutheran Welfare Society chaplain asking if I would hold Bible classes at Oquoquan, the women's reformatory. He felt these women had special needs that only another woman could minister to. I willingly accepted the challenge and began a program of regular Bible classes there. A favorite chorus of the girls at the prison was, "Let the beauty of Jesus be seen in me." They would go back to their confinement singing that chorus. As I saw faces that had come in set and disgruntled leave relaxed and beautiful because of the power of

135

God's Word, I quietly prayed, "Give us discerning eyes, Lord, to recognize soul beauty. Help us to see, through all the tinsel and wrappings, the beauty of your love. Amen."

On one of my weekly visits to Oquoquan, the chaplain asked me to visit a Margaret Dunbar in her cell, saying, "She wants out of our world. She keeps talking about suicide." Peg's police dossier revealed more than 100 jailings for alcoholism. She had thrown in the sponge in her struggle with an enemy whose power to destroy grew with each defeat she suffered. "What's the use?" Peg groaned. "My sentence is soon up, and do you know what will happen? The district will put 50¢ in my pocket and then bus me to the district line. There to meet the bus will be all my old drinking pals. What other alternative is open since I'll need a roof over my head? Then the whole ugly thing begins all over again. There's no use talking, Mrs. Nelson. Death is the only out for me."

I realized this poor woman's willpower was shattered by her alcoholism. She needed more than a few Bible verses; she needed prayers that had legs. "Peg," I said, "I'll meet that bus. You come home to us. We'll do everything in our power to get you started right again. I'm sure God wants something better for you, and maybe he can use us to help."

On my 25-mile ride back to Washington I wondered, "What have I done? I haven't consulted Clarence about this. Mary is still at home. Is this fair to her?" Then I remembered what had happened just a few days before. Without warning, Clarence appeared at noon with a man obviously in need of help. He needed not only clothes, but food and a chance to wash. While this new-found friend was in the bathroom, Clarence explained, "This man came to church today, and after I heard his story, I took him into the chapel and knelt in prayer with him. While I was on my knees, God said to me in the words of James: 'What does it profit, my brethren, if a man says he has faith but has not works? Can his faith save him? If a brother or sister is ill-clad and in lack of daily food, and one of you says to them "Go in peace, be warmed and filled," without giving them the things needed for the body, what does it profit? So faith by itself, if it has no works, is dead.' So here he is, and we'll have to keep him over the weekend so I can help him get started fresh on Monday morning."

The upshot of this adventure wasn't without humor. Clarence thought his clothes would fit the man, so he went into his wardrobe to find a pair of pants. The only pants that fit were his very best pair he had hardly worn himself. The next morning this needy friend accompanied us to church in my husband's "gladdest rags."

All this passed through my mind as I guided the car homeward. Anticipating an understanding heart to greet my commitment, I burst into the living room and explained this new challenge to Clarence. How thankful to God I was when he said, "Of course we must do it."

Clarence and I met the Oquoquan bus with its sad clutch of women, and it was just as Peg had described. Waiting at the district line was a tag end of red-faced men, their life-style plainly written on their faces and clothing—a welcoming committee eager to help these women to another whirl on the merry-go-round of despair that would again fling them back into the pool of misery that was Oquoquan.

Once under our roof, Peg walked about as if in a dream. "One thing is certain," she said, "God sent you into my life. I've done nothing to deserve this. God is here. God is in this place." She shared her life story with us. As a secretary she'd had one promotion after another, finally becoming circulation manager for *Vanity Fair*, a job that took her across the country and even to Europe. But it was also a pressure cooker, and liquor became her easy way out. At the end of this road was Oquoquan where, with the other women derelicts, she could dry out. Released, the sad cycle repeated. Her family had long ago given up on her. But our oft-repeated theme was, "Listen, Peg, God hasn't given up on you. He's got a fresh start for you."

We arranged for eyeglasses, friends helped collect a scant but adequate wardrobe, and Dr. Robert Van Deusen, Lutheran public relations director in Washington, got her a job using her magazine experience to get out the monthly newsletter to Lutheran servicemen. This job became a door to a new life for Peg.

We helped her find a modest apartment, unhappily still in the midst of the broken-down and floaters, but close to Augustana. One night Clarence was preaching at the Gospel Mission and took

Peg along. After sharing the Word with them, the presiding chairman called for testimonies of the reborn. Peg was immediately on her feet, boldly witnessing that she had been plucked like a brand from the burning. Powerfully she quoted Psalm 40: "He drew me up from the desolate pit, out of the miry bog, and set my feet upon a rock." Peg religiously attended Alcoholics Anonymous (AA), but we discovered that a certain man frequently made those meetings a stalking pad where he could single out the next victim to coax to his bed. Not long after, Augustana began its own AA meetings.

"God is ever right here by my typewriter," was the way Peg put it. She truly walked hand in hand with her Lord. Her happy disposition and bubbling spirits spread joy and cheer. But taverns were never farther than a block or two away, and to pass the open doors was a fresh test daily. Finally the familiar smells and sounds nudged her in for that first drink, and she was tobogganing downhill on that fast ride so well known to alcoholics.

Clarence, searching for her, found her in a gutter, woebegone and dirty. Once again we opened our home to Peg. But it is ever so difficult to dry out an alcoholic. Sneakily, clever beyond imagination, they inevitably find some way to get out for that next drink. While I was gone on an errand, Clarence had an emergency call. He hid Peg's clothes above the furnace pipes, sure she'd never look for them there. But she was gone when I returned.

After a few days she called, drunk and loud, giving away her hideout in a nearby hotel. Enlisting the help of a fellow pastor, Clarence loaded Peg into the car, drunk, dirty, and cursing. She was devil-possessed when liquored up. When they arrived at the parsonage, Peg refused to budge from the car. Realizing their predicament, I came out to help. When pleading proved of no avail, I sternly said, "Peg, we have no other choice but to call the police to take you to Oquoquan unless you let these men help you in to get a hot bath and some black coffee."

In her leering, drunken way Peg answered, "Yes, and I suppose these two preachers will even help me with the bath." This was too much for our pastor friend; he broke into loud laughter which was ever so good for all of us. Peg came in to be with us yet again, a preacher at either side supporting her. In a jiffy I was tubbing her, and soon thereafter had her tucked in bed. Grateful beyond words, a sober Peg vowed she would never again be tempted by drink. She knew now that even one drink could be her undoing. Together we gave thanks to God.

Then a tragic incident nudged us into a program for senior citizens. Clarence had gone only a block en route to a luncheon when to his horror he saw a woman fall to the sidewalk from the sixth-story window of the apartment kitty-corner from the church. He rushed to her side and arrived just as she died. From her excited sister and neighbors he learned she'd been ill and greatly depressed. The uneventful days a burden, she simply chose death. Clarence came home distraught. "What are we at Augustana doing to put meaning and joy into the lives of these folks right at our door?" he asked. We called together some of our leaders who helped us conduct a survey of the close apartment buildings, inviting seniors to a luncheon meeting. An amazing mix responded, and we launched Augustana's "Young in Heart" program.

God was truly guiding us in meeting the challenge of Augustana, now with its open-door policy, Operation One Mile, Young Adults, Boy Scouts, Brownies, and Young in Heart. Our efforts were rewarded.

Each summer we enjoyed a vacation back at Koja. We drove our Chevrolet jam-packed with needed clothing and bedding. Ole positioned himself with his paws on Clarence's back, his wet nose resting on Clarence's shoulder. We ate at modest, small-town restaurants or hamburger stops to keep costs down. We never needed to ask Biz what she wanted to order; she hot-dogged her way across the country regardless of what tempting dishes we offered.

The weeks at Koja were pure delight. The children swam to their hearts' content as the sun copper-bronzed their skin. One day, however, Mary got into some poison ivy and a painful infection puffed up her face like a balloon, even closing her eyes. That night Jon's bedtime prayer was, "Dear God, please heal Mary's poison ivy in four hours." When I protested he was dictating to God, he said, "There! You didn't believe he could do it, did you?"

A ready-made circle of friends waited each year to pick up

where last year's summer fun ended. We had rollicking sings with folks gathered from all around the lake. On Sunday evenings from 10 to 15 boats would congregate out on the lake as the sun set in its glory. We sang until our voices were hoarse, always concluding with "Silent Night," promising each other we'd remember these delectable moments at Christmas.

OUR
WORLD
FAMILY

10

In 1953 we expanded our horizons, embarking on a world tour with Luther and Irene. We sailed on the Swedish liner *Gripsholm;* the voyage was beautiful, with time to reflect and converse. As Vinga Fye, the lighthouse just off Sweden's southern coast, came into sight, we exclaimed, "Just think, we will be walking on the soil that was home to our parents." We saw the quaint, well-preserved church built in the 1100s where Clarence's father was baptized, visited the old farmhouse, still in the family, and shared dinner with numerous relatives.

As a United States district judge, Luther had prearranged contacts with the American embassies as well as with the International Christian Businessmen's Association. Thus, distinguished staff people often met us as we deplaned in each country. In Stockholm, General Youngdahl, ex-chief of the army, greeted us, flower bouquet in hand. We enjoyed a day's yacht tour on Stockholm's famous *Archipelago,* owned by a successful industrialist Luther and Irene had entertained in Washington. Aboard with us were Prince Carl and the editor of *Svenska Dagbladet.*

One afternoon Luther and Clarence were billed to speak

through interpreters at St. Jacob's Church's midweek vespers in Stockholm. Clarence was listing the medical treatments Louis XIV of France endured just before his death. The last item was the application of a large bloodsucker to his foot to bleed him. Confused, Clarence's interpreter turned to ask, "Ja, men, Pastor Nelson, vad ar en 'bloodsucker'?" I was sitting just under the pulpit and said in a stage whisper, "Skip it, Clarence, skip it. Get on with the rest of it."

We also visited Agneta's home in the beautiful rural town of Molndahl, set on a rocky wooded hillside. Agneta had returned to Sweden determined to bring to her church the people-to-people concern she had experienced in America. She enrolled at Uppsala University and graduated with a theology degree. While attending school she spent vacations working in a home for the aging and also became a leader for a youth camp program that brought groups of Swedish youth into other countries—a hands-across-the-seas program.

In Denmark we were dined at the Yacht Club by a fabulous little old man driving an early vintage car. He formerly had vast holdings of forests and lumber mills in Russia and Europe, but lost all in the Great Depression and the Russian Revolution. He was now contentedly rejoicing in what he called his riches in Christ.

Our days in Cologne permitted sight-seeing in depth. We took in the nearly restored cathedral with its noble windows and art treasures. Our guide told of the city's total prostration at the war's close. One-third of Cologne lay in ruins. The cathedral had suffered a devastating direct hit. The city fathers decided that rebuilding the cathedral had to be the first step. A singing procession of celebrants took the sacred treasures from their hiding places and brought them back to the cathedral. The result was electrifying. Hope was born out of the ashes, and rebuilding began in earnest.

A similar story was related to us in Hamburg as the mayor told of his people's numbing despair. The harbor, once Europe's busiest, had been a tangle of broken ships and gutted warehouses. Rubble lay mountain-high in the streets, the buildings unheated, water and electric systems only partially restored. Here the decision to hold the International Horticultural Exposition had galvanized the people.

In Berlin an American embassy aide escorted us into East Berlin, its streets wide but nearly empty of traffic. He took us high up into the Staatshus belfry to view the famed Freedom Bell. From that high place we saw the seemingly endless line of ill-fed East Berliners who, having received permits to enter West Berlin, had lined up to receive gift packages of food to take back across the border.

When visiting Prague, we wanted a firsthand view of the famous cathedral at the top of the hill. Told that the trolley that passed by our hotel went very close to this historical edifice, we confidently boarded it. As we passed through the city and across the bridge, we thought we must be close to our destination, so we got off and began walking toward the towering steeples. We walked, and walked, and walked, winding around and around up the hill. When we came to the place we thought was close to the cathedral, Clarence said, "We're lost. I don't even see the steeples anymore." However, knowing we were heading in the right direction, we pushed on. As we rounded the next corner, we came upon a gate. Beyond it was the cathedral. The buildings close by had completely obliterated what could readily be seen from afar. I thought to myself, "So it is often in life. God's wonder and reality are lost in the pressure of the needs about us. We neglect the long look."

It was an exciting day when we first met face to face with the Polsters in Stuttgart-Rohracker. Theirs was a humble second-story apartment in a refugee section of the city. Mrs. Polster's greeting was unlike any I had ever known. She patted my cheeks and said, "You're beautiful! You're beautiful!" I felt an overwhelming closeness to this woman. I had grown up envying beautiful girls, those who were small and well-proportioned. I had seen the overt glances they received from the opposite sex and had asked myself, "Why didn't the Lord make me like that? Why did I have to be built like a powerful Katrinka, with a size larger shoe than most stores carried, and with the Youngdahl nose that held such a prominent place on the map of my face?" As an adolescent, I secretly groveled over this ignominy. But here was someone whom I knew only through letters saying I was beautiful. When you look at another person through the eyes of love, you see beyond the appearance to the real person within. We had a gala meal in their little apartment with laughter and song filling the rooms, concluding by lifting the rafters with "Ein Feste Burg Ist Unser Gott" ("A Mighty Fortress Is Our God").

From there we went to Damascus, Amman, and then over the desert to Jerusalem. We were hot, dirty, and tired as the car started climbing the hill to the ancient city. We drove past the little town of Bethany, where the Lord stopped with Mary, Martha, and Lazarus, and on up the road to the city set among the mountains. Our guide had said we would find relief there, but we had not anticipated how tremendously refreshing that cool mountain air would be. The world was veiled in the rose and tawny gold of evening as Clarence took out his Bible and read from Psalm 125, "As the mountains are round about Jerusalem, so the Lord is round about his people, from this time forth and for evermore."

Arriving in Jerusalem we learned we were to dine at Prime Minister Sharrat's home, a delightful experience. Table talk ranged the world, always coming back to the troubles and triumphs of Israel. One day as we walked the streets of Jerusalem, we saw a young lad carrying a flat tray of rising bread dough on the top of his head, headed for the community baker. Unfortunately, the flies had discovered the rising dough, and it looked exactly like raisin bread. Unforgettable sights.

Bethlehem was one of our favorite spots in the Holy Land, perhaps because it fulfilled our imaginings so well. As we drove down the hillside from Jerusalem to this city of Jesus' birth, we saw flocks of sheep and shepherds in their characteristic garb, exactly the dress I had struggled to devise many Christmases at home for our little shepherds in the church school. Around a corner in the road, with olive trees lining the way, was the little city of some 2000 homes, set like an amphitheatre in the hollow of the hills. The streets were lined with little shops selling mementos, but so it probably was when our Lord was born, for Palestine was a trade center and crossroads for the then-known world. We had to bend low to enter the Church of the Nativity because the door was cut down in size during the Crusades so horsemen would not ride their steeds into that sacred place.

We made our way down to the grotto designated as the place of Christ's birth. Although ornate trimmings surrounded the place, we closed our eyes and remembered the simplicity of that first setting and the humility of the one who changed the course of history. The streets of Bethlehem were filled with ordinary people talking and going on their various errands. It was an ordinary Palestinian town, yet Scripture tells us how extraordinary it was. Rachel was buried right outside this place. Here Ruth and Naomi came. From here King David had come, then only a poor shepherd boy with his kingly days ahead. God chose this ordinary place for the most extraordinary event of all time.

Nothing could eclipse the feelings engendered as we visited the holy places sacred to the memory of our Master—Galilee, Gethsemane, the garden tomb, the Church of the Holy Sepulchre, the Church of the Crowing Cock, the Via Dolorosa, and finally, the hill to Golgotha and the cross. As a mother, I tried to envision the agony, hopelessness, and awful injustice his mother must have felt. And the poor, defeated, frightened disciples—what a way to usher in a new kingdom. As I stood there, I could see him looking down from the cross, his eyes finding mine, and hear him say, "This I have done for thee; what hast thou done for me?"

In Rome we visited the Scala Sancta, the "Holy Steps" brought from Palestine as a shrine for pilgrims. The penitent made their way up these steps on their knees, saying prayers at given intervals to erase years from their stay in purgatory. Martin Luther, seeking peace, started up these very steps, but halfway up he rebelled, saying, "No, this can't be God's way. There is no peace in this." As we watched, we saw a crippled man painfully pull one knee up after the other and young folks going through the ritual and then skipping away. My heart was heavy at the blind way these pilgrims were going when the Lord has provided an open door. It was these man-made devices for salvation against which Martin Luther protested; throughout the Scriptures he discovered that salvation is a free gift of God.

As Irene and I were flying from Athens to London, we were expressing our disgust that our husbands had kept us so busy sight-seeing we didn't have a chance to shop. The seats on the plane were in threes, and the third woman sitting with us joined our conversation. After introducing herself, she said, "I couldn't help but hear what you were saying. I'd like to tell you of my experience. My husband has been in the foreign service for many years. As we traveled the world, I gathered many beautiful things I prized. But when the last war broke out, my husband telephoned saying, 'Gather whatever you can into one suitcase. We must flee quickly.' In those next minutes I did some tall thinking. What would mean the most in this emergency? I assure you they were not the baubles that had been my pride and joy. They are gone, and never again will I concern myself much about anything material."

For some time after that we sat quietly. I remembered having to sort out things after the passing of loved ones. We cannot take our material possessions with us when the call comes to make the last great journey. Why, then, should we become so fond of these trifling toys? I silently prayed, "Dear Lord, so much of our life is

*A family portrait
taken during our
Washington years*

146

spent in pursuit of perishing things. Give us again a sense of values that has the long look of eternity. In Jesus' name. Amen."

Upon our return to the United States and Washington, the Augustana congregation turned out in droves to share our trip through words and pictures. The international flavor of our religious life did not end with the world tour. Shortly after our return a delegation of Russian churchmen were guests of the National Council of Churches in our city. About 70 of us gathered in the church parlor to break bread. As we shared the concerns of our hearts and our longing for peace through interpreters, we found that our allegiance to Christ was the answer. Before we parted, we formed a circle around the room, joined hands, and sang "Blest be the tie that binds our hearts in Christian love."

Every Christmas in Washington found our home filled with folks from around the world

Another international religious experience occurred at a World Day of Prayer observance at the Cathedral. We had prayed that this meeting might witness to our oneness in Christ. Mrs. Eisenhower and her mother were part of the prayer chain that encircled the world. When I greeted the First Lady's mother, Mrs. Doud, I mentioned that my people had come from Sweden as hers had. Her eyes lit up as she asked me if I spoke Swedish. Just then, however, we had to process in to the service. People of all colors and nations were one in God that day. As they bade me farewell, Mrs.

Doud, with tears in her eyes, said, "All I could think of was, 'Trygaaare kan ingen vara,' the Swedish hymn translated as, 'Children of the Heavenly Father.'"

With the first lady, Mrs. Eisenhower, and her mother, Mrs. Doud, at a World Day of Prayer observance

We were very soon back into the full swing of making calls on church members and attending meetings. One Sunday evening as we were leaving church after a busy day, I was anticipating the comfort and relaxation of the fireplace at home. Clarence, however, said, "I can't get Lenore off my mind. I think we should stop at the hospital to see her."

"But," I protested, "you just saw her last night. She was getting along nicely then. Besides, it's way past visiting hours." Then, realizing my protests were foolish, though exceedingly human, I agreed, and we made our way to the hospital.

Although it was 10 o'clock at night, Clarence's clergy status admitted us, and we proceeded to Lenore's room. As we entered, she cried, "How did you know I have been praying you might come? How did you know how desperately I needed you?" and broke into convulsive sobs. I went to her bedside and held her until she calmed down enough to tell us what was wrong. She was there for a biopsy and had been fearing the worst—cancer, the dread disease that took her mother. That afternoon the husband of a woman patient across the hall came to visit Lenore. She told him the doctors had assured her the biopsy indicated no malignancy. But this well-meaning man responded, "Don't believe them. That's what they told my wife, and here she is. Don't believe them."

After he left, Lenore was beside herself. Were they hiding something? It must have been at this point that the Lord put it into Clarence's heart to change direction and head toward the hospital. As he read to her from Psalm 37, "Commit your way to the Lord; trust in him, and he will act" and then from the 23rd Psalm, speaking the meaning of every sentence, her tense, taut body relaxed. We left her at peace.

When we arrived home, the phone was ringing. It was Lenore's husband. "I don't know what you did," he said, "but I want to thank you. Lenore just phoned to say she knew she would have a good night's sleep and maybe she would be home for Christmas. Thanks a million."

Lenore was home for Christmas, and her three-year-old son Keven was all smiles. When a visiting neighbor asked, "Aren't you glad your daddy brought your mother home for Christmas?" Keven replied, "Not my daddy. God did it."

One day our tradition of taking birthday cakes to the elderly took us to a nursing home in Maryland to visit a special little lady, Martha Mulvey, a Swedish woman who cooked for five presidents in the White House, but who was now confined to a wheelchair. It was her 90th birthday. After we had everything set up for the festivities, Martha said, "Wait a minute. I have something I want you to read, Mrs. Nelson. It's from Mamie Eisenhower." The president's wife wrote she had learned from White House records that Martha had served as chief cook in the White House all those years, so she wanted to send her warm regards on this special birthday. This letter brought such joy to Martha. We left feeling the celebration was a great success.

Our trip home, however, was quite the opposite. It was spring, and winter ice and snow had caused deep ruts to form in the twisting road. There were places where sharp rocks jutted from the hump between the ruts, and one pierced our oil pan. The flashing red on the dashboard warned us we had lost our oil, but it was too late. Our pistons were burned. We ground to a stop, telephoned for repairs, and then called Luther for a lift home. When Clarence described where we were, Luther retorted, "Say, Clarence, how far into Maryland does your parish extend anyway?"

During this time I was literally belting the country with speaking engagements, rewarding experiences in witnessing for my Lord. Countless times a mother would come forward to thank me for having had her son or daughter at our home for dinner. When my name appeared in the news, I often received letters from the youth themselves, now matured and in responsible positions, telling how memorable this experience had been.

Traveling allowed for renewing many friendships and for making new friends. One night in Jacksonville, Florida, I shared the platform with Mary McLeod Bethune. As this great Negro woman thanked God for the progress in race relations and poured out the ache of the lonely hearts of people who are not accepted for the eternal souls they are, I thought of Mother and the heartache she felt as a stranger in New York, shunned, alone, ridiculed. I was one with Mrs. Bethune in the great yearning for a world where God's love knows no strangers.

We taught our children to accept and love others, but this was not always without its hazards. One evening Mary, then in high school, was home alone studying. The doorbell rang, and when she answered it she found a very disturbed, drunk marine standing on the stoop, demanding to know if his wife was hiding at the parsonage. Naively, trustful Mary invited him in, assuring him no one had come to the house while she was home and suggesting that he wait for her father. She then went to the piano and played every hymn she knew, all the while saying, "Just wait. I know my

150

dad can help you." The music worked. But when Clarence came home, he was very concerned that Mary had been so trustful. He drove the marine back to his apartment and together they knelt, asking God to turn the steps of the wife homeward and to help this couple make a fresh start with Jesus as the cornerstone of their life and home. The man, now sober, his body shaking with sobs, gave his heart to the Lord. When his wife returned, he told her that he had given his life into God's hands. His confession of carrying a concealed butcher knife when he had burst in upon Mary made us realize how God watches over his own.

This same message was graphically illustrated when we received the warning of Hurricane Ione heading directly for Washington. We were told to expect winds up to 90 miles an hour. As we began preparing to brace ourselves against the storm, I thought, "Men know all about many things, but as yet they are powerless to stay the storm or to control the wind." Recollections of that frightening afternoon huddled at the lake place as a child while a tornado raged outside flashed through my mind, and I silently thanked God for watching over us.

About this time my dream of sharing my favorite hymns and scriptures with others became a reality. For months I had been working on a book of meditations. This book, *God's Song in My Heart*, was published in 1957. As noted in the preface, it was written in a variety of settings:

> In the mountains of Livingston, Montana; by the sands of Daytona Beach, Florida; in the rich, Pennsylvania Dutch country; in a motel in Birmingham, Alabama; on the coast of southern California—and then in the parsonage in Washington, D.C. and at Nelson's Koja at Moose Lake, Minnesota—these are some of the places where the writing has been done. In the midst of a speaking schedule, in the whirl of the demands of keeping house, and in between trying to serve as a pastor's wife, have these meditations been born. Only by the grace of God has the drawing apart been possible, and only because of His wonderful answer to prayer has the work been finished.

Also in 1957, Clarence and I celebrated our 25th wedding anniversary. It hardly seemed possible we had shared a quarter of a century together—it seemed like only yesterday I was walking down the aisle with stardust in my eyes and a song in my heart.

Shortly after that Peg entered our life again. She had been doing so well, but once again she stumbled, and once again we took her home. This time she would have to share a room with Clara Toller, another desperate alcoholic who also was drying out at the parsonage. When Peg complained of sharp pains, I got her a doctor's appointment and drove her to his office, also offering to pick her up. But Peg refused, insisting she'd call a cab.

She didn't make it home on her own. Instead she called Clarence's office in the late afternoon. By the noises in the background and her slurred words, he knew at once that Peg was in a tavern. He immediately drove to the bar and managed to coax her into the car. At the time I was out at Bible class. When I returned home, Peg and Clara were sitting in front of the fireplace with Clarence, talking over a cup of coffee. I prepared the other twin bed in Mary's room which Peg would share with Clara. (Mary was away at Gustavus.) When I joined them about the fireplace, Peg was saying, "I know one thing. No matter how much I have sinned, Christ forgives me. I am in the hollow of his hand, and no one can take me from there." After a while I suggested we should all get some rest, and we retired.

Next morning I decided to let the women sleep as long as possible and so made no effort to arouse them until after the morning chores were done. When I knocked on the bedroom door, breakfast tray in hand, Clara responded, "Come in." As I entered the room, she whispered, "Peg has been resting so quietly, I didn't want to disturb her." But one look at Peg's face, turned to the wall so Clara couldn't see it, told me that her boat had pulled in on the shore of eternity. There was a momentary shock, and then joy as I remembered her witness the night before.

We went through her effects for anything to pass on to her family. Tucked into her billfold was a typewritten card, dated the week after she first came to our home, which read, "Dear God, thank you for sending a Good Samaritan into my life to help me when I thought all hope was gone. Thank you for showing me that your love never gives up. Thank you, Christ, for being my

Savior. Bless this home and everyone in it. And continue to let your love shine through it. Amen." That one thing I kept.

Then we summoned Peg's family from New York. They were very grateful that Peg had died in the refuge of our home rather than in a gutter. Four pastors who had figured redemptively in her last years carried her casket from Augustana Church to her grave. A sizable group of her new friends in Christ attended the victory service celebrating Peg's relinquishment of the cross for heaven's crown.

That summer Clarence and I set out as usual for our vacation at Koja. Mary, however, returned to Washington for a government job to help pay her tuition at Gustavus. One Sunday after worship, Mary noticed a young girl standing quite alone. Always sensitive to a stranger, Mary hurried to her side. Drawing out her story, Mary learned that this young girl, Elsie Gibson, had recently come to Washington from Costa Rica and was employed as a judge's domestic. They had advanced her money for a plane ticket and were eager for her to be at home in Washington. The judge, having read of Augustana's Operation One Mile and its open-door policy, drove Elsie to our church. Mary immediately made Elsie at home with our youth. As soon as we returned from Koja, Mary introduced her saying, "Mom and Dad, Elsie here hasn't a soul in the world to call family. This is what you must be to her."

So Elsie became our Costa Rican foster daughter, or, as she dubbed herself, our "smoked Swede." We gave her a key and opened our home to her on her day off to do whatever she pleased. She became an active member of the choir, offering up her beautiful coloratura soprano voice. She also volunteered as a visitor at the Lutheran Home for the Aged.

When the big day arrived for Elsie to become a United States citizen, we really celebrated. That night after choir rehearsal, members congratulated her with coffee and a large cake inscribed with "Proudly We Salute You, Citizen Elsie!" Each slice had a miniature United States flag.

In 1959 our family had another wedding as Jon took Juni as his bride. He met Juni on the Augustana College campus. She was a sophomore, he a second year seminarian. Juni was a blue-ribbon girl, born and reared on a farm in Boxholm, Iowa, as at home on

153

a tractor as she was in the kitchen. The tantalizing fragrance of her delicious Swedish rye bread baked when he visited the farm home, her down-to-earth capabilities, and her creative artistry, in addition to the attractive young lady that she was, completely captured Jon's heart. What defense did he have against such a combination? She quickly became a part of the family, bringing to it her spirit, loyalty, and faith.

One afternoon we received a letter from missionary friends in Taipei, writing on behalf of a student soon to arrive in Washington for a year's study in government finance. They wrote: "Paul is a new Christian and we fear lest being caught up in the Washington milieu he will lose touch with his faith. Could you recommend a Christian home where he can find supportive Christian fellowship and an introduction to a Christ-centered and lively church family?"

Clarence and I said in concert, "Why can't it be our home? We have room." Since our children were away at school, their rooms stood unused. The bus went right past our corner and could take him where he needed to go, and Augustana had a wonderful mix of internationals. In our integrated congregation the color of one's skin or the slant of one's eyes meant less and less. We sent off our letter immediately, welcoming Paul to our home.

We loved Paul T. King from the very first day. Despite all he'd gone through, he was optimistic. He always had a cheery "Good morning," took immediately to American cooking, and added ever so much to our table conversations. His good mind was very apparent when he was singled out for a special seminar under Dr. Walter Heller, University of Minnesota economist. Dr. Heller offered Paul a teaching fellowship at the end of his studies, but Paul declined, having promised his government that he would return home to use what he had learned for his country's betterment.

Paul was separated from his wife and children when he had to flee for his life after the Japanese invaded mainland China. As mayor of a large city, he was marked for death. When he could finally arrange to have his family join him via the underground railway, his wife refused to leave. Persisting in the hope that someday they would be reunited, Paul wrote frequently. Finally, he received word from the mainland. As he approached us, his step,

154

characteristically light and tripping, was now measured and heavy. He said to us in an anguish-filled voice, "There are only 46 words. She says for me never to write to her again. This isn't a separation, it's a divorce. I tell you, Pastor and Mrs. Nelson, I'm at heart a married man. I love my children and wife. It's hard, so very hard, for since my mother and father are both dead, I'm all alone. I have no family. No one." Then he blurted out, "Will you be mother and dad to me?" In an instant we were in each other's arms, our tears answering his cry and cementing a new tie for the three of us. He became a son to us in the same way that Timothy was to St. Paul. On his return to Taipei, Paul remarried. His new wife was a widow, a committed Christian with a daughter. The two children born into this marriage were named Clarence and Ruth.

During our Washington years our family was expanded not only by the addition of Elsie, Juni, and Paul, but also with grandchildren. Lorraine and Win had Anne in 1951, Karin in 1954, Berit in 1957, and Christopher in 1960. Juni and Jon had their first child, Kristin, in 1960. We thanked God for the richness of our home.

Surely I would be remiss if I gave the impression that there were no difficult times, no times of heartache and stress; yes, even of despair. The pressures our children were under while working their way through college and the seminary (the doctors called it "student fatigue")—making life-changing decisions involving continents; matching the idealism of their Christian faith with the hypocrisies of practice and daily living, even within the church—produced times of nerve-wracking tension! In the midst of all this, some of our children suffered periods of mental depression characterized by an agony of spirit that was indescribable, and had to take time out for treatment and recuperation. These were grueling, heartbreaking days and months.

Clarence and I searched our hearts and cried out in despair. Where had we failed? What had we done to have caused such agony? We felt people were pointing their fingers at us, saying, "Look at those pious people. See what their demanding faith has done to their children!" We groveled in prayer and begged God for mercy.

The Lord heard. He delivered us out of the troublous times

155

and restored his joy in our hearts. Each child, in turn, came through this refining fire and regained a sense of purpose and strength to face a continuing struggle. As we looked back, we realized that these times in the valley were a part of life that God used to help us better understand the struggles of others.

One day the phone rang. It was Harold Hansen on the line asking, "Pastor, can you meet with Tore H. and me this noon? We've a proposition to make." Over lunch they offered a bold new move for Augustana Church, saying, "Pastor, you're working too hard. We'd like to lighten your load. You're aware of the contracting firm Harold and I have launched, Triangle Construction. Our goal is to set aside one-third of all future profits to the third partner in our firm, God. We want our church to seek out an assistant for you. We'll cover the costs for the first two years while the budget gets adjusted, anonymously of course. We feel deeply that Augustana is in for a period of growth, and we can provide the seed money."

Clarence was overwhelmed and speechless. Now he would have help to follow up the growing list of prospects. There would be a pastoral team with an input of fresh new ideas. The lunch ended with a brief prayer of thanksgiving and a solemn exchange of handshakes.

They began the search for the right man. Pastors recommended by conference authorities proved to have run into problems in the parishes they presently served, and by the statistics in the yearly conference minutes, hadn't been too ablaze with enthusiasm. Whoever came to Augustana must be open-minded on the race question and be ready to pull up his sleeves and plunge into the work. One of our best friends, Dr. Robert Van Deusen, suggested Pastor Wayne Woods, saying, "Clarence, he's already on the Washington scene, has been without a call for several months, and his background plainly suggests that God has been preparing him for Augustana."

Pastor Woods had succeeded his father in a parish in an older section of Pittsburgh that was experiencing change—blacks were moving in. Wayne welcomed the opportunity to broaden the horizon of the otherwise smug congregation. The first black to apply for membership was a teacher of religion in the release

156

time schools. Surely no one would be so insular as to deny such a person Christian fellowship. But the board voted him down. It almost broke Pastor Wood's heart, but he shouldered the blame, saying, "I just haven't prepared my people for it." He began a family-to-family visitation program to help them get the Christian perspective. But a second vote was also negative. His idealism shattered, Wayne resigned his pastorate and moved his family to Washington, D.C. He resolved to take secular employment rather than continue as a pastor if it meant compromising what he felt was right. The only job open was selling pianos, but Wayne just didn't have the "killer instinct" to press for a sale when he knew the family needed their meager income for food and shoes. With his slender cash reserve almost gone, the road ahead looked bleak.

As Clarence weighed Wayne's credentials, he knew this was God's answer to our prayers. Wayne was a Phi Beta Kappa student, had served as a pastor for a year in Berlin, and had a heart for the blacks who constituted so large a part of Augustana's neighborhood. He was a humble, unselfish servant of the Lord and singularly gifted. Clarence had him to lunch for an interview, fully persuaded in his own mind that he was the man sent from God for Augustana. When he asked Wayne how he felt about the possibility, Wayne answered, "My heart leaps up within me. My whole being says yes."

After an interview by the Augustana Board, their answer, too, was, "Yes, he's just the man for us." On the Monday after the special meeting of the congregation that extended Wayne Woods a call, Wayne began his ministry at Augustana. It became Wayne and Clarence's custom to have staff prayers in St. Eric's chapel each morning. Wayne's prayer that first morning was, "Thank you, dear Father, that you have put me in this post. I can hardly believe that I can walk out from this place and extend my hand to blacks, inviting them to fellowship and to work with us and to assure them that skin color makes no difference. Thank you, Father!"

Wayne had an infectious deep-down laugh and was great fun to be with. One morning when Clarence and I were teaching at a Camp Tremper Youth Retreat, we had to leave at an ungodly early hour to keep another commitment. We saw a flashlight beam

157

guiding its owner among the sleeping cabins on the mountainside. It was Wayne, come to bid us farewell and offer his prayer for our safe journey.

Finishing college at 20, Mary received a scholarship toward an experimental cram program at Brown University that would permit her to receive an M.A. and a teacher's certificate in one year. After finishing her master's, she offered herself to the church and was assigned to the Ashira Girls' School in Moshi, Tanzania. Following an orientation quarter at the Chicago Lutheran School of Theology, she would have a two-year assignment on the slopes of Mount Kilimanjaro.

Elizabeth, en route to her post in Indonesia as an English teacher at Nommenson University, was greatly impressed by the amazing relief program the Lutheran World Federation sponsored in Hong Kong. There was a staff opening, and some of the missionaries urged Elizabeth to encourage us to apply. Inspired by the global challenges taken on by our daughters, Clarence and I had discussed earnestly seeking a foreign assignment. Since we were both pushing 60, it would probably be now or never. So when the request came from the Lutheran World Federation, Clarence wrote saying we were available.

We were invited to New York for an interview and believed we'd be recommended. The board of the National Lutheran Council, however, stipulated that the appointee must have a social worker's degree. We were out. Knowing how eager we were for a foreign post, the New York office passed our dossier on to the Department of Overseas Churches of the National Council of the Churches of Christ in the U.S.A. Not long after, Clarence was interviewed by the director of that department. Our first offer was an immediate post in Teheran, Iran. Unfortunately, I had already promised to do a series of meetings in Europe and Africa for the Protestant Women of the Post, a mission to the wives of our military. I couldn't renege at so late a date, so we turned down the Iran opportunity.

We drove to Seattle for David's ordination, discussing our hopes for a foreign assignment. The day we arrived in Seattle a cable from the Protestant Fellowship in Dhahran, Saudi Arabia, reached us, informing us that Clarence had been called as pastor to that far place. The hand of God, we said to each other, surely was active in arranging this. We applied and answered the pages of questions, sent on pictures, and even taped a sermon. But just before the signature blank was the notation, "No one over 50 need apply." I scoffed, saying, "Send it in anyway, and add that we both water-ski!" Soon after we received a cable informing us, "By vote of the three congregations, we have changed our constitution to read: 'No one over 50 need apply except under unusual circumstances.'"

On what a tiny hinge a radical shift in one's destiny can move. A swim across Lake Independence and we get married. A skill in waterskiing and our work for the Lord picks up at a desert outpost. Although I always said, "My name is Ruth, and I'll go anywhere my husband's ministry leads him," I couldn't help asking, "Where in this wide world is Saudi Arabia?" Even though Dhahran was halfway around the world, we cabled our acceptance. We would be there by the week of Thanksgiving.

That fall was difficult. Mary was at our Lutheran seminary in Illinois, preparing to go to Tanzania, Africa, as a missionary teacher at the Ashira Girls' School. I flew to Europe to begin my four weeks of widely scattered meetings with the Protestant Women of the Post, returning just days before our departure. The impossible task of moving was Clarence's. If we were to become tumbleweeds, out of necessity we had to trim down our files and possessions, taking only the essentials. Moreover, sundering ties that had been aweaving these 15 years added a sweet-sad dimension to it all.

As we prepared for our move, we became concerned about Koja. It required constant maintenance, and we knew how busy our family members were. Koja could literally fall apart. But when we suggested selling it, each of them protested. In fact, Dave insisted, "Dad, if you sell Koja, I'll quit school and get myself a job so I can buy it." We knew he meant it, so we relented.

When the letter of call arrived from the Dhahran Fellowship president, one mystifying line read, "There must be no newspaper write-ups of your accepting this assignment." This meant a personal visit to the religious editors of the Washington papers and a long-distance phone conversation with a feature writer from

The Lutheran. Because Arabia was in the Muslim holy land and one of the king's titles was Defender of the Holy Koran, the church in Dhahran was kept under wraps. This was the reason behind the strange request; the oil company for whom many of the members of our new fellowship worked was jittery lest publicity endanger their concessions.

It was fortunate for Augustana that Wayne was already strongly rooted in their affections when we made our move. At the congregation's farewell, as Wayne rose to speak, a baby's cry was heard. Said Wayne, "The cry expresses how we all feel today as Ruth and Clarence leave us for a post halfway around the world."

Slipping unheralded out of Washington without one line of explanation in the news media made some of our friends ask, "What terrible breach of conduct did Pastor Nelson commit?" Nonetheless, an immense crowd of Augustana folk showed up at the airport to sing us off. The music resounded through that lofty plaza. Even an hour departure delay didn't scatter them; they remained until we took off on our new adventure—a mission for the Lord in Saudi Arabia.

A DREAM FULFILLED

11

En route to Dhahran we stopped off to visit Biz in Indonesia. We set down at Medan and spotted her in the waiting crowd. Customs were touchy—Clarence was temporarily divested of his billfold and I had to undress in a booth. But Elizabeth cornered a high government official to vouch for us, and in minutes we were in each other's arms. The short drive to Siantar had us squealing with delight as Elizabeth skillfully wove around buffalo, groups of squatting women leisurely sipping tea, and merry children at play.

Biz's bachelorette quarters on the Nommenson University campus were airy and spacious with high ceilings and wide doors. The bamboo furniture was well suited to the jungle clime. Bowls of exotic tropical fruit and splashes of flowers freshly gathered from the blooming shrubs outside the door made it home-beautiful. We were immediately introduced to Cassi, the cook and substitute mother, who prepared a fabulous 20-course Indonesian dinner.

Biz inveigled me into teaching one of her English classes of seminary men, and we were entertained by a student group

161

where we were each formally invested with a handwoven *ulos* ("scarf") as the students expressed their welcome in a native dance. We toured the Goodyear rubber plantation, swam in their pool, and were hosted at a dinner by the Lundbergs, the plantation managers.

The steamy heat had us down at first, but Siantar served as a good decompression chamber from our temperate American climate to the sizzling heat of Saudi Arabia. If Biz could take it, we were determined to do likewise. We traveled to Lake Toba and stayed at the vacation cottage maintained for the faculty's use, recalling globe-trotting Reuben's description of its breathtaking beauty as "the loveliest spot in the world." We made a pilgrimage to the Nommenson grave and also to the monument built to memorialize these early missionaries who were cannibalized by the shore of this idyllic lake.

Biz introduced us to Dr. Walter Lempp who was sent out from Germany by the Rhennish Mission Board to teach Old Testament Bible and Hebrew. We sensed a deep bond between Biz and Walle. All too soon, however, we were excitedly enplaning for the last leg of our journey to Saudi Arabia.

We overnighted at Bahrain in a tiny, overheated hotel room. Against my fierce objections, Clarence drank from the water carafe at our beside, insisting that since the hotel was British-run, the water should be safe. But it wasn't, and he arrived the next morning in Dhahran with a bad case of "the runs."

Dhahran was a godforsaken spot surrounded by unending stretches of sand dunes. Airport customs consisted of two shacks made of unpainted boards set apart with barriers of chicken wire. No one was on hand to welcome us, and having no Saudi riyals in our pockets, we stood in the blazing sun at a complete loss as to what to do. Within minutes, however, several cars of folks from the fellowship wheeled up in a cloud of dust. Our plane had arrived a little early, much to their and our discomfiture. But the warmth of their welcome soon dissipated all this. Grabbing our bags, we were off to our new home set down in an oil community halfway around the world.

The first days included a round of welcome dinners in the hospitable homes of our parishioners, a real trial for Clarence whose enteritis persisted. Our residence was a row house with a tiny patch of grass surrounded by a high concrete-block wall. It was furnished with surplus furniture and decor solicited from our members. We were very comfortable until our own household goods arrived a few months later.

Our congregation was made up primarily of young families; most of the adults were university graduates. They were totally committed to Christ and they assumed their roles in the church's activities with dedicated skill and enthusiasm. They were the church in action. The congregation gave missions (almost all centered in the Middle East) more than half its budget. Moreover, not one dollar went into real estate. Our services were held in the company movie theater which was available for our use free-of-charge, as was the well-equipped company school building. Clarence's modest salary and that of the part-time secretary were practically the congregation's only expenditures.

Once settled in, Clarence was off each morning to his tiny office in the senior staff recreation building. The Indian section of the

Our Dhahran fellowship included many Indian members

fellowship added an exciting dimension. I had long wanted to serve as a missionary in India. Now, at long last, I was fulfilling my dream. Most of the Indians had been trained in India's mission hospital as nurses or pharmacists. They were also devout believers. Their colorful saris and raven-black hair added quite a flair to our services.

One Indian nurse who stood out was Arjun Chauhan, a Mennonite, who was often in our home and came to call us Mom and Dad. He became deeply involved in our Sunday evening fellowship and also gathered with other Indian nurses each Saturday for a Bible study in their recreation building. Arjun enlisted the Indian children for our Sunday school, suggesting that a bus be hired to bring them in to the Fellowship Friday School (Friday was the Arabian sabbath). Arjun often took Clarence's place as the Bible teacher when Clarence was called away for other services.

Because the geographic area of mobility was so limited (a one-mile perimeter) some women struggled with claustrophobia and/or boredom. Many, however, turned their talents to working with music, ceramics, painting, sculpturing, gardening, and cooking. Some of the local artists achieved great renown. To own a painting by Reg Strange or Mrs. Shirlee Blank was to have a piece of authentic Arabiabilia.

Clarence and I became involved in "potpicking" and soon were familiar with sites of ancient villages among the dunes, now wholly engulfed by sand. With the shifting of the dunes in a *shamal* ("sand storm"), the sites were scrubbed bare. Their rubbish heaps became places to hunt such treasures as blue and red and tan pot shards from Persian cooking pots. Bits of ancient jewelry, broken perfume bottles, and coins were prizes when found. We would drive out early in the morning with sandwiches and coffee stashed in our VW to search or *shuf*, as the Arabs said. Usually there were no signs of human habitation, but it wasn't long before we were surrounded by curious children who popped up from behind the nearby sand dunes. They offered to sell curios they'd picked up and would ring around us when lunchtime came, hungrily watching each bite. Eagerly they accepted the invitation to join us in our lunch.

Clarence used many of the treasures from our "potpicking" to make collages. The first he made was a sacramental cup astride a Persian-blue world. The Chi Rho (the Greek letters for Jesus Christ) on the cup made clear his meaning: the poured-out life of Christ for the world. To the right of the cup was a lily of the valley, to the left a rose of Sharon worked out with broken glass, shells, and beads. Near the top was a representation of a fish, the first century symbol of the Christian. He became so engrossed in his work that I teasingly called him a "collageaholic."

I used some of my time to accompany an employee of Aramco's medical department on expeditions to nearby villages where young mothers assembled for classes in food preparation and child care. The company provided liquid refreshments that I augmented with Swedish spritz or pepparkakor. We women also spent many hours amusing little Arab children who were hospitalized, many suffering horrible burns from the open cooking fires set on the sand floors of the tents.

Exciting travel opportunities were another safety valve against boredom. Charter groups availing themselves of the Muslim religious holidays were organized for such places as Isfahan, the Holy Land, Cairo, and even to such out-of-the-way places as the Mount Sinai Monastery.

We also had visits from several members of our family. We sponsored a visit from Luther and Irene so Luther could give a lecture. Reuben stopped off on one of his annual global tours and went wild shooting pictures, some 800 in all.

Mary brought her missionary sidekick Glenice with her from Tanzania for a much-enjoyed Christmas stay. Christmas in Arabia was special, even though we were separated from many of our loved ones. We made every effort to keep traditions. We held a midnight service with the choir processing with candles. We decorated our meeting place with desert tamarisk and palm branches, and gathered the "loners" to a festal dinner we prepared. Some of us with Scandinavian background decided on a joint dinner with sylta, meatballs, rice pudding, sill, lefse, and cardamom breads. When we bewailed the fact that lutefisk would be missing, a friend spoke up saying, "I'll cable a friend to pick up some. He's just enplaning from New York." Then he did just that. His poor friend combed the New York delicatessens, all the while running up an astronomical taxi fare. At the last place he stopped, the butcher persuaded him to take a goodly piece of fresh cod saying it probably was what the Scandinavians called lutefisk. When it finally arrived at our home, I was given the task of preparing it, although I had no experience whatever with the smelly stuff. Once on the stove the smell became so offensive that Clarence rushed it out for a quick burial in the desert sand.

We also led a youth group of singers and instrumentalists to serenade the American consulate compound and the hospital with Christmas carols. The Aramco Women's Club asked me to present the Santa Lucia as done in Sweden, replete with the train of lovely young girls in long white dresses caught at the waist by wide crimson sashes. One of our skilled shop people made a genuine crown for the lit candles. The girls and their St. Stephen attendants carefully memorized the Lucia song, and I presented the story. The filled-to-capacity auditorium made the efforts well worthwhile, and everyone seemed to enjoy it immensely.

One day while Mary was still visiting us, an Aramcon said he'd like to introduce us to two Christian Arab friends out in the desert. We enthusiastically took him up, marveling that such were to be found. We left our car on a spot entirely bereft of any visible habitation and followed our guide over the intervening sand dunes. Suddenly he stopped short and, pointing to the sand, said, "Here they are." Two human skeletons were exposed in the sand just ahead. Then he explained, "I'm certain they were Christian. Their heads are toward Jerusalem. Every Muslim gets buried with his head pointed to Mecca."

While Mary was visiting us she developed a deep friendship with Amal Boody, a Syrian nurse who worked at the large Aramco hospital. Amal was a Christian whose dream was to one day open her own mission hospital deep in an unreached part of the Great Desert. She soon became like one of the family. The night of Mary's farewell party, Amal asked if we would mind picking her up on the way to the airport so she could say good-bye. "But the plane leaves so early," I protested, also thinking to myself, "and it will already be crowded what with the three of us and all Mary's luggage." But Amal insisted, so plans were arranged.

We picked her up the next morning while it was still dark. When we arrived at the airport, they asked for Mary's passport. A crisis. Unfamiliar with company rules, we had failed to post Mary's departure plans with the company's travel department, so they had not returned her passport to her. At this early hour the office would be closed. In panic Clarence turned to a high company official who was flying out on the same plane, but he said, "There isn't a thing you can do about it. Mary will have to take the next plane that leaves in a few days." The problem was that someone was driving long miles across country to meet her in Arusha. Such an upset in schedule would greatly inconvenience many people.

Then Amal, who had insisted on coming along, volunteered, "Give me the phone. I know the travel director personally, even his phone number." In a moment she had aroused him from sleep. He offered to pick up the passport and come posthaste to the airport. Now our problem was to delay this international flight until the papers arrived. The flight expediter, an Arab, joined us as we anxiously watched the road from Dhahran. Finally he said, "I'm sorry, it just isn't possible to delay leaving any longer."

I pleaded, "Oh, please. Allah will bless you." Just then we saw headlights break out of the gray morning. Clarence ran to intercept our friend and, shouting our thanks, grabbed the passport. The counter clerks quickly stamped it and Mary ran up the ramp. Apparently her plight had been made known to the folks aboard, for they clapped and cheered her down the aisle.

As we watched the plane soar out of view, I smiled warmly at Amal and thanked God she had been there. What a witness for Christ she was in spite of some derision she received, especially from a young internist, an atheist who often sought her out during coffee breaks to jest at her Christianity. He would ask, "If Adam and Eve were the first humans on earth, where did Cain and Abel procure their wives?" Or, "If God is love and all-powerful, why is the child of praying Christian parents struck down with crippling polio?" Amal's strong faith was more than a match for this "Doctor A." When he would twit her with, "Amal, you seem to be on personal terms with the Almighty. Have you ever seen him?" Her answer would come back, "Indeed, I have, with the eyes of faith. Moreover, I know his Son Jesus, and Jesus is the spitting image of God as he said, 'He who has seen me has seen the Father.'" Or when he belittled Christianity by saying, "Look at the long centuries Christianity has been in the world and then look at the mess we're still in." Her quick answer was, "You remind me of the heckler in London's Trafalgar Square who, with a dirty face, made fun of a Salvationist using these same words. Well, sir, the Salvationist said, 'Fella, look at the eons water has been in the world and then look at the condition of your face.' Christ hasn't failed. We've simply failed to apply his timeless truths. And doctor, I'm praying for you that God will yet be permitted to get through to your needy heart."

Imagine our surprise when not too long after that, late at night, our doorbell rang and there stood Doctor A, still in his white uniform. He said, "Excuse me for coming so late, but I've got trouble. Bad trouble. A colleague suggested I seek you out for counseling when I shared with him some of the dark thoughts I've entertained. He said I shouldn't delay." Then Doctor A told of how he had contemplated poisoning his wife and children because his wife was threatening to divorce him; she felt that he totally neglected and disregarded his family. As a doctor, he knew he was on the verge of a breakdown and could lose control of himself at any time. His body was torn with stifled sobs as he uttered, "Oh, I need your help and that of God Almighty."

As Clarence read from the Bible, never did a heart reach more avidly for the great promises of Scripture. He committed himself to Christ. Clarence went home with him that night to speak with his wife—she already had recognized that their home needed to be built on a more solid foundation. The change in Doctor A was reflected in a change in the entire medical staff. The doctors greeted Clarence as he made his sick calls, and they began to phone him to ask his help with depressed patients.

The first time Biz came to visit us she was waiting to hear from Walle. He had gone back to Germany to seek release from a vow of celibacy which he and several classmates had taken together, hoping to vicariously expiate their nation's war guilt. We were shocked at how thin and depressed Biz was as she flew into our arms at Dhahran's airport.

Now a continent apart, Biz just wasn't sure the marriage was right, much as she admired and loved Walle. She spent the day looking through the family slides, talking of days gone by. Burdened as we were for her, we knew that any attempted persuasion from us was wrong. We tried to keep her very occupied. She flew with us to Riyadh, the capital city, and we did many other exciting things. One Sunday she gave an illustrated talk on "The 100 Years of Christianity in Indonesia," capturing the people's hearts. With time, Biz gained perspective. When Easter arrived she asked us to hold a private healing service. "God has touched and renewed my life," was her simple statement. So when Walle's cable arrived announcing that he was free to ask for her hand, she, too, was ready. She and Walle were engaged. Soon she was off to Germany, her heart bursting with joy.

I flew to Stuttgart a week early to help with wedding preparations. Clarence arrived the day before. He was almost late to the wedding, however, because he first went to the wrong church and then got lost. As he was speeding to the right church, a policeman stopped him. "Mein toehter verheiratet" ("My daughter is being married"), Clarence explained, and the policeman waved him on. Despite the stiff, awe-inspiring setting, the wedding itself was informal with no processional of bridesmaids. The whole party simply moved to the church front, Biz and Walle to chairs set for them. A former colleague from their ministry in Indonesia gave the sermon. Afterwards we went to a local inn for a family dinner. Amazingly, the president of our Dhahran Fellowship was there. He presented the couple with a sizeable check so Biz could take her husband to America to meet the rest of his new family and they could get to know firsthand this humble, gifted man.

The lengthy program consisted of contributions of poetry and drama cleverly worked out in German by Walle's many nieces and nephews. A tremendous gathering of friends and great conversations followed the program. Agneta had flown in from Sweden to be an attendant, standing in for Mary who was unable to leave her assignment in Tanzania. Frau Polster was there too, with the two of her children who were still at home—Pfarrer Polster had died. He now walked with Jesus in the light, close to the one who sustained and guided him through all those perils. All their children were being educated and were giving their lives back to their Creator in service to their fellowmen.

Walle not only captured the hearts of our family in America, but those of the Dhahran folk as well. When they visited us in Saudi Arabia, his natural humor broke out as he responded to their welcome. Knowing how carefully everyone had been looking him over, he said, "Folks, this is the way I look to the front." Then, turning his back, added, "This is the way I look behind." His sermon on Sunday, given in clear English, was well received. We hated to see them leave us, knowing it might be quite some time before we would be back together.

Soon, however, we were enjoying a charter flight to Jerusalem. When the plane landed we piled into buses which took us to our hotels. Each evening we held a briefing on the next day's schedule. We gave scripture background and heard historical and archeological lectures given by people steeped in the lore of the Holy Land. Among these was Mrs. Bertha Vester who Lowell Thomas discussed as "My Most Unforgettable Person" in *Readers' Digest*. Although she spoke from a wheelchair, her mind was razor-sharp as she recalled the exciting saga of the years she spent ministering to the needy people of Jerusalem, many times caught in the crossfire of contending armies.

We knelt for prayers at Gethsemane, gathered devoutly in the rain at the garden tomb just below Calvary for an early morning service, sang Christmas carols at Bethlehem in the cave where the manger child was birthed, and drank water from Jacob's well in Samaria. It was a prayerful pilgrimage in Jesus' footsteps.

One day we were with a party of Jerusalem pilgrims from Arabia on World Day of Prayer and thought it would be wonderful to have a Mount of Olives experience. The only time it could be arranged was the early morning hour of 5:30. Having set our alarms for 4:45, we awakened to a cold, drizzly day, but went on with our plans, undaunted. We joined some 60 intrepid souls gathered at the top of that sacred mount. A colorful company, Indian women in their saris, Lebanese, Syrian, and Jordanian, joined us Americans in the fellowship of prayer.

170

At first we huddled together in the cold, but as we lifted our voices in "Holy, holy, holy," the rain ceased, and we experienced an hour of scripture and prayer such that our warmed hearts dispelled the chill of our bodies. Just as our service was drawing to a close, the Master Electrician turned the switch, and a glorious shaft of orange, gold, and crimson light broke through the clouds in the east. Spontaneously overflowing hearts broke into song, "Jesus shall reign where'er the sun, does its successive journeys run," followed by "He's got the whole world in his hands." As we returned from the mountain to the hotel, we were met by those to whom the warmth of their beds meant more than this visit with the one who ascended from that very mount. However, the glow in the early risers' eyes conveyed what had been missed.

Later, using the three-week vacation granted every other year, we visited Mary in Tanzania at the Ashira Girls' School high on Kilimanjaro's mountain slope. That Mary was highly thought of was quickly evident. Early we were interviewed by two shy girls asking about our life together. They were completely amazed at the idea of a minister's wife actively working with her husband and giggled when we unabashedly shared some of our more romantic chapters.

Mary arranged for Clarence to preach on Sunday. Their largest assembly room was the school's physics laboratory, and all 400 girls plus a sprinkle of faculty from nearby schools were crowded in. Their singing of the hymns was as if an organ were played with all stops pulled out, and the words stood out as if sculptured. The service over, Clarence was about to lift his hands for the benediction when Mary tugged at his sleeve, whispering, "Not yet, Dad. The service doesn't end here." Singing "Why don't you love my Jesus?" the 400 girls filed out, row on row, and assembled in formation on the grassy square of the schoolyard. The brilliant sunlight in that pure mountain air created a nimbus over each black curly head. What a sight.

Mary and Glenice shared a comfortable staff house with their own cook who made each meal an experience. Early one morning I slipped out to enjoy the sunrise on the mountain and beheld the most magnificent sight. There stood the snow-covered mountain peak, unshrouded, in all its pink-white splendor—a very rare sight.

171

I dashed back into the house exclaiming, "Kili's out! Quick! Quick!"

When we returned to Dhahran, things went on very much as before. Then one morning I woke up with double vision. An Egyptian friend on the medical staff said a virus had attacked my optic nerve, so a specialist was called for consultation. The verdict was that I be put to bed; I was housebound for several weeks. During this time the fellowship members brought our dinners, an outpouring of love that deeply touched me. The greatest deprivation was being unable to attend worship.

On one of those housebound Sundays I was paid a visit by Tom and Imogene Allen and their two little girls, Terry and Jean. Imogene had made a lamb cake that Terry and Jean proudly bore on a silver tray. They spoke excitedly about their upcoming trip to visit the place where Jesus walked, a fulfillment of one of their life's deep desires. They were leaving in a week. Their original ticket called for them to return on Sunday night, but because they had been able to expedite their Jerusalem visit, they would be returning two days earlier. They promised to come by to see me as soon as they returned.

They never made it. Their plane, flight 444, came in for a landing during a shamal and disappeared. A fruitless search of the desert surrounding the airport offered no clues. Finally a search plane spotted the wreckage in the nearby waters of the Arabian Ocean at Half Moon Bay. The company called for the clergy to stand by as the bodies were brought up one by one by deepsea divers. All 83 bodies were eventually found, and the entire community went into mourning.

A joint memorial service was held in the school the following Monday. The Catholic priest and the Protestant ministers conducted the service, and their joint choirs sang. The resurrection words of the victorious Christ brought their powerful witness from the lips of each. The closing hymn sung by the united choirs was, "A Mighty Fortress Is Our God." In this hour of tragedy we joined hands to seek the comfort that only God can give. There was triumph in the lives of those who knew the reality of the words of our Christ, "I am the resurrection and the life; he who believes in me, though he die, yet shall he live."

A half hour after our return from the service, Clarence received a phone call from a company official who said, "A miracle happened at that service. Before it, the camp was filled with fear, tension, and uncertainty. The seeds of faith planted at that service have made all the difference in the world. How grateful I am."

The crash of the 444 wasn't the only disaster that weekend. Our Protestant Fellowship had an annual Oasis Day, a time when missionaries were brought in to share inspiration and insights. We were anticipating a visit from Bishop Chandu Ray, whom we had met at a retreat at Green Lake, Wisconsin. This humble, great Christian had a story to tell that we were eager to share with our parishioners. He was due to arrive at 1 A.M. Thursday. Clarence had picked up a virus and had a rising temperature, so I insisted he go to bed. I joined the president of the council in meeting the bishop. Circumstances at the airport delayed our getting him released for two hours, and it was almost four when I finally fell into bed. The reasons for the bishop's delay were a real cause for concern, so we lay in bed discussing them. At about 5:30 I finally fell into deep sleep, only to be awakened at 6:30 by the ringing of the phone. A nurse from the hospital told me that one of our Indian women who had been "care-taking" some American children while their parents were in the States had been stabbed by a prowler and was bleeding to death. Immediately Clarence arose and went to the hospital to be with the distraught husband and to pray for Surim's healing. He spent the entire morning there as again and again they fed blood into this frail little woman, hoping to get her blood pressure up high enough to operate on her slashed liver. Finally the doctors decided their only hope was to go ahead and operate. Her gallant fight and sturdy faith, the skills God gave the physicians and nurses, and the power of prayer combined to result in her recovery.

We scheduled our first long vacation so we could return to Koja. Before leaving Europe we picked up a VW to use during the two months at home. Arriving in the States, we overnighted in New Jersey. Then we set out for Washington, D.C., where Clarence had promised to preach the sermon at the ordination of one of his confirmands, Jim Wiberg. Augustana opened her arms to us —Pastor Wayne Woods saw to that.

Wayne's years came to an end all too early. A vicious cancer that meant ever-increasing pain and a withering of the body took over. Yet he bore the pain and the sufferings that not even medicine could smother with such courage and faith that all who knew him recognized God was truly with him. In his closing months, some of his final words to his beloved congregation as he preached from his wheelchair set in the sanctuary crossing were recorded by his wife Margaret. Sensitively, with scrupulous honesty, she recorded in a book entitled *We Lived with Death* his struggles with suffering, how he took on pain and drew from it spiritual gain and his ultimate victory.

We did our program "Nights in Arabia" for Augustana, enjoying the opportunity to renew these friendships. Then we headed for Minnesota and family. What joyful reunions. Sand Lake's cool

Relaxing at Koja

174

northern waters to swim in, the flora and fauna—we reveled in Minnesota's verdant beauty after our two desert years.

We returned for our second Arabian desert term by way of the West Coast. This allowed for a visit to Clarence's forester brother Art and his wife, Ethel, in Phoenix. We also visited Jon and Juni in Olympia, Washington, reveling in the time we could have with them and their growing family. There was Kristin, born in 1960, Leah, born in 1961, and David, born in 1962. Biz and Walle had just had their first child, Karl. We would be attending his baptism on our way back to Saudi Arabia.

During a stopover in Hawaii we swam in the beautiful waters, visited the Lutheran church, and toured the pineapple acres of this volcano-created island. Then we headed for Japan over the wide blue Pacific. We had not taken into account the day we would lose when crossing the international date line, so according to our schedule, we arrived a day late. Pastor Hoaglund, our missionary friend who was to have been our guide and host, had to return empty-handed from the Tokyo airport to his home in Bofu. Painfully aware of our oversight, we made our way as best we could through the people-packed airport and finally found the information attendant who arranged a hotel room for us. We called Pastor Hoaglund to express our regrets and got instructions for a train in the morning. Then we taxied to our hotel. Once settled in the room, we struck out for our Lutheran Student Center. The chaplain took us in tow, and we shared happy hours with fellow Christians.

The next day, after a delightful train ride, we were at last with the Hoaglunds. While in Japan we stopped at Hiroshima and saw the horrible scars left by the American-triggered atom bomb. Our hearts bled for the tens of thousands of victims. We bowed prayerfully at the eternal light, kept forever burning at the commemoratory monument to the dead, and prayed for forgiveness for our nation and that the world take note of its tragic lesson. We there resolved we would do whatever was in our power to work for peaceful solutions of international problems.

A special treat was our overnight stay at the Three Sisters Inn, with its incomparable food and its steamy sauna bath. We slept that night on straw mats.

Back in Tokyo we reconfirmed our Indonesia flight from Jakarta to Sumatra and cabled Biz and Walle as to our arrival time. Taiwan was next on our agenda. Once again our beloved missionaries were on hand and received us with open arms. With them were Paul T. M. King, our D.C. son, and Mr. G. Nelson Yu, who had been an enthusiastic member of Augustana as an exchange student in government finance.

Paul and his wife Lillian hosted our stay, installing us in a regal suite at the Grand Imperial Hotel, the nicest hotel Clarence and I ever stayed at—it had an onyx grand staircase and storied carvings. Our spacious room had white marble wainscot and a balcony from which we could look across the sprawling city to the mountains beyond. We felt like modern-day Alices in Wonderland. Paul joined us every morning for breakfast, and then Mr. Yu would take us sight-seeing in his chauffeur-driven limousine. We drove to Madam Chiang Kai-shek's mountain retreat where she held her Sunday Bible classes.

It was amazing how many people we met in Taipei who had been guests in our Washington home. We counted at least 12, each demanding to return our hospitality, but there simply weren't enough days. So they combined efforts for one big dinner.

It was hard saying good-bye to Paul. He wanted with all his heart to take up studies at our Lutheran seminary and become a pastor. Clarence had written to Dr. Bergendorf, who readily opened the seminary door. Senator Hubert Humphrey, too, had gone to work through State Department channels, seeking to have Paul's earlier commitment to return to work for his government waived. But the door remained stubbornly closed. Although bitterly disappointed, Paul had resolved that his investment in Christ's kingdom need not be that of a pastor. He had asked for grace to give his life totally to Christ in whatever role he found himself—exactly what he was doing now.

Our next stop was colorful Hong Kong. Again, missionaries were ever so helpful. We swam in the South China Sea, addressed the Bible school and the seminary, visited the Christian Buddhist Center, and the Freedom Bridge, the border with mainland China where so many refugees had shed the repressive yoke of communism. A cablegram from Biz reached us in Hong Kong asking us to bring along a case of Similac infant formula and some needed polio inoculations packed in ice for Karl. Friends helped us with these purchases. The cluster of friends seeing us off held a prayer session on the airport tarmac. Since our luggage was overweight, Clarence carried the heavy, bulky case of milk on board and put it under our seat. I clutched the thermos with its iced inoculations.

We flew to Jakarta where we were to transfer to a plane for Medan, Sumatra. The ticket agent there declared we didn't have reservations on that flight despite the fact that we purchased our tickets weeks before and had confirmed them by cable while in Japan. Only one plane a week made this trip. Clarence pleaded with the agent, but with little success. Then I drew from my purse a recent snapshot of baby Karl and said to the agent, "This is our grandchild. We have come all the way from America for his baptism. Surely there is something that can be done." Hope sprang anew when he replied, "Let me ask my boss." After a wordy consultation, he was back. He told us to be on hand the next morning at departure time. Some passengers might not show.

We were there early the next day, in time to see our U.S. consul general at Medan personally supervising the loading of case after case of liquor and mixes onto our plane. We knew immediately that it wasn't space that was at a premium, but weight. The threat was that we might displace the cases of whiskey. We were greatly relieved when they said we could enplane. Finally we were on our way.

When we set down at Medan, however, no one was there to meet us. Our letters and cable had not arrived, so Biz and Walle were still in Siantar, 70 miles away. We phoned a friend of Biz's who offered to drive us. Soon we were in the arms of two very happy people who had given up on our making it at all. The next morning we were off to church for the baptism. More than 30 infants were dedicated to God that day. After the service we lingered in the churchyard for greetings. The Indonesians were warm and friendly, looked us straight in the eye, and were not in the least overwhelmed by us white foreigners.

We visited the church's Bible school and its school for the blind. Our respect for this emerging young church grew with every one of these visits. At the leper village we admired the neatly kept grounds and cottages. Just the day before, more than two dozen lepers had been released as arrested cases and returned to their respective villages to live a normal life. Back once again at the seminary at Siantar, we felt that the Christian church in Indonesia had deep roots in the hearts of these islanders.

In addition to teaching Old Testament Bible, Walle also was writing a three-volume commentary on Genesis in Indonesian. It was his magnum opus, his gift of himself in pure love to the Indonesian church.

Soon we were facing another difficult departure. We were feted by the faculty at a reception. Although the faculty was truly international, it was heartening to note the number of Indonesians qualifying—a quantum jump from the day when the Dutch ruled these islands. One woman told of how during the Dutch rule the swimming beaches had signs warning Dogs and Indonesians Strictly Forbidden.

It was hard to say farewell in Siantar. Once seated on the plane, I shook with stifled sobs as we waved farewell to our Indonesian family. Then it was back to the desert for our second two-year term.

The last two years in Saudi Arabia we settled in a remodeled dwelling that had earlier been a dormitory for single workers. We had three bedrooms, two baths, and an L-shaped living room and dining room. In addition, under that one roof were the church office and a sizeable hall for use by youth groups, Bible classes, and women's groups. I usually taught the regular Sunday morning women's Bible class that could draw upwards of 50. We started a business women's group and a children's group, with the Bible as our chief text.

Neighbors to us in our new location were the Episcopal rector and the Catholic priest. We shared our Christianity in every way, clearly evidenced when we held a joint memorial service for President Kennedy after his tragic assassination. The Episcopal minister took the scripture and prayers, Clarence the sermon, and the Catholic priest the requiem, translated into English so all might understand. Every able-bodied Aramcon attended this deeply moving service, as did the families of the American consulate located a mile beyond our compound. Following the service, a company official commented, "It's amazing what this service did for us all. Each of us came to it deeply shaken and heavy of heart, but we left with the trauma lifted. Once again hope took over and we could thank God for all the good this young president was able to accomplish in his short time in office."

The isolation of that far place could get to us at times. We fixed Tuesday as the day for getting out the family letter which Clarence carbon-copied to make the typing less burdensome. The return letters from family were great boosters. We kept a sharp lookout for the green flag that was hoisted on the post office flagpole when the mails were distributed.

We were keeping a pretty fast pace—in addition to his regular duties, Clarence was filling a vacancy in the neighboring oil village in the interim between pastors. One day we had traveled over 50 miles across the hot desert to this town, held a service, a Bible class, a children's group, and then a young people's group in the early evening. We returned to our compound around nine o'clock. As we were turning down our street, I noticed a couple of friends heading for the movie, and the thought occurred to me that it would be nice to relax at the cinema. I mentioned it to Clarence, saying, "I wonder what is on at the movies tonight?" His tired response was, "Well, you know how to find out. Ask the recreation office." That really got my dander up. I thought, "As the man in the family, if he cared enough, wouldn't *he* do that?" But I didn't give up. When we got into the house, I went to the phone to make the inquiry, feeling very abused. The title the man at the other end of the line mumbled didn't sound very interesting, so I was about to forget my request when I saw Clarence, already in his pajamas and dressing gown, snuggled in the most comfortable chair, ensconced in *The Christian Century*.

This crowning touch of cooperation almost undid me. What if it had been a movie I really wanted to see? Hadn't I tried to be helpful all day? Weren't we here, halfway around the world, together? Hadn't my whole life changed due to the patterns necessitated by this isolated place? Other mothers had their children close by. The grievances piled up thick and fast. I stomped into the bedroom to put on the best pout I was capable of.

Then God gently knocked. He reminded me what I had been

179

teaching the women in the Bible class that day, that instead of thinking of what I wanted, why spoil this evening? There was our comfortable home and a million things to be thankful for. I didn't capitulate immediately—I'm too stubborn for that. But God didn't give up. He put it into my mind to answer two letters from elderly friends who had blessed my life that past week. (Little did I know that while I was writing the one letter, God was calling her home.)

By the time I had finished one note, the poison was seeping out. When I completed the second, I went into the living room and asked, "How about a game of Scrabble?" This is what he had wanted to do, finding it great relaxation. We played our game, and I went to bed. (I wonder if there wasn't some self-righteousness in me yet!) The next morning I awakened early and began reviewing the preceding evening. Ashamed of my childishness, when Clarence opened his eyes I said, "Forgive me for being foolish last night. I should have thought of what you needed." We had a great day.

We made a point of daily outdoor exercise. Sometimes it was tennis, ignoring the heat as best we could. Almost daily we went for an evening swim in the olympic-size pool. Frequently we'd take the perimeter hike, following the path along the five-square-mile tornado fence that ringed our community. And just about every day, summer and winter, we'd slip out to Half Moon Bay for a noontime dip. I'd pack a lunch for this one-hour outing. Old-timers of the community looked on us as two polar bears, but we considered the winter dips here easier than those late summer swims back in northern Minnesota waters.

We kept ourselves busy with the women's Bible class each Sunday morning, the afternoon Bible groups, the early evening Youth for Christ group, an adult evening Bible discussion group every Monday, the Indian Bible class on Saturday, and a weekly noon luncheon for the Aramco secretaries. One day during an after-school children's Bible group, an Arab lad in a white ghutra stood in the classroom doorway, curiosity glueing him to the spot. When Clarence motioned for him to join in the game, he turned and fled. Afterward the Arab janitor asked, "Do you know who that was? He is one of our princes, a son of King Ibn Saud."

180

On Friday afternoons during the winter we preempted two or three volleyball courts for couples from church. We also had a theater group, a group of square dance enthusiasts, and a group of artists, concert pianists, painters, and sculptors. Something for anyone who truly wanted to relieve boredom.

From time to time we'd plan picnics on the sandy beaches of Half Moon Bay, sometimes staying overnight. We would drive to the slip side of a dune and unroll the sleeping bags on the yielding golden sand of the bay. Some of our friends had boats moored at the company-operated marina, so we could fish and even water-ski.

Each year the Sunday school held its picnic at Half Moon Bay. Although our group was primarily Americans, it also was quite international with Indian nurses, Arabs, Europeans, Orientals, and even Icelandics. No effort was spared to delight the children and parents with races, games, and gobs of hamburgers served with beans and potato salad, free ice-cream cones, and pop. The day concluded with all of us seated on a gentle dune for a sing and concluding devotional. The setting sun over the water and the breathtaking beauty of undulating sand and dunes made a scene hard to surpass.

Just at sunset the children formed a line at the top of a sand dune whose 60-degree slope ended abruptly at the water's edge. Holding hands to form a human chain, they ran at top speed down the slope and into the sea. It looked like such fun that Clarence and I joined in. But just before reaching the water, the soft sand enveloped my feet, and my momentum threw me onto the hard-pan created by the heavy salt content of the water. I distinctly heard a sharp crack and felt myself falling into the water, then blackness. Clarence dashed to my rescue, holding my head out of the water while the youth ran to fetch help from workmen nearby. They were afraid I had broken my back, so they took a picnic tabletop and carefully eased me onto it. Then they bore me to their pickup truck for a fast ride to the hospital.

Just as they were starting out, I came to momentarily and said to the children surrounding the truck, "There's a pan of brownies in the back seat of our VW. You go ahead and have your spread while these men run me to Dhahran." Then I slipped back into unconsciousness. Coming to again, I asked, "Clarence, what happened?" I never heard the answer though—I slipped back under.

What a pitiable sight I must have been, still in my rubber swimming cap, my bathing suit covered with beach sand. Finally we arrived at the hospital and skilled, loving hands took charge. I had a broken arm, a difficult fracture close to the shoulder. The doctors were deaf-eared to my plea to be allowed to go home once they set it. I did get to go home the next day, wearing my arm in a sling, to preside over our mother-daughter banquet.

Some Fridays Clarence exchanged pulpits with the pastor in Abqaiq. We greatly enjoyed our friendship with Pastor Cecil and Betty Johnson who served this fellowship just 50 miles over the desert. Cecil was a pastor from the Covenant church with a warm loving spirit who also enjoyed his Swedish background. His messages were heartwarming and evangelical. Betty was outstanding at training children's choirs, and they both related very well to the Indian nurses and other employees.

Our routine for these Fridays was to leave Dhahran in the early morning when the heat was less oppressive. We would drive in our bathing suits in order to save our good clothes. Arriving at Abqaiq, we'd jump into the pool for a vigorous swim and then pull our clothes on. We would breakfast at the air-conditioned dining hall and afterwards present ourselves at Sunday school. An hour later Clarence would lead the service held in the cinema. Some beautiful friendships grew out of these visits.

Our usual round of sight-seeing meant taking the 100-mile desert road to Hofuf. We dubbed a certain oasis just this side of Scribner's Canyon our "Howard Johnson's." A cluster of palm trees afforded a shady spot to spread our lunch on an Arabian straw mat. Hofuf was untouched by "progress," vying with Damascus as the oldest continuously inhabited city in the world. Aromatic spices filled the air. Here were moneychangers' booths manned by merchants with chiseled, hawklike features. Here also was Brass Alley where we could buy all sizes of beak-nosed coffeepots so characteristic of Arabia. The women's market with its dates and other foodstuffs was fascinating. The main attraction, however, was the camel market. One day each week these vile-smelling but patient beasts, "ships of the desert," were auctioned off. We never tired of gawking at the critters at close hand, noting their supercilious expressions. Muslim legend explains it like this: "There are 100 names for Allah. We know 99 of them, but only the camel knows the 100th. So he keeps his nose in the air and wears that superior look." Never does he look funnier than when folding or unfolding his awkward legs to squat or arise. Aramcons often said, "This creature surely was designed by a committee."

On one of these trips we came upon a horrid sight in the city square where five beheadings had just occurred. There on the sands only yards away lay the truncated torsos of five youth, their severed heads rolled to the side with the sand drinking up the spilled blood. In Arabia the exposure of this gruesome sight substitutes for our newspaper coverage in conveying the message that crime doesn't pay.

Reuben visited Saudi Arabia as our sponsored guest. (No "tourist" could get an entrance visa to this Muslim holy land.) He was terribly excited about this picture-book land. One of the photographs he took recorded a horde of flies on a quarter of camel meat hanging on a butcher's hook. In fly season this was a common sight indeed. When we saw little children who did not even bother to shoo away the clusters of flies in their nostrils, their eyes, and at the side of their mouths, we knew why the average life span of an Arab at that time was only 27 years.

Another activity that helped relieve the boredom of our confined community was a quarterly trip of some 1300 miles along the Tapline, the pipeline that carried the oil, ending in a three-day holiday in Beirut. We visited four oil pumping stations located at intervals along the way, having written ahead to notify the children and adults of the upcoming class and worship. As many as a score of adults often showed for the worship and hungrily took in the hidden manna of the words. One time, however, a pipeline leak drew off all but one worshiper. Clarence told him the story of a Methodist circuit rider in Texas who arrived at one of his preaching stations to find only one person there. He expressed his disappointment and said, "We'll skip today, hoping for better next time." The man who had come to worship responded, "Sir, I'm only a cowhand and know nuthin' 'bout preachin'. But if I had brought a load of feed and only one critter showed, I'd be dang-busted if I'd go off without having thrown him some." The preacher accepted the implied rebuke, turned back to the pulpit, and went through the full service, complete with sermon. Expecting commendation as he shook the Texan's hand at the door, he was instead met with, "Sir, if I did throw that critter some feed, I'd be danged if I'd throw him the whole load."

Some deep friendships developed at these stations set in the utter desolation of the drab, rock-strewn landscape. We greatly cherished some of the gifts pressed into our hands such as the heavy Arabian brass pestle and a Qaisumah diamond we had Beirut gold workers make into a necklace.

The brief stay in Beirut was a welcome break from our strenuous schedule. We heard a symphony concert out under the star-studded canopy of the heavens, the soft breezes and the unbroken stillness enhancing every note sounded. Another favorite run was to Baalbeck on the eastern edge of Lebanon to see the storied ruins of the Temple of Venus with their row on row of huge stone monoliths.

On another of our short vacations we toured our LCA mission stations in Tanzania and met friends of many years as well as some more recently made. We stopped to visit Anne "Sunshine" Hall at Kiombi, a school for missionary children. Anne had come from our Augustana congregation in Washington, the first black missionary to be commissioned.

On the morning we enplaned to return to Dhahran, we were hardly airborne when the pilot announced, "We've a fire in one of the wheels." The sand had created enough friction to ignite the greases. But in minutes we were safely down again and the fire quickly smothered. Careful inspection determined that we could go on. It made a big difference to us that this pilot, even with all his RAF flying experience, never got into his cockpit without first kneeling in prayer to ask God to be with him at the controls.

We were also able to visit Mary's Ashira cottage a second time as well as the Lutheran Theological Seminary in Madras, the city of Calcutta, and the Taj Mahal, a site even more breathtaking than we'd imagined.

Swifter than a weaver's shuttle, our desert years drew to a close. The nudge that brought us to a decision about our plans for the future was a call from the Lutheran World Federation. Its executive director wanted us to consider serving the church at LWF headquarters in Geneva, Switzerland. It seemed well-timed since we were nearing the close of our second two-year stint. The abrasive climate and the constrictions of such a closed-in community could have an impact on our health. Even though we dreaded severing the ties that by now had deep roots, we made the decision to answer the call.

Soon the company movers were upon us. Some half dozen or so spent days sitting on our kitchen floor carefully crating our things. They worked in slow motion, gently enjoying each separate article of household gear. Before wrapping an item, they would hold a conference as to its possible use. Often they quizzed us to settle the argument. I was kept busy making tea for these happy Arabs. Finally a mountain of boxes stood stacked in the basting sun of our front yard, waiting to be taken to the ship. The few items we did not take along were quickly sold.

The several farewell parties pulled heavily at our hearts. At the parting communion service, Clarence and I together sang "I Look Not Back"—all eight verses. Our eyes overflowed as did many another's. Over 500 came to bid us good-bye at a reception held at the company guest house.

It was hardest to part with the Indian personnel who had their own special party for us. They literally clung to us. There was Arjun, calling us Mom and Dad and presenting us with beautiful gifts, including gold cuff links for Clarence. And there was Hassan, our Arab gardener with whom we had developed a deep friendship. One day we drove 30 miles into the desert to visit his village and meet his family. Sometimes he would come to work carrying a handful of dirty, bantam-sized chicken eggs. When the news percolated through to him of our departure, he stood at our door. First he embraced Clarence and then ceremoniously rubbed his nose on each cheek and for full measure added a kiss.

185

The Indian personnel held their own special party for us

Taking Clarence's hand, he put it over his heart and spoke two carefully rehearsed English words, "My brother."

Once our departure plane was airborne, we circled back over the beautiful new Dhahran airport, a noble example of the skill of Japanese architect Yamasaki. Dhahran had changed since the day we arrived four years ago. It no longer was a hostile, barren place, but home.

FROM DESERT TO MOUNTAIN: SERVING GOD IN THE ALPS

12

As we deplaned at Geneva, the sun was shining on the majestic Alps and a band of church members was on hand to greet us. They were most helpful in seeing us settled into our apartment nestled in the Alps. A table, a few chairs, and a bed with blankets were our furnishings for the first weeks while we waited for our shipment from Arabia.

The church building, constructed under the aegis of the German church, was nearly 200 years old. It was not allowed to look like a church; only the Calvin-established churches could stand out visibly as places of worship. Inconspicuous boards with small gilt letters gave notice that a congregation gathered here each Sunday for worship. Otherwise it appeared to be just another ancient apartment building, built of stone and facing the main square of the old city. The German minister and his family lived on the second floor. A third-floor apartment had been rented for years by an elderly woman who stoutly maintained tenant rights by virtue of city law. High on the hill just above it reared the proud towers and lofty nave of the Cathedral of St. Peter and St. Paul with its flying buttresses and thick walls.

The worn stone stairs leading up to Clarence's tiny library office were evidence of many feet through the centuries. The sanctuary was studied in its plainness. It had a freestanding marble altar and a wine glass-shaped pulpit with canopy and worn wooden steps centering the front wall, declaring the importance of God's Word. A balcony ringed the three sides, and an ancient tracker-action organ occupied the rear wall. The hand-fabricated pews were painted white with a brown trim; the colonial-style windows were of clear glass. The only decor was the Beatitudes lettered in German.

We began our work with a winnowed band showing for services, but rejoiced as the pews began to fill. Soon a volunteer choir bolstered the hymning and liturgy and enriched our worship with anthems. Choir practices and the monthly meetings of the women's groups were held at our apartment. Our best cups and silver and fresh flowers always crowned the table for such gatherings. Each Sunday morning adults gathered here for Bible discussions. Our biggest problem was finding housing for our Sunday school. The inadequate quarters of the German day school were the best available. We kept looking, but to no avail.

Since we shared the German congregation's sanctuary, we were represented on their council and divided the building maintenance costs with them. Each month Clarence sat on this committee and had his bout with the German language. Our other representative directed a whispered translation in Clarence's ear, keeping him aware of what was being said. We had our own council, too, with subcommittees covering the usual areas of concern. The follow-through and interest these men and women displayed were a source of great encouragement. Many had jobs that called for much travel, but whenever they were in Geneva they pitched in and helped.

We established excellent relationships with the American Episcopal Church, the leader in the English-speaking community. We kept cordial ties with the Scotch Presbyterians, the Church of England, and the English Roman Catholic church. Each month the clergy from these various churches met in one or the other's hcme. The day they gathered at our apartment, Clarence served Swedish pancakes, a tremendous hit. Each Christmastime we joined for an English carol sing that was exceptionally well attended.

We strove to extend ourselves to the folks among whom we lived. We drove the aged to the weekly party arranged by Protestant churchwomen, picking them up at their ghettolike apartment homes. Although they spoke only French, they made every effort to communicate. The songs we sang on the way, our laughter and smiles, breached the language barrier. In no time we were friends.

Each Sunday evening we had a fellowship group in our apartment to study the Word and to seek God's will for our lives, a truly international mixture with missionaries from Tanzania now working at headquarters in Geneva, a Swiss engineer and his British wife who had served 20 years in India, a woman from Russia, a fine young couple from Norway, an American nuclear scientist and his wife, and many others. A special member of this group was Peter Sing, a loyal Christian who entered into worship with all his heart, but who remained closemouthed about his errand in Switzerland for his country, the Republic of China in Taiwan.

The first Sunday we had Peter to dinner he took a great interest in our library. We love sharing books and had accepted the fact that a book on loan might never return. But Peter always brought his back, and each week would choose another one or two to take with him to his rented quarters. One such book he kept an unusually long time. When he returned it, he apologized, but with a broad grin, saying, "Please forgive me for keeping this book so long. Maybe you will be pleased to know that I have translated it into Chinese so my friends back home can read this thrilling story too." The book was *Monanga Paul*, the story of the life and tragic murder of Dr. Paul Carlson, a physician who had labored untiringly in the African Congo and was senselessly slaughtered, clearly illustrating that the blood of martyrs is the seed of the church. The book was later published in Taiwan, and we were amazed and pleased when we saw it to discover on the jacket an enlarged photo of a collage Clarence had fashioned from pot shards we gathered in Saudi Arabia—his first, centered around the large chalice with the Chi Rho.

189

Deep friendships formed from this international prayer fellowship. Sometimes our group visited an ancient convent that stood on the shores of Lake Neuchâtel, a charming place with stout stone walls and delightful storied rooms.

Another Geneva challenge was to relate to the single secretaries employed in the offices of American firms. One such secretary from England had just had surgery. Not wanting her to have to return alone to an empty apartment, we brought her to our apartment to convalesce. The outpouring of her gratitude was almost embarrassing. A beautiful Danish serving dish among our things is a reminder of this sweet girl.

There was also a capable American secretary who was desperately lonely. Visiting with her at church one morning, I got the telltale signals that she was near the end of her tether. She was very much on our hearts, so immediately after dinner we drove to her apartment and invited her to come back with us. Then she unraveled her sad tale. Wallowing in her black depression alone in her apartment, she had wrestled with the thought of jumping from the bridge into the swiftly flowing Rhone close by. "You have saved my life!" she exclaimed. Another deep friendship had formed.

We were often asked to help with tour groups and travelers from the United States. Our wide circle of acquaintances meant frequent houseguests and the sharing of our table. We delighted in showing beautiful Lake Leman, Castle Chillon, and the walled village of Gruyères perched high in the Alps, a scant 15 minutes from our apartment. In 25 minutes we could cross into France and visit Yvoire, a showplace among ancient villages with its narrow twisting streets and flower-bedecked balconies on the shores of Lake Leman. Then there was Chamonix at the foot of Mount Blanc. Many times we wheeled our VW there to share its beauty with friends.

G. Nelson Yu, still moving in his international banking circles, visited us in Geneva, as did Elsie, our Costa Rican daughter. She was with a tour group seeing themselves about Europe, proof of the reality of the American dream. A black girl from Costa Rica, raised in utter poverty, her job as a domestic in the home of a Washington judge permitted her both time and money for this opportunity. We loved taking her about, listening to her ejaculations. It was as if we were seeing everything for the first time ourselves.

In addition to family and friends, our home was also open to strangers. More than one American youth vagabonding through Europe called on us for help. One morning the phone rang early. A girl sobbed, "We're at the youth hostel. My traveling partner has just fainted. What should I do?" The girls were from a Lutheran community near our cabin, and their mothers had given them our address should they need help. Clarence told the girl not to panic, that he'd be right there. It was plainly an emergency for the hospital. Soon the girl and her wobbly pal were in our VW. Clarence drove to the hospital emergency entrance only to find it locked. A bit high on the wall, yet within reach, was a polished brass button with a placard in French. Unable to decipher this, he pushed the button. Immediately a loud gong began sounding within. In seconds the door opened wide, and doctors and nurses appeared with hospital carts. After Clarence explained their plight, he was given a sharp scolding, "You pushed the panic button that is reserved for only civic emergencies." Clarence, greatly embarrassed, mumbled an apology. After examining the girl, the doctor said she would be all right but that she was greatly undernourished, probably from seeing Europe on a pittance, eating prunes and peanuts rather than square meals. We took her home and put her to bed. A few days of nourishing, home-cooked food and she was a different girl, able to rejoin her friend and resume her travels.

Another night we received a frantic call from a young friend attending a fashionable boarding school. She said her roommate had tried to kill herself by slashing her wrists. Could they come to our house? Would we help? "Of course," was our immediate answer. What a tragedy, a brilliant 16-year-old turned off on life. Yet it wasn't to be wondered at. Her father, a prosperous lawyer, and her mother, an outstanding psychiatrist, were separated. The girl had been sent to school in Switzerland with her own car and everything money could buy. But she felt rejected, unloved, unwanted. This made her life intolerable.

Clarence spent hours counseling her as he tried to make real to

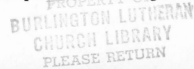
191

her that there was a love that never would forsake her, a heavenly Father who cared. She returned to school, but a few weeks later the school called and asked if we would meet her at the train and put her on a plane for the United States. She wanted to return home, but they were concerned that she might make a second attempt at taking her life if left alone. Clarence readily agreed, and the short ride between conveyances was packed with prayer and loving concern.

Three months later we received from her as beautiful a letter as has ever been dropped in our box. She had laid her life in God's offering basket and was finishing school, preparing for a life of service to mentally retarded children. The letter breathed gratitude and praise to God:

> . . . Pastor Nelson, you were one of the rare persons in this world who was able to open my eyes to something as important as religion. After our talk and the short time, yet so long in my memory and heart, I spent with you and your wife, I did a great deal of soul-searching and thinking. I had my doubts and questions, but continued the struggle to find my way back to God. I took small outward and inward steps such as continuing the fight against the threatening desire to return to drugs and turning to my father with an attempt at love in my heart instead of the bitterness I had felt since the divorce. Each small thing I did was difficult, but rewarding. I had a good, long, look at this world of ours and all the people that occupy it. I saw everything in a new light and was filled with an inexplicable and growing desire to be useful, appreciative, and sharing with everyone and everything I had been running and hiding from most of my life. This, however, included God, and him I feared most of all, for I was afraid he might not want me back. . . . I prayed as I have not done in two years, and the tears that streamed down my face were the first I'd ever had of peace and happiness, instead of pain.

> When I awakened the next morning, I felt completely refreshed, but knew that I had much more to face in my life, for I am quite young. Still, I am lucky to know, now, that *he* will always be with me through the doubts, the tears, the questions, and the darker years. But those years will not be as dark as they

might have been without him in my heart. He was always there, but I have just now been able to recognize him.

I wanted you to know all this, Pastor Nelson, because you were the one who started me anew on the right path. It will be hard, I'm sure, and I'm not completely there, but as the years come and go, I want to let you know that there is always an unforgotten place for you in at least one small heart. I am certain there are thousands like me, but I want you to know that this young soul of mine, that was stunted so early in life, has learned to bloom again and would like to sincerely thank you for the important part you played. . . . All the little things you took time to do, out of your way, I am sincerely grateful for. Wherever the path of life may lead me, there will always be a warm spot in my mind and heart for you and your wife. May the Lord bless you both.

A grateful young person

More than once we hosted visiting U.S. college choirs. Although we had great difficulty delivering anything like a packed house, they blessed us for our efforts. One such choir was the Golden Valley College Choir from Minneapolis. Among its singers were youth from families whose friendships went back to churches we had served many years ago. Many tour groups also checked in with us, and we thrilled to see how many elderly people were venturing out on world travel.

In the midst of our Geneva stay, a riot broke out in Dhahran. The oil company immediately flew the women and children out, distributing them at various points of safety. One group landed in Geneva. We made ourselves as helpful as we could finding quarters and arranging outings to help pass the tension-filled days while they waited for reassuring word from their husbands.

While in Geneva, I also found time to complete work on my second book, *Where Jesus Walks*. I tried to lead the readers into the many life situations—illness, prison, poverty—where true faith compels Christians to go. It included dramatic incidents from our travels to Tanzania, Beirut, Jerusalem, Pakistan, India, Indonesia, Taiwan, and Japan. The inscription reads, "This book is lovingly dedicated to the Saturday Evening Bible Class of the Dhahran Protestant Fellowship."

It was also while we were in Geneva that Reuben died. We flew back to the States for his funeral, experiencing the mixture of joy and sorrow that the homegoing of a loved one causes. After we returned to Geneva, we received an illustrated letter from our seven-year-old granddaughter Kris, who wrote, "I wish he did not die. But he went to be with Jesus and that is good. I loved Uncle Reuben, but I am happy that he went up with God."

Granddaughter Kris' letter of sympathy

At Christmas Biz and Walle spent a few weeks with us while they were on furlough. We got to really know our grandchildren from Indonesia. Eager-beaver Inga (born in 1965) was always trying to add hours to playtime, wanting to turn night into day. Shushed and put back to bed by her mother, in minutes she was up again while it was still dark. This day, entering her parents' bedroom, she pulled aside the drapes and commandingly said, "Mother, God says it is morning."

Mary and David also broke away from their demanding Chicago jobs to visit us. We crammed those days with sight-seeing and plenty of togetherness time. Some friends shared sleeping room for Mary. The rest of us just hunkered in our apartment, finding it jolly good fun, even though a bit crowded.

We introduced Inga and Karl to their first snow, taking them sliding in the Alps. "Grandma" and Inga fashioned a huge snow lady that Inga never tired telling about—Mrs. Lezinski, the snow lady. One winter day we took Dave, Mary, and Biz and family to enjoy the wonders of the Alps at Christmastime. Clarence and I amused Inga and Karl with a sled while Biz, Walle, Dave, and Mary took the cable car to see the dazzling beauty of the snow-crowned heights. A delay occurred when the cable car malfunctioned, leaving them swinging in the icy blue above the valley. Our children, deeply moved by the wonder of the scene spread before them, broke out in the spiritual, "Go tell it on the mountain." Their fellow passengers, diverted from panicking, demanded more. Biz suggested they all sing Christmas carols, each in his own tongue—quite a songfest. Soon they were moving again, landing safely on terra firma, visibly exhilarated by the unusual experience.

We hated to see them all leave. We missed being close to family, and we missed our beloved United States. We had been gone from America for seven years, and at a time when the church was embattled as never before. We felt the nudging of the Spirit in answer to our prayers. On word from our David, Dr. Robert Marshall arranged for a call to Tabor Church on Chicago's South Side. Here was a church facing rapid change with a day-by-day erosion of its congregation. That Dr. Marshall wanted us to step in here was a trust. We could only take heart in receiving such a call at our time of life.

Another uprooting. We would miss our dear Geneva friends, but we were firm in our resolve to return to America. One afternoon we were having tea with an American friend from Dhahran who asked what arrangements we had made to ship our furniture and personal things, most of which we had purchased while in Arabia. The oil company had shipped it at their expense to Geneva. Having already priced such moving services and knowing it was totally beyond us, I quipped, "Perishing things of clay, born but for one brief day. . . . We're not going to lose any sleep over a few sticks of furniture." My friend replied, "When I get back to Dhahran, I'm going to have my husband call this to the company's attention."

True to her promise, she did exactly that. Shortly after we received a letter saying that, in recognition of many valuable services rendered, Aramco would assume our shipping expenses to the United States. We were to select a reliable shipper and make the necessary arrangements so that all our household things could reach Chicago in first-class condition. The speedy skill and care of the Swiss women packers were a marvel. We thanked God for Aramco's generosity and the Swiss women's loving help.

The day of our departure we drove to Le Havre, France, to board a boat for our transatlantic crossing. We stopped on our way at the home of some missionary friends for breakfast, and to our delight, Peter Sing appeared to bid us farewell. We were greatly moved by the deep appreciation he showed and by the generous contents of the envelope he slipped into our hands as we got into the car. It all seemed a little backwards—we were the ones who had been so richly blessed by his friendship. When we reached Le Havre, we boarded our vessel and were soon steaming toward America.

BACK IN THE U.S.A.: THE TUMULTUOUS 60S

13

Finally we were back in the United States, and it looked ever so good to us. Arriving in Chicago, we stopped at the skyway bridge to call the chairman of the Tabor Church Council, arranging to meet him and the church treasurer at the parsonage. The well-maintained, inviting parsonage was a turn-of-the-century model built next to the church. The board members were cordial, expressing their hope we would be happy at Tabor despite the changing community. They even had a check ready to cover our shipment costs, a token of trust and welcome.

Tabor was a real challenge with a special bonus of closeness to Dave and Mary and their work. We moved right into the empty parsonage. Dave supplied cots, and we fetched dishes and pots from the church kitchen next door. In brief hours we were settled in. Our shipment wouldn't arrive for several weeks.

Dave and Mary warned us how difficult it would be to get a white church to accept black neighbors. They both had faced tremendous prejudice in their work. Dave had been sent to Country Club Hills south of Chicago. After some 1200 survey calls, he gathered a group to organize House of Prayer congregation. At first they met in a school, but later built a lovely sanctuary. Then came the opportunity for inner-city work. Dave became pastor of Bethel Lutheran Church in Garfield Park.

On the Sunday he was installed as pastor of Bethel rioting had already occurred, and during the service troops and tanks were outside restoring peace in the community. On the Friday evening before his installation, Dave and Mary, without knowing it, had driven right into the heart of the riot. Dave had to push Mary under the cowl as a huge stone smashed against the car.

As Dave walked the streets and saw the lives of his people, the injustice and the seeming hopelessness of the ghetto overwhelmed him. He sought advice from three other pastors in the neighborhood, and soon the four joined forces to launch an ecumenical cooperative ministry. After more than 10 years of growth, 12 churches were involved in providing such economically redemptive services as job placement, consumer protection, a sheltered workshop, a second-chance alternative high school, Bethel Chris-

Students at the Bethel Christian School

tian Elementary School, and a host of child development centers. An entire city block was set aside for a human development center that housed a nursing home, medical clinics, a child development center, and other related agencies. A documentary film of the work was made called "Ashflower of Hope." God's blessings on committed lives was the only explanation for the growth of this ministry. The motto over the entrance was: God Is With Us.

One day as Dave was coming out of his ministry's headquarters on Madison Avenue, a woman screamed, "Get those guys! They've stolen my money!" She had just cashed her weekly paycheck. Dave, seeing two young men running away, gave pursuit. Since it was summer and warm, he was coatless and his clergy shirt was very obvious. After they crossed a parking lot, the two thieves separated. Dave dogged the one who ran across the lawn of a senior citizens' home. The occupants sitting around on benches called, "Get him, Preach! Get him!" The thief charged between two buildings, little realizing that he was headed down a cul-de-sac. Soon Dave was upon him, but the thief shouted, "Here's the money. Let me go!" and flung down a fistful of bills. When Dave stooped to gather them, he lost the thief in the crowd on the sidewalk. Dave returned the money to the amazed woman who asked, "Didn't he pull his gun on you like he did on me?" Dave thanked the Lord for leading him to follow not only the one with the money, but also the one who was unarmed.

Often Dave's little parsonage was broken into, so the congregation put bars on the windows. When we visited there, Clarence dubbed it "Fortress David."

David and Mary worked closely together on many projects. Mary was lured back to the United States after reading of the riots and burning back in the States as blacks tried to break out of the confining trap they had been put into because of their skin color. She returned and became part of the work in West Garfield Park just at the time David became Bethel's pastor. It was under Mary's guidance that the alternative academy developed. This second-chance high school for dropouts received national attention for its redemptive work with students the public schools considered uneducable. Accredited by the Illinois State Board of

Education, it had a record of 65% of its graduating youth going on to higher education.

During this time Mary worked for and received her Ph.D. in urban education from Antioch College. As director of development and planning for a community project, she developed a solar energy roof garden, multifaceted senior citizen programs, and sheltered workshops. She became adept at putting together the impossible. She also became involved in many citywide advocacy programs. In addition, she taught Sunday school at Bethel Church and participated in many other church activities, even substituting at the organ when an emergency arose. She often wrote the festival programs for the church school. Her apartment was constantly filled with a variety of people who shared her warm hospitality and were refreshed with genuine friendship.

Dave and Mary's ministry was assisted by Agneta, our Swedish miss, who became aware of their inner-city work in Chicago and challenged her Swedish young people to adopt Bethel as one of their causes. They sent generous offerings to help the program, and Agneta returned to spend a summer as a staff worker in that west side ghetto.

Since Dave and Mary knew the scene intimately, they were of tremendous help to us as we attempted to fulfill our mission at Tabor. For example, Dave advised his dad, "You'll first probably have to preside over the death of old Tabor." Heeding his advice, we dug in with the thought that with patience and hard work, a mixed congregation could yet come alive on the corner of 80th and Escanaba South.

As a starter, Tabor's secretary welcomed her new black neighbor, calling for her personally and bringing her to visit Tabor. Mrs. Hubert Harris, a woman of great inner beauty and strength, was in church the very next Sunday. Shortly after we enrolled her two boys, Hubert and Bennye, in the Sunday school, and later Clarence baptized baby David. Once again God had driven a wedge into an all-white church family. Soon other new black neighbors came to Sunday school and vacation Bible school. With our membership ranks thinning, it was a constant marvel that teachers could be found for the classes.

Confirmation instruction was also difficult. Parental support was so lacking that Clarence had to telephone each pupil an hour before class time to urge them to attend. Home lesson preparation was out. Clarence had to be content with one brief hour a week to share in simplest terms God's great truths. It was quite a comedown from the eager, keen-minded, accepting youth in Geneva. But he kept reminding himself of God's promise, "My Word shall not return void." He stayed with it until the harvest—Confirmation Sunday.

As Dave had warned us, "The Chicago schools are a jungle. Anything like inner motivation is out." This was a hard fact. We now understood why Dave mingled so much activity with his confirmation instruction, busing his classes to the Chicago Planetarium, keeping them hepped up with picnics, a swift motorboat ride, and touring other churches. He led his students that stayed with it on a canoe excursion into northern Minnesota's canoe country.

We worked diligently to establish Tabor's many-faceted programs during those three years. We held Lenten services of the lighted cross, but because many were afraid to venture out after dark, we held the service in the morning each Lenten Wednesday. Each month the church women gathered in good numbers. We presented an annual series of morning Bible studies for their enrichment and fellowship. We also arranged cars to pick up and take home those too infirm to make it on their own. Being able to leave the constricting walls of invalidism was so rewarding for these people. The monthly luncheon we initiated for senior citizens also caught on. Clarence and I arranged for volunteers to serve, and we set our table with our treasures gathered from around the world. No matter how bad the weather, we had a good turnout.

Our proximity to the Chicago Lutheran School of Theology provided great resources. During two of our three years in Chicago, Clarence was assigned a student. Although expected to be with us for only three months, each one stayed on a volunteer basis for the entire school year and was extremely helpful. One happy result was the close, warm involvement we gained with the seminary, "the school of the prophets" as it was sometimes called.

I kidded Clarence a lot about the altar guild, the most efficient group we'd ever worked with. They held monthly meetings to check on their calendar assignments and other duties. If only they had showed a like concern for visiting the shut-ins and bringing cheer to those in the hospital. When one or the other of the three on hand for the usual dressing of the altar and placing of the flowers would get ahold of Clarence and say, "Time for us to dress you, Pastor," I'd become irked and say, "Honey, can't you pull that robe on yourself?" Could it be I was jealous? Or was it simply that there were so many other important things requiring the time and talents of devoted Christians? Maybe a little of both?

We regularly visited the aged, shut-ins, and hospitalized, keeping a careful cardex on the visits to be sure no one was overlooked. Clarence offered each monthly Communion. Besides the devotions we assiduously tried to share some of the beautiful, encouraging events that were happening at church and in the family in order to open some windows in the walls of their constricting prison of pain and confinement. We also alternated with the pastor of a close-by Missouri Synod church to bring a weekly prayer service to a nearby privately owned nursing home. The residents of the home truly doted on these devotionals. The Missouri Synod pastor was a sweet singer and a polished guitarist. Clarence brought his Autoharp, I my ukulele, and we had wonderful songfests. We also frequently visited Augustana Home, and the more often we visited, the longer grew the list of those who pleaded for us to stop in their rooms.

We were aided in our efforts by so many. Whenever our daughter Elsie was near any one of our churches, she was willing to sing a solo. She was introduced to and welcomed by Dave's congregation at Bethel. Then one Sunday she was with us at Tabor. The neighborhood had changed dramatically, with many whites leaving because of color hang-ups. When Elsie first rose to sing, the audience stiffened, but as her beautiful voice rang out, first in Spanish, then in English, the words of a hymn which was a favorite of many Swedes in the congregation, "Om jag agd alt men icke Jesus" ("If I gained the world but lost my Savior"), she won them one by one. Eyes misted and hearts went out to her.

Unfortunately, not everyone was helpful. We often faced pettiness difficult to understand within a Christian setting. For example, when Clarence asked the council to approve a request from the South Side ministers that Tabor host the joint sunrise Easter service for youth, he was turned down. It involved serving a simple breakfast of coffee and hot cross buns after the early service but the council balked. Did they fear a fully integrated audience or were they siding with the sexton in his antipathy to serving food? Embarrassed by already having promised the date, Clarence said, "Ruth and I will serve it in the parsonage." To which came the angry retort, "No you won't, unless we agree. This is church property." In our nearly 40 years of serving the Lord together, we had never had to face up to such pettiness. It hurt terribly. Right then Clarence decided to ignore the council. We hosted the youth in church, and there were no repercussions.

Where arose this hard-knuckled intransigence? Was it the hard competitive pace of life in Chicago, the morning and evening rat race on the expressways, the sheer bone-weariness they had to shake off merely to attend their meetings? Or was it related to the many changes that were occurring in the community and the tensions these caused? I came to empathize a little more with the seemingly petty reactions to everyday occurrences when I found myself reacting in the same way.

Clarence was taking me to the Chicago airport to catch a plane for Colorado where I was to participate in a retreat. The Kennedy Expressway on which we were traveling was a moving parking lot. Beside myself for fear of missing the plane, I became Clarence's helper, directing, "Turn this way. Look out, there's a truck. Speed up. . . ." Finally my ordinarily patient husband turned to me and shouted, "I'll drive this car." Was I ever hurt. A cold silence followed. How could he be so unfeeling? I was only trying to help. But what a way to part—not speaking to each other. I looked out the car window until the Holy Spirit finally got through to me and I could turn to Clarence and say, "Forgive me, I didn't mean to make it hard." His response was, "I accept your apology." That, too, hurt, but I realized for such a thing to occur we both must have been caught up in the rat race ourselves. I resolved not to let it happen again.

Not many months after we were established in Chicago, we were faced with another homegoing—that of my sister Mabel.

What a gal she was. She brought laughter and fun with her wherever she went. I remember, as a little girl, counting the days until she would come home for vacation from teaching in the country. She had the gift of making everyone feel important. With a swing of her hand (a special gesture she had), she would say of our children, "Ruth, they're the greatest!" Of course, she said this about all the other nieces and nephews too. We were told that just days before she died at the Mount Olivet Home at age 79, she had delighted a visiting group of entertainers by leading in three cheers for them after their performance. She thought the applause had been inadequate. She was such fun to be around. How we would miss her.

Within two years, my brother Ben joined those of my family who had gone home. Many honors were accorded Ben in the years he was dean of the graduate school of social work at Washington University in St. Louis. He had served on White House commissions and had been national president of the leading social workers' organizations. Yet the most moving tribute was the one connected with the Lasker Award from Columbia University. Clarence shared it at Ben's memorial service. It read: "He was a friend of the poor!"

Now only Luther and I were left of our parents' eight children.

One night as we were preparing for bed, the phone rang. It was Dave, frantically explaining, "I'm at the hospital. Mary has been brutally attacked on leaving headquarters. She wasn't violated, but she is still unconscious." Our response, of course, was, "We'll join you at the hospital as soon as we can." Hastily pulling on our clothes, we were on our way in minutes. In that half-hour drive our minds conjured up all manner of possible horrors. Was Mary's face slashed by some crude weapon like a broken beer bottle? Would she be scarred by the trauma? It was a memorable, prayerful ride, tearing from Chicago's South Side to Lake Shore Drive, and then, via the Eisenhower Expressway, to the community hospital at West Garland Park. There we learned she had been moved to another hospital, St. Anne's, so we hurried there. Clarence rushed to her side through the waiting room where a clutch of grim-faced friends sat weeping. She had not yet received a thorough medical examination. When her eyes opened, Clarence said, "Mary, you've just got to get out of this area at the earliest." She answered, her first words since the attack, "Dad, I'm going to be back at my desk before the week's out." Then back into the coma she slipped.

Her assailant had brutally, repeatedly kicked her. She had fought back like a tigress and remembered saying, "You can kill me, but you'll never take me." Her head was matted from an ugly gash that took 16 stitches to close. Her arms and breasts were an angry purple from the bruising of leather heels. Clarence and I joined the group holding vigil in the waiting room. Here we learned the details of the attack.

Mary had expected to drive the director home. When they came out to the car, they found the lights had been left on, and the battery was too low to turn over the motor. Mary went back into the building to call her housemate for a lift. As she left the dark building, and turned the lock, her back was toward the street door. Suddenly she received a sharp blow on the head. Blood flowed freely, blinding her. The assailant demanded she reopen the door. Then he dragged her from the lobby to the back hall which was screened from the street by a wall and fought with her, choking her. Mary's last recollection was feeling a knife against her throat. Then she blacked out.

Probably at that very moment her housemate opened the door. Not seeing Mary, she called out several times. When she turned to leave, she heard a low moan, ran forward, and found Mary in a pool of blood. All this time the director was being detained and interrogated by two policemen who wanted to know what he was up to in the parking lot at this late hour.

Dave was notified at once. He called a number of ambulance services for help, but on learning the address, the answer was, "Our rigs are on calls." So Mary's first ride to the hospital was in a police paddy wagon. From that emergency room, Dave had rounded up the money to call for a private ambulance that brought her to the nearby Roman Catholic hospital. It was here we had finally come.

The doctors told us that Mary had severe body bruises, but would be all right. Soon she was in her hospital bed. I stayed at her side that night. Unconscious, Mary now and again would call out, "Oh, God, help me!" But she kept her word. Before the week was out she was back at her office, her head still bandaged, huge black-and-blue areas over the side of her body, and the ugly red imprint of a man's hand still on her throat. When Curtis Foster, a member of Bethel, learned of the attack, he walked the streets in search of the man, vowing to kill him in cold blood. And he probably would have. "She's been like a sister to me" were his oft-repeated words.

We had many happy days in Chicago, too, like our annual mother-daughter banquet that the men cooked and served. They even marshaled a corps of singing waiters to delight the group. We had a beautiful 70th anniversary celebration of Tabor's founding, with a festive banquet and a worship service with our synod president in the pulpit. Each Holy Week the women held a Maundy Thursday Communion followed by a frugal breakfast celebrated at tables assembled in the form of a cross. The decorations were the instruments of the passion, including the crown of thorns, the cat-o'-nine-tails, the chains and lantern, Pilate's basin, and the like. It was amazing how many they were and how vividly they recalled to each "how much he was willing to bear." We also put on a big rummage sale and supper despite our thinning ranks. If Tabor was sinking, it was with its bands playing and its flags waving.

One hot summer Chicago night we shared an evening with our long-time friend G. Nelson Yu. Dave and Mary relished giving him a ride in their motorboat to the heart of Chicago's financial row by night, and Mr. Yu delighted in telling how refreshing this ride was. It was so good to see him again.

Although we tried our hardest, things were still not going well for Tabor. It was symptomatic that the pastoral act Clarence most frequently officiated at was the funeral—at least one a week, a sad, heavy duty. One of these funerals was for a woman who had been dead for three days in her apartment without even her next-door neighbor being aware of it. That's living anonymously—for which the service conducted in Chapel B for Case #412 was final proof. Time was running out for Tabor.

For nearly a year Clarence had been corresponding with Dr.

206

William Berg who wanted him to consider being a part-time assistant at Augustana Church, Minneapolis. We met at his hotel in Evanston where he was visiting his brother and talked over in some detail this possibility. It greatly aroused our interest. At first Clarence pleaded for another year at Tabor, but at least he had the call in mind. We both felt God's hand was in it. At his age, Clarence needed to reduce his agenda, and I loved the idea of returning to the church where I had been baptized and around which my earliest Sunday school memories clustered. For both of us it would mean a return to family origins and a wide circle of dear friends.

We decided to accept the call to Augustana, and yet another time came for tearing up deep roots and the pain of parting. Those last days as we were packing and waiting for the mover, everything seemed to fall apart. Clarence's secretary at Tabor had a nervous breakdown and several others on the staff were hospitalized with serious illnesses. It seemed utterly impossible to break away. When again the mover disappointed us by not showing up, we left the overseeing of the loading to David and headed for Minneapolis where we were to be installed the next Sunday at Augustana.

COMING FULL CIRCLE

14

It was hard to believe all the old friends who showed up for our return to Augustana. Somebody asked us which place we liked best of all the places we had lived: Minneapolis, St. Paul, Duluth, Washington, Saudi Arabia, Geneva, or Chicago. We replied, "Each one at the time we lived there. We have learned so much from those with whom we have shared our lives. Each has been a rich chapter!" Now that Clarence was serving at Augustana each Sunday I sat facing the very font where my parents brought me to be baptized. How good God is!

We began our work at Augustana in earnest. Clarence's list of shut-ins and nursing home residents went past 50 almost at once. Sometimes as many as five were residents in the same high rise, but others were in scattered nursing homes, most on metropolitan Minneapolis' periphery. Clarence fulfilled his ministry as he brought them Communion and shared the Word, making them know they were a remembered and a meaningful part of our congregation. Nursing home patients required that second mile of faith. Life could be so mundane for them, bedridden as they were, often pitied because of their debilities and functional problems.

For some, every last friend had died and the last draught from life's cup was bitter. To still affirm God's goodness and mercy in the face of all this and to point to better days ahead demanded a robust faith and the patience to listen. As Clarence noted, "That's where the morning watch the staff held paid royal dividends. To read together such passages as, 'It is of the Lord's mercies that we are not consumed, because his compassions fail not. They are new every morning: great is thy faithfulness,' and then to share the proof garnered from each of our firsthand experiences was all the equipment needed."

Clarence cherished his partnership with Bill Berg. To Clarence, Bill was a son of Barnabas, always encouraging and hardworking. He never missed the 8:30 staff prayer huddle, and often he slipped to a hospital bedside for late prayers. Many times they went together to hold a healing service for a sick person, and Bill's messages at funerals were always personal and consoling to the family.

One special charge Clarence undertook was the Pioneers. With this group of oldsters we had free rein to introduce variety and excitement. We loved to get them singing together as the miles sped by when we took our bus trips together. These efforts garnered a tremendous harvest of appreciation.

Trips with Augustana's Pioneers were full of good times

In the summer of 1972 we returned to Koja. For over 40 years this had been our family rallying place. Every summer as we left, I thought regretfully that it would be a long time before we would be together again in this blessed spot. Then, almost before we knew it, that long time had gone by and we were headed for Koja again. Young folks smile when this white-haired lady says to them that it seems but yesterday she was a little girl with long hair, squealing while her mother braided her pigtails. Some of my obliviousness to the fact that time has passed is evidenced when my friends and I refer to each other as "girls." But we *are* still girls at heart. And it was having a place like Koja and fun-filled family times that kept Clarence and me young.

Koja was special to our children too. Once Jon wrote from the seminary, "You know I think that when the day comes for me to report to St. Peter at the pearly gates, I'll hear him say in greeting, 'Welcome, Jon; just look around to the first turn of the golden street. You'll find Koja right there.'"

Each summer the ladies of Hope Lutheran Church held a "Mrs. Nelson Night," arranging for me to speak to the women gathered from all the village churches and the surrounding communities. It was an honor and privilege to witness to the Lord's goodness with these wonderful neighbors.

It was at Koja that the children helped us celebrate our 40th wedding anniversary. They took over Northwood Cafe at Barnum, and the grandchildren acted out a play highlighting scenes from our lives together. During the play little Inga lifted her head up from the floor and said, "Tell me once again, who am I supposed to be?" She was playing the part of Carlson of Omaha, a free-loader who moved in on us in D.C. thinking that preachers were supposed to be given to hospitality. After about two weeks I had said, "Clarence, either you get Carlson on his way, or you'll be without a wife." They also presented us with a marvelous banner summarizing our 40 years together.

One day an old neighbor from our St. Paul days set about to nominate me for Minnesota Mother of the Year. Dr. S. H. Swanson, 80 years old, went to work on this project contacting notables for recommendations. He enlisted Dr. Berg of Augustana Church,

The banner celebrating our 40th anniversary

who willingly agreed to sponsor me. I tried in every way to discourage Dr. Swanson, but he brushed aside my objections with, "Ruth, if you don't get it, I'll eat my shirt." To which I responded, "And since I think you'll have to, I'll gladly frost it." But it happened; I was named Minnesota Mother of the Year. This was one of the last of Dr. Swanson's many good deeds before he went to be with his God.

In May 1973 I represented Minnesota at the National Convention of American Mothers in Denver. We each had three minutes to present the story of our lives. I chose as my theme the words of Apostle Paul, "I am a debtor." Believing to the depth of my being that I was there through God's grace, the debts I owed were easy to enumerate:

I am a debtor to a loving God and Savior, Creator, and Redeemer who has put such rich meaning into my life. I am a debtor

Speaking at the
National Convention of
American Mothers in Denver

to parents who taught me and the nine others of their children that life is a stewardship, that we are born to serve and love God by loving and serving our fellowmen; that if we permit Christ to live in us, each of us can make a difference; that we are our brother's keeper, and that life will find fulfillment only as we remember this. I am a debtor to my church which nourished and inspired faith and love and taught me that a Christian must grow. I am a debtor to my country in which I could get an education, in which I'm free to worship according to my conscience, in which I'm free to criticize it because I love it. I am a debtor to a husband who is fun to live with, whose first desire is to serve the Lord, who has helped me to grow and dream and love. I am a debtor to my children who have shamed me by their dedication, whose compulsion, understanding, and love are beyond anything I ever knew, who have stimulated and inspired me to press on and enlarge my plans and gifts, who have

212

put their lives on the line again and again in serving their Lord and sharing his love with others. Our children by birth and our foster children have enriched our lives beyond words to describe.

I am a debtor to countless friends whose love, companionship, and inspiration are a constant joy and encouragement. I think of the little prayer groups in Washington, D.C., in Saudi Arabia, in Geneva, Switzerland, and now in Minneapolis. What a fellowship.

Imagine my amazement when I was selected National Mother of the Year. Again, that such an honor should be mine was possible only through the grace of God. I was challenged to witness to what the Lord can do with one person, to witness to how each individual can make a difference in a home, an office, a school, a community, a country, the world, if people permit the presence of Christ to so live within as to mold opinions, motivate actions, and spur them on to translating his love into human relationships. Some of the most beautiful mothers are women who have never given physical birth to children, but are mothers of the heart who care for lonely, destitute children.

In late June of 1973 Clarence was hospitalized for prostate surgery. During the surgery, the doctors discovered a malignancy. What a shock! In his 43 years of ministry, he had never missed a Sunday preaching because of illness. He had never been in a hospital except to visit others and had never really known what it was to be ill. We had to face it, calling to mind Dr. Anna Mau's statement in *Who's Afraid of Birthdays:* "We often hear it said, 'where there is life, there is hope.' It is even more correct to put it, 'where there is hope, there is life!'" As Christians we had this beacon of hope, no matter what the outcome.

The first days after the surgery were trying, but fortunately Clarence could convalesce at Koja; he was even allowed to go swimming. Mary had just acquired the ramshackle log cabin next door. At first she thought about renovating it, but after looking closer at its swaybacked shackiness she knew it would be a waste of money. She decided instead to build her dream cabin. Cost what it may, there had to be a full basement so her dad could have an all-weather workshop. Local contractors dug the hole and masoned the cement blocks. Then, with 78-year-old Carl Franzen as our boss, the entire family joined in raising the walls and setting the rafters in place for the roof. Many of our friends came to help.

As the work progressed, a running battle ensued. Clarence insisted they use the lumber and nails from the old structure as the subflooring. Jon, backed up by Mary, was the toughest opponent to the idea, saying, "Let's use only new stuff." But Franzen agreed with Clarence that the reclaimed flooring would do. The tensions grew with neither side willing to give in. There were outbursts of hot words. In the end, Clarence won; the old boards were used for the subflooring—but not the nails he had so carefully saved, the bent nails.

That fall we moved to an apartment in Edina, and Clarence began a series of cobalt treatments to reduce the cancer threat. The malignancy had been only decimals away from the bladder. For many, the cobalt treatments had side effects such as loss of appetite, headaches, and listlessness, but Clarence felt none of these. He reported each weekday at 7:30 A.M. to strip himself and climb onto the table for the few minutes the treatment took while the nurse manipulated the huge overhead apparatus from her safe post behind a ray-proof shield. The machine had its own peculiar buzz like a jet plane lifting off its pad. You could almost smell the ozone released by the invisible healing rays.

Clarence told of the thoughts that went through his mind as he took the first in the series of treatments. It was a marvel to see the skilled hands direct the huge, impersonal machine that generated the powerful healing rays. There also was the dedicated teamwork of doctors and nurses. And, enveloping all, there was the presence of the Creator of heaven and earth and the awareness of the countless prayers being said on his behalf. In its depth, it became a hallelujah experience. He could now personally identify with the people at whose bedside he had shared the reality of faith that can transmute rugged suffering into the gold of God's love.

Our move was made easier by the help of my nephews, Pastor William Youngdahl and Pastor Jim Anderson, who insisted on giving us a hand carting boxes. Clarence remained strong, and we were soon established in our new niche. We loved our compact third-floor apartment. It was a new experience to be able to leave for the lake or a vacation by merely turning a key behind us. We easily agreed on this apartment from among the many we looked at because this one had a sauna and an indoor pool that afforded us both exercise. However, it was hard to decide what personal possessions to keep now that we had limited space. Some of the decisions, put off for a more convenient time, were never made, and those possessions still jam up the ever-so-limited storage space of the apartment.

One day, after his 28th cobalt treatment, Clarence was walking at his usual swift pace across Elliot Park when he felt a slight pain in his left calf. The next morning at therapy, he asked the attending doctor about it. The doctor took one look at it and immediately ordered Clarence into the hospital. Electric hot packs were applied, the usual treatment for phlebitis, and the condition of his leg soon improved. After nine days he had responded to treatment sufficiently to go home, rejoicing that he was out in time for Thanksgiving and Christmas.

Clarence helped serve communion at Mount Olivet's altar over the holidays, and Bill and Eileen Youngdahl, my nephew and his wife, had us to Christmas Eve dinner. This was most thoughtful of them since we were without family at home. We could be more than a bit lonely with yesteryear's memories of family piling home, their cars loaded with fellow students who otherwise would have been stranded on campus.

That Christmas we had a long-distance phone call from Indonesia, the other side of the world. Biz and her family in Jakarta called to ask how Grandpa was. We were practically speechless at the joy of it. Each talked to us except 10-year-old Karl. We missed his boyish voice on the phone. A week later Biz's letter explained the reason—Karl had been overcome with tears. When his sobs finally quieted, Biz asked him to explain why he wept so. "There were three reasons," he said. "First, Grandpa and Grandma and all my uncles and aunts gave me so much, and I have nothing to give back. Second, I cried because my grandparents in Germany are dead. And I cried when I thought of the summer spent at Sand Lake cabin with Grandpa and Grandma and all my cousins." Biz talked with him and proposed that he make something to send us. He and Inga made us an amazing calendar. Then she asked him what he thought would make Grandpa and Grandma the happiest of all. Together they decided it would be if he would give his heart to Jesus. That, he said, he wanted to do.

A day or so after Christmas, Clarence began having problems with his other leg. This time we tried home therapy, applying hot packs as best we could. But Clarence simply couldn't make it. Walking became so painful that he'd crawl on hands and knees to the bathroom. We finally admitted defeat, and once again, in January of 1974, Clarence was hospitalized. His legs were so swollen and angry that a specialist was called. He was confident, however, that he'd have Clarence back on his feet in a short while. Indeed, in a week he was walking the corridors, shuffling along in the oversize blue slippers I had gone from store to store to find.

Never a complainer, Clarence made the most of his hospital visits. He wrote in "Bent Nails":

I was amazed in each of these hospitalizations to experience the meaningful fellowship one could have with the several room-mates. Suffering ,breaks down most barriers. And it was natural and easy to witness to one's faith and to share in prayer. I had some difficulty sleeping, but many of those waking hours got laced with intercessory prayers as I personally tucked one or the other of family and friends under the protecting wings of God. Then also I blessed those midnight disc jockeys who filled the air waves with good music. Lest I disturb, I kept my ear glued to our faithful little FM receiver picked up while we traveled in Germany. The nurses were ever so skilled and watchful; they were truly angels in white, and the camaraderie and rapport that developed was something. Ruth spent so much of her time with me that I could only wonder at such loyal devotion. And so often my dearly beloved stepped into the breach for me. Again and again she took over the Bible study series, shared regularly in the Wednesday Renewal Hour, and filled in for me at the monthly Pioneers. She so endeared herself that her name appearing in the Bulletin's "Week in Prospect" was enough to fill all empty chairs. In addition, the church staff and members and other pastors and friends, new and old, brightened the hours of each day.

216

Clarence was ever so appreciative of the mountains of support he received. A special blessing was the patience of Pastor Berg and Augustana. They pleaded with Clarence to take plenty of time for healing and insisted on keeping the monthly salary checks coming in. Sometimes during the night watches, the thought of all the goodness and the many Augustana prayers moved Clarence to tears.

My nephew Dick Youngdahl and his lovely Kitty were most helpful in Clarence's convalescence by making their Florida home available to us. On doctor's orders, we flew to Florida, a costly business since it meant not only air fare for the two of us, but also a car rental. But the healing that came to Clarence from those days in the sun made the cost seem as nothing. The Youngdahl home, set down by the water's edge on a quiet, dead-end street in a lovely country club addition with flamboyant flora and fauna, nudged all the healing forces within him. Friends could seek us out and vice versa. In only 10 minutes we could be at the seaside beach to laze in the sun and picnic. The heated pool just off the front patio teased us into its healing waters at least a couple of times a day. We felt as rich as Croesus without all his worries about holding onto his piled-up wealth. We also had time to catch up on our reading, frequently reading aloud to one another as we came across favorite passages.

Once again at home in Minneapolis, Clarence picked up his calls as Augustana's visitation pastor, a work he dearly loved. Many deep attachments were formed as a result of his ministry. It was also about this time that my book *You Can Make a Difference* appeared in print. I dedicated it: "To my husband Clarence whose commitment to the Lord has made such a difference in our lives!"

One day I was called by the Internal Revenue Service to have our income tax reviewed. They thought our list of contributions was vastly padded and asked that I bring documentary evidence to support our figures. As I flashed those receipts one by one, it was my turn to witness to the blessings that had accrued to us in that giving. Clarence and I had started our habit of tithing back in Duluth. And always, whatever we gave was returned and then some. It reminded me of a conversation between two friends.

"Man," objected one pal to his tither friend, "you're crazy giving so much. First thing you know, you'll have nothing for yourself."

"That'll never happen," came the answer back, "for as fast as I shovel out, God shovels in. Only God's got a bigger shovel."

Not many days later, evidence of God's big shovel arrived in a letter from our son Paul, in Taipei, who wrote:

> We have in Taipei a Sunday fellowship of Christians who gather for witness and prayer. The man chiefly responsible for this is our capable minister of finance. Lillian and I are wont to attend. Yesterday evening we had a Mr. Sing, and the title to his witness was, "We Must Live the Scriptures." As he began his testimony he read from Acts 20:17-38. Then he told us that many years back he was sent by the government to engage in some undercover work in a French-speaking country. He said that the pastor and his wife were both kind to him. He could find all the good Christian virtues in their daily living, and he was greatly touched by their love. This alone made his work and living in a strange land bearable. But the time had come for the American pastor and his wife to leave to go to Chicago where they had accepted a call. Then he movingly described how he parted from them with tears. The pastor's wife called him her son, although she was at most 10 years his senior. At this point it suddenly became clear to me who this American couple was. They had to be the Nelsons of my life too! And, of course, this Mr. Sing would be General Peter Sing, whom you had mentioned to me some years ago, but whom I had failed to locate.
>
> After the testimony, I introduced myself to him. He knew my name long ago. So we finally met. Mr. Sing is now an elder and works full time for a Lutheran congregation affiliated with the church of Norway. . . . What a dramatic setting for our meeting. . . .

Bread upon the waters—returned a thousandfold!

Then came our summer weeks at Koja. The night before the Fourth of July, Clarence awakened with sharp stomach pains and repeated visits to the john. His only relief was when he applied an ice pack to his stomach. The next morning he had a temperature, sharp stomach pains, and loose bowels, so I insisted we check with a doctor. Mercy Hospital had an outpatient clinic, and there

218

Clarence was checked. The doctor suggested it might be a combination of muscle strain and stomach flu. He suggested rest and some aspirin, but should the problem persist, we should go to Minneapolis for our own doctor's diagnosis.

Clarence's sharp pains decreased, but he still didn't feel well. Refusing to let the flu keep him down, he moved piles and piles of dirt by wheelbarrow and did many odd jobs around the cabin. However, his temperature was above normal each evening. At Mary's and my insistence, we were off to Minneapolis. Dr. Lindgren did a cursory examination and diagnosed a ruptured appendix. In minutes Clarence was undergoing a follow-up by Dr. Farley who, before the hour was up, had him in a hospital bed booked for surgery the next morning. It was, indeed, a ruptured appendix, and Dr. Farley said, "It was a tiger of an operation. The pus-filled sac had been encapsulated and for a while I thought that the intestines were involved. We also checked out his prostate and found no further sign of cancer. That's a plus!"

For 10 days Clarence was on intravenous feeding. When he finally could take solids, he found food distasteful because his tray was tabbed "No salt." I had to coax the food into him. At last he was released and we drove back to Koja. We had feared the doctor would rule this out of bounds and wavered in asking his approval. Amazingly enough, he OK'd it, but his inner reservations registered on his face.

How we flavored those first days of freedom with those idyllic scenes of forest and lake to every side. Koja never was more cozy. We were surrounded by children and grandchildren. Kristen, Jon and Juni's eldest, loved pairing up with Grandma to go blueberrying, sharing stories in the deep forest. Clarence had Dave and Benjamin working with him in his basement workshop or in the yard.

Benjamin was a tireless fisherman, and we loved his offerings of sunfish, always well cleaned and ready for the fry pan. There was time to draw out Heather's shy but ever-so-sweet smile or to listen to Elizabeth on the piano or answer her questions such as, "Grandma, do you and Grandpa ever quarrel?" Lovely Leah put her culinary skills to work in preparing exotic oriental meals, and Joshua, with his intriguing, gravelly voice, would sidle up to Clarence and say, "I love you, Gramp." Micah would come on the scene to work his magic tricks or to show his prowess of walking on his hands with his legs, paralyzed from polio, dangling in the air.

One of those first days we were afraid a new outbreak of phlebitis had hit Clarence. We talked by phone to a nurse who, after carefully weighing the symptoms, suggested that she saw no reason to panic and that we should wait it out, elevating Clarence's legs whenever possible. What a relief. Soon the scar was wholly healed, and he felt good enough to work in the yard.

One sunny day Clarence was transplanting wild ferns from the forest. The roots clung stubbornly to their dank bedding amidst the shrubs and trees. Suddenly breathing became difficult for him, as if he'd stepped off a high cliff. He cried out, and we hurried to his side. In minutes we had him in Moose Lake Community Hospital's intensive care unit, his life in balance. Soon he was bedded down in the newly installed coronary care unit with a sophisticated heart monitor attached to his body that showed at a glance the pattern of his heartbeat. A young heart specialist directed the fight to bring him back, and specially trained nurses watched over him around the clock.

That first night, disregarding strict orders, Clarence reached to attend to one of his needs. In a trice his night nurse, a tall, handsome former navy man, was bending beside him saying, "Don't you do that again, Clarence. Follow your instructions to the letter. You've been given just one more chance to make it. Don't you blow it."

Family was permitted to visit him for only five minutes. Jon and Juni's plans called for setting out for Seattle so the children could report for school opening. They were torn about leaving since it was still touch and go for Clarence. Hot tears streamed down Jon's cheeks as he knelt by his father's bed and asked forgiveness for the time they had disagreed about using the old timbers and rusty bent nails on Mary's cabin. Clarence answered, "I forgive freely and, Jon, I need yours for all the times I tried to bull my way. Your place is with your family. With the children enrolling in new schools, it makes no sense for you to delay. You have my blessing."

Just as Jon turned to leave, Clarence said, "Jon, I bequeath to you the three buckets of bent nails." A burst of laughter cleared the air.

The roofing on Mary's cabin was finished as vacation days were done, and we dubbed the place "St. Mary's by the Lake." We hated dropping those hammers—we had such fun working together as a family. Carl Franzen was engaged to finish the interior during the winter. It turned into a real dream house. Clarence and I were wont to say, "The Kennedys have their Hyannisport, but the Nelsons have their Sand Lake." We were happy with Dave's and Jon's earlier purchases of their cabins, and now Mary building hers only added joy on joy. These cabins have made for us some wonderful togetherness times. We can hardly wait for the long winter months and the intervening weeks to be over so the family can gather again. What satisfaction we have in seeing the changes a year makes in Jon's and Juni's brood of eight. It gave all of us a special thrill the year that Micah, lately of Korea, was introduced to the beauty of forest and lake. He took to the water like a seal, and we felt good about the effect that friendly medium would have on his thin shanks.

Clarence was progressing well, but, nonetheless, he dictated to Mary what he wanted to be included in his memorial service. He was right in his inner conviction that his heart attack was not going to lead to his homegoing, at least not yet. He finally persuaded the doctor in Moose Lake to release him, but only after promising to check in at once with Dr. Lindgren. To his chagrin, Dr. Lindgren's verdict was that he had heart failure. With that, Clarence was back in Metropolitan Medical Center. Once again the nurses were taking daily blood tests and monitoring him closely.

After this second hospital stay, Clarence was finally at home under strict orders to act as if he were still in his hospital room. He puttered about the apartment, thanking God with every step. He kept repeating to himself, as if it was an incantation, "Clarence, you've got one more chance. Don't blow it." By doctor's orders he frequently did a simple breathing exercise to keep his lungs fully inflated. As he drew in the fresh air, he opened his heart and life to the living Christ and his energizing spirit. He sought for his heart and life a total renewal, saying, "That battery of pill jars can't do it alone."

How he thanked God for the prayers of friends. As if with a sweep of a magic wand, a virtual network of remembrances had been stitched together, people covenanting to seek God's healing for him. More surely than he knew his own name, Clarence knew that God was hard at work in him to make this "one last chance" suffice to put this servant of his back on the firing line for the kingdom. "Don't give up on Clarence," he often prayed, "not even for one day."

Clarence's convalescence lasted through our one-month Florida stay in 1975. While at Dick's, we became interested in the possibility of a six-month residence in the warm climate and then a six-month stay at Koja. We began looking at some mobile homes advertised in the paper, but then a phone call changed everything. Lute and Irene had driven up from Fort Lauderdale when the call came. On the line from Minneapolis were Dr. Berg, Chaplain Vernon Johnson, and Mr. Alvar Nelson, each at a phone. They thrilled us by offering Clarence a position as an assistant chaplain at Augustana Home. It was agreed upon, and this, of course, ruled out any action on a Florida residence.

This assignment was within the limits of Clarence's present strength, and he rejoiced at once again being useful to the Lord. He described making a call on a little birdlike octogenarian spinster named Mamie who kept punctuating his conversation with, "Pastor, do you think I'll ever make anything of myself?" He knew much joy in assuring her that we've got it made in Christ and that he has wrapped his arms about us and claimed us as his sisters and brothers.

In 1976 our book *Cast Your Bread Upon the Waters* was published. Although my name appeared as the author, this book was truly a joint effort as clearly evidenced by the preface:

> This isn't "my" book; it is "our" book in more ways than one. My beloved husband has written much of this book and he has also encouraged and helped me in my writing. Even to the time before the writing, it has been our work together, our teamwork that has played a large part in making possible the sharing of the bread. The fact that we were of one mind in this regard

made the extra work easy, and somehow the good Lord always provided the wherewithal, scant though our resources were. Which brings me to the basic "our" relationship!

Because we wanted Christ to be the head of our house, because through his Word we sought to know what a Christian home should be like, we were enabled to have an open door into open hearts! The Lord is the most important part of the "our."

It was thrilling for us to read in the April 1975 church bulletin the following account of Clarence's new position with the Augustana Home entitled "Of Prunes and Pulpits and Prayer":

Many Augustana members and friends will never forget the powerful and Spirit-filled message shared from our pulpit by Dr. and Mrs. Clarence T. Nelson last Sunday morning. They stood in the pulpit together—a great sight. Jesus was there with them. It was a moving experience to hear the closing duet; "I Will Not Be Afraid."

We also cherish the closing moments of the service when we gathered at the altar for the "recommissioning" of the Nelsons for continuing ministries at the Augustana Home and in many places. They have been on the go and on fire for God in many places, St. Paul, Duluth, Washington, D.C., Saudi Arabia, Geneva, Switzerland, Chicago, and Minneapolis. But their greatest and most fruitful ministry is NOW.

I recall a favorite story about Dr. and Mrs. Nelson. Ruth, as many know, speaks often at group and mass meetings. Pastor Nelson often accompanies her, and often they give great programs together. On one occasion, as Ruth was speaking, Pastor Nelson was sitting in the balcony reading a book. He was wearing his clerical collar. A little lady in the balcony was looking at him disapprovingly. Following the sermon this lady met Pastor Nelson and discovered that he was Ruth's husband. She said, "Well, that's a relief. When I saw you reading in the balcony instead of listening to the speaker, I thought to myself, 'That poor stick of a preacher could learn something from that woman.' "

We have surely learned much from the Nelsons. God has enriched and inspired us through them. Why? Because they listen to Jesus and learn from him. Then they share with us his words of life.

We are grateful and reassured that they will continue to worship and serve in our midst. Here is a note of thanks from Pastor and Mrs. Nelson:

Our heartfelt thanks for last Sunday's outpouring of love. Nothing we ever did deserved this explosion. This is the outshining of pure grace. That's the long and the short of it. And Ruth and I stand back with deeply grateful hearts wondering at it all.

From two wrinkled prunes

Another day we were being used in a Lenten mission at First Lutheran Church in St. Peter, Minnesota. Palm Sunday morning we had shared in two services and had a beautiful experience. We thoroughly enjoyed the hospitality of the evangelism committee in one of the member's homes and sensed the splendid dedication of these young couples. There was an evening presentation, then, wearily but joyfully, we went to nephew Ren Anderson and his gracious wife Sylvia's home for rest and renewal. But there was no sleep that night. Violent pains racked Clarence's back, and he walked the bedroom floor hour upon hour, not wanting to awaken the folks. Ren was up early and tried to get a doctor, but it was hunting season, and he wasn't successful. We knew we had to get Clarence to Minneapolis and his doctor there.

I took the assignment of speaking to the pastors and wives who gathered that morning. Then we headed for Minneapolis and Clarence was immediately put into the hospital. I returned to St. Peter for the evening presentation, knowing Clarence was receiving the best of care. On Wednesday he was to have a biopsy of a swollen gland, so after I had spoken at a women's luncheon, I rushed back to Minneapolis to be with him.

I was tense and nervous waiting in the family room with many other anxious folks whose loved ones were undergoing similar ordeals. It seemed like an eternity. Then my name was called. I eagerly went up to the desk to meet the strange doctor who had done the biopsy. His curt comment was, "It's malignant."

I stuttered, "What—what now? Will it be an operation—or cobalt treatments?" Just as curtly he replied, "That's not my job."

With leaden feet I returned to Clarence's room. I couldn't tell him the truth. Instead I said, "Dr. Martin (our regular doctor)

224

will be coming in soon. It will be good to hear what he suggests next." Whether Clarence was such a good actor he could fool me, or he hadn't caught the innuendo of my evasion, I don't know. He wasn't perturbed. When the doctor came in, he reported that Clarence's cancer had recurred and he would begin a 10-day series of hormone treatments that could conceivably shrink the enlarged nodules and give him some comfort, but there were no promises. On April 26, 1976, Clarence wrote to his children:

> . . . I am to begin the injections next Monday and that's that. You can be sure that all this has made for some reflections on our life together. I'm ready when he calls. In the meantime, I'm going to do all within my power to make what days remain meaningful. I believe implicitly in the power of prayer and faith, but my only demand of God is for grace to take what may be ahead with courage and to extract the most from each day of joy and friendship. Ruth just couldn't be more wonderful in her attitude, and this means so much to me.

Then, during Epiphany of 1977, he wrote:

> We had expected to mail this from Florida, but our plans are still on, only postponed. Because of increasing pains which became almost unbearable, I am back in the hospital for 10 more estrogen treatments. The doctor wants us to go to Florida, anyway, and so we are. Our times are in the hands of a loving heavenly Father. The doctor's directions are "Keep active. Do what you have been doing." That suits me fine. I've made the lines of S. Hall Young my own:

> LET ME DIE WORKING
>
> Let me die, working.
> Still tackling plans unfinished, tasks undone!
> Clean to its end, swift may my race be run.
> No laggard steps, no faltering, no shirking;
> Let me die, working!
>
> Let me die, thinking.
> Let me fare forth still with an open mind,
> Fresh secrets to unfold, new truths to find,
> My soul undimmed, alert, no question blinking;
> Let me die, thinking!

Let me die, laughing.
No sighing o'er past sins; they are forgiven.
Spilled on this earth are all the joys of Heaven;
The wine of life, the cup of mirth quaffing.
Let me die, laughing!

When we returned from Florida, Clarence picked up his chaplaincy work at Augustana Home. That spring we had two great short trips together, a week in Arizona speaking and visiting, and a weekend in Jamestown, North Dakota. While we were in Arizona, Clarence's pains accelerated. Even in this far place, beautiful friends from former years ministered to us. When we returned home, Clarence resigned his assistant chaplain job, and the doctor tried to find how best to alleviate his pain and make the nights less nightmarish.

Clarence summoned everything he had to live as normally as possible. The great anticipation was the arrival of Biz and family from Indonesia. They planned to spend some weeks at Koja before settling in Germany. We remembered with joy the time they spent here with us only two years ago. How Biz reveled in the scenes so dear to her childhood. As for Karl and Inge, they melded right in with their cousins and others of the colony of their own age. The upper room of the boat house rang with the whoops of the boys who used it as their sleeping quarters. Mary was thrilled to turn over her new cabin to her sister and family.

Koja was a natural for the Youngdahl reunions. It was always special when Luther and Irene found it possible to join us. Lute would be sure to read in his inimitable style, "Chicken Neck" and "Kiss Him, Son, He's No Stranger," the ballad of the golfing buff. Earlier reunions when Ben, Reuben, and Mabel were with us were relived, especially that dinner at Hart's when Rube demanded the tab, causing Lute to simulate fainting from shock. Ren and Syb always were sure to be along, generously adding to the larder. Win and Lorraine were there, and Dick and Kitty flew in from the East, bringing such members of their family as were free to come.

The summer of '77 was a summer to top all summers. Each day was a gala event, with one or another grandchild learning to make it on one ski or sailing in our little sailboat. We even had our annual swim and picnic on Lake Superior and Clarence went swimming too. At our cabin, he could make it down the steps to the beach, but not up, so Walle, Dave, and Jon carried him up in a wicker chair. He said he felt like King Knute during this operation. We had a beautiful reunion and shared festive international meals. Biz and family prepared Indonesian fare; Mary, Tanzanian; Leah and company, oriental; Grandma, Swedish and German; and Uncle Dave, the generous benefactor, the American with steaks and corn on the cob. It was like taking a trip around the world— not just in eating (we tried not to make it too elaborate), but in flavoring knowledge about other people and cultures and in sharing things we had learned with each other. For many breakfasts we had Clarence's Swedish pancakes.

To one of the international meals we invited quite a group of friends. As always, singing abounded, and laughter and joy filled the air. One of our guests reported that the next day on the way home her young daughter asked, "Is Pastor Nelson really going to die? How can they be so happy?"

We *were* happy. Hours of great discussions and philosophizing took place during those days. That summer was a very special gift from the Lord, a sort of gathering of all the loose threads to finish the tapestry of a life whose theme was serving the Lord. Each morning Clarence would go to the workshop in Mary's basement where he and one helper or another would work at framing batiks from Indonesia and prints from Tanzania. There would be some rest in the afternoon, and then the beach.

Clarence made it a point to at one time or another seek out each grandchild and relate to that one individually. Kristin was going to Sweden as an exchange student, and he teased her a bit about those blond young men she might be meeting, but in between the teasing were words of wisdom to guide her in her choices. Their parting at the Minneapolis airport was tender.

One day Clarence took Micah on his lap as together from the deck they watched the volleyball game on the lot between our two cottages. Micah was a little downcast—he would have loved to be out there. But his polio-crippled legs eliminated volleyball. Then Grandpa said to him, "You know, Micah, when Jesus comes

Swimming

All the grandchildren

*Clarence as
"King Knute"*

*Clarence
at the piano*

Blueberrying

*Sailing
on the lake*

Inimitable Luther

to take us home, we'll each have a whole new body. We don't know what it will be like, but we know there'll be no more sickness or pain or crippling."

There were also precious hours with Inge and Karl. Their long years in Indonesia had kept them from coming so many summers. But this year they had a chance to flavor their grandpa. Karl spent many hours with him in the carpenter's shop and quickly learned the skills of saw and wood from him. Inge was the helpful errand runner, always ready to assist in any way she could. Both children shared their piano skills and delighted us.

We shared family devotions after the evening meal. One evening we all gathered on Mary's deck where two long tables provided dining space for all. Dad read to us Psalm 130, "Out of the Depths." We touched the hem of heaven's garment that night. Clarence's prayers had a way of breaking through the barriers of earth and putting us in the presence of the beautiful Savior.

We had other spiritual feasts as we worshiped in the village church. One Sunday Clarence and I did a dialog sermon, Jon liturgized, and Elsie sang. At another, three generations of us furnished the music, singing in seven different languages, "I thank the Lord, my Savior," and ending with "In Christ there is no east or west."

The partings were rough as the Lempps left for Germany, Jon Nelsons for Seattle, Elsie for Washington, and then the Johansons for Geneva. Mary and Dave gave us a Labor Day weekend that was unforgettable before leaving for Chicago.

As we returned to Minneapolis, Clarence's strength waned, but he never stayed in bed. He got up every morning as usual, shaved, and gave himself to writing his memoirs. One day he wrote:

There was a little cramped gate alongside Jerusalem's main Damascus gate called the Needle's Eye. A merchant with his loaded camel had strained his every energy to make the safety of Jerusalem's stout walls for his beast and burden through the main gate. But at sunset the gate slammed shut. His only hope was to unload, make his camel kneel, and, summoning every possible hand, push and pull the grunting beast through the Needle's Eye. Thereafter the precious cargo had to be hand-carried with sweat and strain to the safe side. To me a heart attack resembles this whole operation. One learns firsthand Jesus' words: "A man's life does not consist in the abundance of his possessions." One's eyes get peeled wide open to what are life's real values. Battling for breath sheds new light on what really is important. It came out like this for me. Here are the top notches on my life's totem pole:

The rockbound promises of God as found in his Word.
The beauty of a bird on a wing.
The laughter of little children at play.
Dappled sunshine on tree and house and hills beyond.
The unnumbered ministries of a loving helpmeet.
A friend's promise to pray for me.
The sure knowledge that despite ugliness and crime across our shadowed land, the famine that stalks the globe, and all the economic woes, *God is about, and Jesus is Lord!* And time moves relentlessly to his return who will set things right.

Almost daily, at our devotional time together, Clarence would begin his prayers with:

See to thee, I yield my heart;
Shed thy love in every part.
Thy pure vessel I would be,
Wholly consecrated to thee.

We discussed many things together, and frequently played Scrabble as a diversion from pain.

On September 18, 1977, we gave a dialog sermon in our beloved Augustana Church. Clarence summoned every ounce of strength he had to do what he loved best—share the gospel. His opening sentence was, "Maybe some of you think this is the last hurrah of a dying old man; but I tell you, I'm practicing up for the alleluias." We closed the sermon singing together, "Our Times Are in Thy Hands."

The next day Clarence had a doctor's appointment. Again, the report was bad, and he was wheeled from the doctor's office into the hospital where he immediately was given oxygen. It looked as if he were responding to the treatment, and the doctor held out the hope of his coming home in a few days. Pastor Berg brought up the tape of our dialog sermon on Thursday, September 22. Clarence thought he'd like to sit in a chair and listen to it. I was helping him swing his legs over the side of the bed so he could get into the chair. It happened in my arms. In the twinkling of an eye, in less than a second, the light went out here—and on there. He was with the Lord.

VICTORY CELEBRATION

15

Would that I could give an adequate picture of this man I loved! That he was privileged to be an undershepherd of the Great Shepherd of us all was the overwhelming fact of his life. Being a minister was never a burden, never an intrusion. It was an all-consuming fire! It was his great joy and challenge. Being a father was an extra gift from God. How dearly he loved, and how tenderly he shared in the presentation of each child. He surrounded them with his prayers. And, loving God, he loved people. He accepted them where they were, even though they might oppose him in things he wanted for the kingdom and the church. He didn't give up on them. He taught me patience with people. He taught me love. Oh, how I would miss him!

Three years prior, when he had his first heart attack, he had planned every detail of his memorial service. Mary had kept the notes so his every wish was fulfilled. We began the service with "My Faith Looks Up to Thee." This was followed by many of the same prayers Clarence had prayed the previous Sunday and then by the five scripture passages he had selected. After the scriptures, the singing of "Amazing Grace" set the stage for each family member to say a few words.

David spoke first:

These moments together are not just a funeral, they are a memorial, a celebration. We'd like to share, as a family, some remembrances and reflections. We together want to express our thanks. First to Pastor Berg for the call that you and the people of Augustana extended to Dad after his ministry had encircled the globe. And we're thankful to all of you here today. The Youngdahl and Nelson clan whose traditions are so rich and whose witness in the faith has touched and empowered us all. You know how much Dad loved every one. From around the world some of you have come . . . and we get a little bit of the flavor of the wonder of God's family as it stretches across the miles and the continents and through all time and space and makes us one people together. But mostly we're grateful to our heavenly Father for the gift of Dad, a heritage of love that we've all been touched by.

It was on occasions like this that Dad would really shine. His voice would get deep and come from his, well, his guts. You could tell that his heart was in what he was saying.

This summer Dad was aware that his time was short, and he was preparing us for the time when he'd step across the border and his suffering, his pilgrimage, and his joy of this life would end. I'll never forget the last letter he wrote. It started with these lines: "As I come sliding towards home base, the richness of these moments of life gets even greater." I remember last summer after one of Pastor Berg's visits, Dad reflected on the visit and commented on the close relationship with God evident in him and how he had thought about asking Bill to place his hands on his head as the Scriptures have commanded and pray for healing for him. But then he thought, "What more can I ask out of life than God has already given? How much more full and rich can I expect life to be?"

Sometimes Dad was a saint, but there were other times when he was a pretty ornery human being. He had a lot of grit. For example, he worked for an entire week leveling dirt with a burst appendix; that's grit. And he worked finishing making frames out of scraps of wood that last summer. When he could no longer stand, he sat. He stuck with it until every last picture was framed. That's grit.

But most of all I remember the worship services at Augustana. I'll never forget throughout all my life Dad giving the benediction.

Mary spoke next:

Dad, I know you're here. Your spirit is hovering among us, and I know that you're going to be with us the rest of our lives. Dad was always trying to teach us things, and one of the things he was always telling us was not to waste anything. He didn't like us to waste energy long before the energy crisis. He was forever running around the house turning off the lights, mumbling about how we kids were leaving them on. . . . He didn't like to waste time. . . . Dad didn't like us to waste anything that was broken. . . . I remember typing his autobiography that he had written on little scraps of paper that had been used before because he didn't like to waste a thing.

But most of all I remember that he didn't want us to waste any opportunities of any kind or shape. When it came time for me to decide if I should go to Germany, it was Dad who said, "Don't waste that opportunity; take advantage of it." Or if there was an opportunity to share his love for the Lord and his faith, he didn't want to waste it. He shared with us the opportunity of visiting the sick and the shut-in. And he never wasted the opportunity to invite somebody home for dinner, whether it was a lonely soldier boy, an alcoholic, or an ambassador.

Finally, and most importantly, Dad didn't like us to waste the opportunity of sharing the goodness of what God had given to us. I'll never forget the day Dad came home in his stocking feet. When I asked him what happened to his shoes, he told me that a man had come into his office seeking help. Dad noticed his shoes were almost like nothing, so he gave the man the shoes off his own feet. I only hope and pray as I live out these years of my life that I can follow in Dad's footsteps, and Dad was so wanting to follow in the footsteps of our Lord, I only hope that as I walk closer to that great "getting up morning" that I'll arrive at that day in my stocking feet too.

Lorraine's tribute was brief, but moving:

I talked to my foster father, Clarence, just a week ago yesterday on the telephone. One of the things he said was, "I just wrapped a package for you. It's going to be put in the mail today." That package came later in the week, and the curious thing about it was that it was addressed to Lorraine Servheen. As I looked at it I thought, I bet that as he wrapped that package his mind went back to the day when he took into his family a 15-year-old girl who had lost her parents. He has been my father for 43 years. There's a lot that wells up in my heart when I think of him because of his gentleness and his kindness. Of course, what meant the most was what he gave to each one of the family, and I feel like I should speak for Paul and Elsie. I think that what he gave us three grafts onto the family tree as well as his own four children, he gave us that wonderful nosegay that we all hold today and that is: "Whether we live, we live unto the Lord; and whether we die, we die unto the Lord: whether we live therefore, or die, we are the Lord's" (Rom. 14:8 KJV).

Biz picked up on Mary's theme as she began her tribute:

Mary mentioned Dad's concern about lights. I can just see him, too, walking around turning off lights. But light was very important to him. I remember Dad's love of getting up early in the morning, in the earliness of the sun's light. Whether it was to brew that good Swedish coffee or to make his incomparable Swedish pancakes or to dig into the next Sunday's sermon.

I think we all share today the light that was most important to him. The day we heard of Dad's passing, the verses that met us in our daily reading were: "No longer will the sun be your light by day or the moon be your light by night; I, the Lord, will be your eternal light; the light of my glory will shine on you" (Isaiah 60:19 TEV). So Dad's not worrying about turning off any more lights. He's with the eternal light.

When it came my turn, I began with a tremor in my voice:

I'd like to speak a word, first of all, on behalf of Clarence, and that word is a big word of thank you. Thank you for this wonderful family of God that received so richly and with whom we've had such beautiful times this year. He would want to say thank you to the family for all the joys that they have brought and for the beautiful friends over the years from the many places. Again and again, he'd say thank you to God for the wonder of the life we've been able to live, for the joys we've known amidst the sorrows and the difficulties.

Many, many times he was my encouragement and would go with me when I went on speaking trips. He always upgirded me in prayer. And when he went with me, he would make such friends among the folks with whom we were that it was just a beautiful experience. I can't be thankful enough to him for all the encouragement and enrichment that he brought to my life.

And just one other little word, if I were to pick out a single strand wherein our life has grown richer and richer (and that's what happens when you grow together in the Lord), it would be this matter of praying together. Oh, how rich our lives have been, entreating for our children in the kinds of work in which they were engaged. When things were tough, and evil would stalk and try to prevent the Word of God and the love of the Lord from working, to be able to lift them up in prayer to the Lord and ask him to get in there and let his wonderful will of love be known. To pray for the world. He was so aware of the distressing sections of the world and often carried them in his prayers. The power of prayer to unite people is the greatest power that I know. Whatever happens, we could meet it, unafraid. And that's the way, in my eyes, he met the Lord last Thursday night.

Next Jon spoke, lovingly, forcefully:

C. T. was really off his form when he organized this service because he doesn't have a collection. That, for my Dad, was highly unusual.

Last time I talked with him there was a fellow in his room with a hypodermic ready to give him a shot, he was sitting on the bedpan, and the chaplain was just coming in the door. I said all I wanted to do was greet him, and he said, "Beautiful, Jon, beautiful." That's Dad in the midst of a tough situation.

Then there's another moment I remember. My wife and I and our family were adopting one of our children at a ceremony in the judge's private chambers out in Missoula, Montana. It happened Mom and Dad had made a trip through and were able to be with us for the occasion. I didn't like the judge's attitude.

236

He seemed to think that we hadn't considered fully what it meant to adopt a child. "Do you know," he asked me, "that this child will inherit a share of your fortune alongside and the same as every other one of your children?"

I was irritated when I responded, "Your honor, she can have everything I've got."

Dad sensed I wasn't paying proper respect to the judge, and he said, "Your honor, she can have a slice of my melon too." I think it carried the day, but if you knew C. T.'s wealth, it was purely a figure of speech. Except that I've turned that one over in my mind—a slice of his melon—a piece of his inheritance—and it's really so. We are all common inheritors in the Christian community; of the inheritance of the lives of the saints of light, of that prize which is above every other prize, of the pearl of priceless treasure, of the faith and gift that had been given Dad in his baptism through Jesus Christ that he had passed along in countless meals of bread and wine and moments of love and encouragement, and shared visions of hope and the sure knowledge that Christ has conquered every foe, even death. I'll take a slice of that melon any day, and thank God for it.

Elsie completed the family testimonials:

I think all of you know the story about the man in the Bible who had a vineyard and said he would pay a penny a day to every worker. When day was over and it was time to be paid, the one who came in last got the same as the others. The others said, "How come? We were here all day and we get a penny?" And the man said, "Well, didn't you say you would work all day for a penny?"

Well, I came late, and I got the same love like the rest of the children. I am his smoked Swede. There is a little chorus that he used to love, and Mom loved it very much. I was trying to remember a verse that goes with it, and, translated, it more or less is, "The night is gone with its shadows. Morning is here, and I am happy with Christ. It is morning."

Then Elsie's beautiful voice resounded with "It Is Morning," sung first in Spanish, then in English.

When Elsie had finished, Pastor Berg spoke to the gathering:

I think the angels of God have been leaning over the balustrades of heaven and rejoicing, saying they're having a great celebration down there. Congratulations to the family on having a part in this kind of service. How glad your Dad would be, and how pleased. And please congratulate us here at Augustana too. One of the greatest things that ever happened to us in our 110-year history and one of the brightest highlights for Augustana was when Clarence and Ruth Nelson came our way to stay with us.

And I believe in miracles when I see the Nelson family and Clarence and Ruth 45 years together in all parts of the world, and where did they end up? At Metropolitan Medical Center. And they were about to listen to last Sunday's tape, and while getting on the edge of the bed, Clarence fell into your arms, Ruth, because you were right there, in the right place, at the right time. But God be praised that you didn't keep him. You put him in the arms of your Savior. And what an ending and climax for a drama-packed, world-encircling story these 45 years together. . . .

The last words I heard Clarence speak, shortly before he went home, were these that came in soft gasps: "I see a little light at the end of the tunnel." And now, my friends, that little light has become the streaming glory of God's presence, as he made it safely through the tunnel to the place of eternal day.

After Pastor Berg concluded, the Hallelujah Chorus resounded through the church. This was followed by a tribute from Clarence's brother, a prayer, the benediction, and then the recessional, "On Our Way Rejoicing"—all as Clarence had so carefully set down three years before.

He had requested that he be cremated and buried at our beloved Koja with a Colorado blue spruce to mark the spot. Early the day after the memorial service, the family headed up to Sand Lake. It was a cold, windy day, typical of the end of September in Minnesota. Three couples, friends through the years, were at their cabins, so we invited them to join us. After the boys had dug the grave, we sang a chorale, shared Scriptures together, and then placed the box of ashes in the ground as we sang the evening prayer that had been ours through the years:

Jesus, tender Shepherd, hear me;
    Bless thy little lamb tonight;
Through the darkness be thou near me;
    Keep me safe till morning light.

All this day thy hand has led me,
    And I thank thee for thy care;
Thou hast clothed me, warmed and fed me,
    Listen to my evening prayer.

Let my sins be all forgiven;
    Bless the friends I love so well:
Take me, Lord, at last to heaven,
    Happy there with thee to dwell.

Then we slipped into Mary's cabin where there was a fire and hot coffee. Jon sat down at the piano and began to play one hymn after the other. For an hour we sang hymns from memory. Our faith was strengthened; one coal upon another keeping the flame warm. Clarence would have loved it.

THE BEAT GOES ON

16

Then came the return to the apartment, the sorting out of Clarence's clothing and personal possessions, the decisions: Where should I live? What commitments should I keep?

The children did everything to help with the immediate decisions and correspondence, but then they had to leave: Lorraine and Win to Geneva, Elsie to Washington, Clara (Paul T. M. King's daughter) to Milwaukee, Dave and Mary to Chicago, and Jon to Seattle. Biz remained, but only for a short while.

As I searched my heart, I knew Clarence would encourage me to keep my appointments. He was always my encourager. So that next Sunday I addressed the young people's forum at Normandale Church. Biz was with me, but she had to leave for Germany that afternoon. The letter she wrote from the airplane is one I have kept. She began, "The hardest thing I have ever done in my life was to leave you standing there at the airport—alone."

Three days later I was on my way to Colorado Springs to participate in a three-day Lutheran Church Women's retreat at the Garden of the Gods. What a blessing is Christian fellowship. What a balm for an aching heart is the love of folks who care. God gave the strength to fulfill that commitment, to witness to his sustaining companionship, to challenge us to remember to "redeem the time because the days are evil." I recalled the haunting couplet, "Only one life; 'twill soon be past; only what's done for Christ will last."

My experience going home was symbolic of what would be happening again and again in the days ahead. Because of the weather, I was grounded in Colorado Springs and had to go by ground to Denver to make my connection to Minneapolis. I was due to speak at Mount Olivet Church that night. I arrived in Denver too late to make my scheduled flight, but was put on a later one that would still see me home in time to keep my speaking engagement. The kind man at the desk said, "Is there someone I can call for you to tell them of your delay?"

I gulped. There always had been! Now it wouldn't make any difference to anyone, so I replied, "No, thank you."

But he persisted, "Isn't there someone we should call?" This should have been a warning as to what I would experience when I came into the Minneapolis airport. You know that feeling of looking in the crowd for the face of the one you love? You see all the reunions, the hugging, the tears, and then the sharing. But now I was on my own. Somehow or other, the joy of all the times Clarence had met me flooded over me. How much we take for granted.

When we still thought there might be a chance of Clarence being well enough to travel, we talked about spending Christmas with Biz's family in Stuttgart. Apparently he had laid it on Mary's heart to go with me, knowing he wouldn't make it. At her urging, we did go. Although Clarence wasn't there in the flesh, he surely was there in spirit. With each new experience, each new flavoring of this country that was now our daughter's home, I'd think, "Clarence would love this." History was his hobby, and he would have reveled in the turning of its pages via the knowledge and sensitivity of our son-in-law.

And when Biz, her two children, our granddaughter Kris who was attending school in Sweden on a Rotary scholarship, and I made a remembrance trip to Geneva, Switzerland, Clarence was there with me, reveling again in the matchless beauty of the

Swiss Alps with their ever-changing panorama. How we had loved our picnics together in the most secluded places we could find. In those special places we'd settle down, each with a book. Yes, he was there as we attended that quaint church in Old Town beneath the shadow of the great cathedral on the hill. He used to thrill to climbing the well-worn steps up to the high pulpit from which he preached as he remembered the chain of witnesses who had preceded him. How long will I live on memories?

This trip was special, too, because Dave was able to join us in Stuttgart after he had a memorable experience at the Taize Retreat Center in France. His presence crowned that trip and made it possible for him to accompany me back to the States.

In May I was scheduled to speak on a Sunday morning to a large youth gathering in Baltimore. Irene, my sister-in-law, invited Elsie and me for dinner that evening. Luther was the only one left in my generation of the Youngdahl family. When Clarence died, Lute couldn't come to the memorial service because the ravages of disease were taking their toll. He had always been such a bulwark of strength, and he and Clarence had enjoyed a beautiful relationship. That spring the law clerks who worked with Lute through the years had honored him and had a portrait made to be hung in the Federal District Court Building in Washington. Justice Douglas, in his autobiography, had paid him splendid tribute for the way he conducted the Lattimore case. The *Washington Post* had an amazing article with a spread of pictures, and the *Minneapolis Star* editorialized. It was like one "Amen" after another. But now he was critically ill, lying on the davenport in his home.

When Irene announced dinner, however, he said, "I want to sit with you." So he joined us at the beautifully appointed table. Then he said, "I want to pray." How I wish I had a recording of that prayer. It brought to mind Simeon: "Lord, now lettest thou thy servant depart in peace. . . . " He began by thanking God for his loving wife, for Elsie and her thoughtfulness, for Clarence and all that he had meant to him, and for all our family and his own beloved children. A beautiful valedictory to an amazingly fruitful life.

From that point on, he was in and out of the hospital. On his birthday, we called him at the hospital from Minneapolis to sing our birthday greeting. He responded, "I sang it to myself this morning." The old sense of humor was still alive.

Then he was back home again with Irene in the apartment they loved so well. In June came the call. The last of my family of 10 brothers and sisters joined those already with the Lord. I was the only one left. "Lord, to whom shall I go?"

He, too, had prepared every detail of his memorial service. The Catholic priest who came from Minneapolis to Washington to participate told how, when Lute was governor, they had worked together to help young people and keep families together. They had an ecumenical movement of their own years ago. With Lute's homegoing, the last anchor of my generation was lost; I was completely alone.

I returned to Minneapolis and tried to live my life as an old farmer quoted in Peter Howard's *Ideas Have Legs* suggested: "Live as though you would die tonight; farm as though you would live forever!" When people commented on how blessed I was to have been where I'd been and to have seen what I'd seen, I'd answer, "I was blessed to marry the right man." Even though he had a stubborn streak as strong as mine, the mellowing effect of God on both our lives through the years is witness to the fact that nothing is too hard for God. The companionship we knew through it all surely was a foretaste of what it is to come by the grace of Jesus Christ. How often Clarence quoted the Swedish proverb that translates, "When iron rusts, it rusts together." This doing things together, this teaming for the Lord, was the warp and woof of our lives.

That was why this temporary parting left me raw and sore. I missed him more than words could tell, yet how could I ever be grateful enough for those 45 years together? And we will meet again—the best *is* yet to come. Meanwhile, according to his wishes, I fulfilled speaking commitments and asked the Lord to guide me as to what the next step should be.

A friend tucked into my memory chest a doggerel I particularly like:

When I am old and pretty well bent
And my "get up and go" has got up and went,
Then will I grin when I think where it's been.

It isn't where the feet have gone that is so important; it is rather where the heart has gone. Of course, the feet follow the heart, and, "As for me and my house, we will serve the Lord."

The instructions God gives are specific: "As you did it to one of the least of these my brethren, you did it to me." Dad and Mother taught us children that to serve the Lord was to serve other people. Clarence and I taught our children likewise, and now they were teaching theirs the same thing. The beat goes on— all our children were serving the Lord.

In March 1979 Jon again stood before the court; he had gone over the wall at the Trident missile base a third time. Facing the judge, he declared:

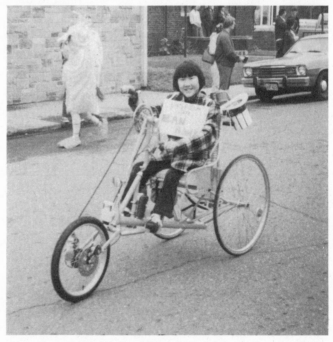

Jon's son, Micah, in a "Ban the Bomb" parade

244

. . . my defense is not before this court, but before the court that ultimately matters to me, the court of my children's future and the future of generations unborn, the court of my conscience before the throne of God.

It is before this court that I say today I have tried to say no to the mass insanity of mutually assured destruction that the Trident weapons system represents. I have tried to speak on behalf of a vision of a regard for a system of international law and peacekeeping and the adjudication of disputes between nations. I have tried to say yes to a belief that if the human species is to survive on this planet, it will have to learn what Jesus himself was teaching, that the key to life is not the considerable courage it takes to lay down one's life for one's own in war, but the courage to give that life fully in pursuit of the well-being of the whole human community.

It is in this behalf that I make my defense.

Jon was sentenced to a second 45-day term in jail. I wrote to him, telling him how much I loved him. How proud I was and how proud Clarence would have been of his actions.

In April Jon sent the following Easter greeting:

Easter Greetings from Prison

4/7/79
King County Jail
Friends in campus ministry,

Mutually
 Assured
  Destruction
   and the aching cursing
cries through steel bars.
        Sardonic iced smile of bureaucratic
guards with impotent hatred in the eyes.

        Jarred slam of metal gates,
and the soothing assurance of our
leaders over the muzak --
        national security comes in
subs two billion apiece -- death
dealing to 80 million enemy.

A counter point -- but not deafening --

to the quiet musical sun rise of the
        Easter morning.

        Greetings this season from the
        felon tanks at the Seattle King
        County Jail.

        Jon Nelson.

In May, when Jon was released, he was greeted by cheers and applause from some 200 persons and was hailed as a prophet for his Trident protest. He embraced Juni and their children and then he and his well-wishers marched several blocks to the First United Methodist Church in a procession led by a cross. At the thanksgiving service they held to welcome him home, Jon delivered an impassioned attack on the worship of false gods and altars of materialism, bureaucratic controls, militarism, and national pride, declaring, "In Jesus Christ lies the hope of the world, not in the strength of armies, but in a spirit of becoming human."

When anyone talks about answered prayer, I think of the lives of our children. From the time they were first born, even before that, when I was carrying them in my womb, we prayed God would use them as channels of his love to others. It really didn't matter in what occupation or profession, only that they would use their God-given gifts to bless others, whether it be as mechanics, engineers, homemakers, or in some other way. We affirmed together the belief in the priesthood of all believers and that everyone is called to be a minister.

How many times Clarence and I would speak of how the children challenged us by their dedication. Now they all were challenging me to face life without Clarence, to continue to contribute.

Paul T. M. King was executive secretary for the Bank of the Republic of China and traveled the world. Several times he called from Blair House in D.C. where he was housed while on government business. He gives of himself as a layman at Truth Lutheran Church in Taipei, setting an excellent example for stewardship. How Clarence would have loved Clara King's wedding. Clara was the eldest child in Paul's family. She had just earned her master's degree from the University of Wisconsin and was employed as a researcher on pulmonary difficulties for the Veterans' Administration. In the wonderful way of the Lord, she met Joe JuGer who was attending the University of Alabama and working on his master's degree. They had been Sunday school children together at Truth Lutheran Church in Taipei! Now they were to be married. I was at Koja and flew down from Duluth for the wedding in Milwaukee, Mary and Dave came up from Chicago, and Joe's father came from Taiwan. Dave, assisted by the pastor of the

Reformation Lutheran Church, performed the ceremony, and Clara was a radiant, beautiful bride.

Then there was Lorraine Johanson, presiding over the parsonage in Geneva, Illinois, with her husband, Win. Bible teacher, dedicated pastor's wife, amazing hostess, gifted artist, mother of four, she constantly spilled out her life in loving concern for others.

Elsie, by herself named our smoked Swede, had given all her free time to helping others. Now she was fighting that ugly disease, cancer, as it wound its tentacles in and around her organs. She had to discontinue her work and live on a total disability stipend. The golden voice that for those many years was a part of Augustana's outstanding choir was now muted by surgery, chemotherapy, and cobalt treatments; yet her strong, simple Christian faith sustained and nourished in her the hope of more time to serve her Lord here on this earth. The Lord called her just before Christmas 1979. She had her plane ticket to join us in Chicago, but instead she celebrated her first Christmas with her Lord.

Jon and his family, too, were serving the Lord. Jon was back at the University of Washington campus, challenging the students through the programs of the ecumenical campus ministry to first make their faith real through study and growth, and then to live it, sharing the concerns of those in prison, the handicapped, and those suffering from injustice. Juni and he were parenting a large family, five now teenagers. Juni, amazing gal, was presiding over a day-care center in their home which substantially supplemented the family income. How fortunate were the parents and children she served in this way, and what a lift that extra income provided when it came to paying the grocery bill.

Dave, after trying another kind of assignment, was back at Bethel shepherding the people of God with whom he had cast his lot, and what a shepherd he was. The concern of each member of his flock was his concern. His unselfish giving of himself followed the pattern of the Great Shepherd of us all. Bethel Christian School continued to be a symbol of hope in the West Garfield neighborhood, and now the church was venturing forth on a housing project to bring new hope to the people who lived in its environs. Dave was also chairman of our national church's committee on world hunger.

Biz, Walle, and their two children were living in Stuttgart, Germany, after having completed some 20 years as missionaries in Indonesia. Walle was heading up a preseminary school in Stuttgart, and Biz was bringing love and life into their home as she poured out her heart in hospitality. Her letters were an interesting chronicle of the people who moved in and out of their home for a few days or even weeks: a lonely bachelor, former missionaries seeking comfort and stimulation, an expectant Indonesian mother in this foreign country. Sometimes it sounded as though the roads of the world converged into that home. And Biz loved it.

Finally there was Mary, who courageously for 14 years had poured her skills and her love into the challenge of an inner-city neighborhood rejuvenation. She was serving her Lord working part-time for a group of Lutheran churches and as director of the Bethel Housing Corporation, a Bethel Church-sponsored pioneer effort to provide decent housing for low-income people. She also served as a deacon on the church council, played the organ for the Sunday services, taught a class of high school youth, served on the Augustana College Board, and was cochairperson of Alternative Schools Network.

Mary had been working with some minority contractors, small businessmen who had quite a struggle even making a living in the swirl of corporations and big business. She helped with the paperwork, managing the finances and making contracts. On this particular evening, having just returned from interviews with legislators in Springfield, she stopped in where four of the contractors were meeting. One of them was working on rehabilitating a church and had just been given $4300 in $100 bills to purchase windows for the next phase of the building. He asked Mary if she would take them and get him a cashier's check in the morning so he could purchase the windows. She zipped them into the side of her purse, got into her car, locked the doors, and laid the purse on the seat next to her. It was 10 P.M., and she headed for Dave's parsonage where she was staying temporarily. It was only a few blocks away.

At a main cross street she had to stop for a red light. When the

248

Lorraine, Win, and family

Biz, Walle, and family

Dave, Mary,
and colleagues

Jon, Juni, and family

Paul T. M. King and family

Elsie

light turned green, the car ahead of her moved on. She had shifted to follow when there was a smashing of glass—her car window had been shattered. Trying to protect her eyes from the flying glass, all she saw was the hand reaching in and grabbing her purse —and then the retreating figure on the run. She screamed, but the car ahead of her had disappeared and there was no one to hear. She drove to Dave's and burst into his home, sobbing. He tried many times to call the police, but only after 20 tries did he get through. It was another 20 minutes before three police officers arrived, and they spent precious minutes interrogating Mary. The thief had all the time in the world to get out of the neighborhood.

The next day they found the purse in a garbage can, emptied of those hard-earned bills. The irony is that through the years both Mary and Dave had learned to carry very little cash with them. The newspaper reported a whole series of such purse-snatchings from cars; the thieves used either a piece of pipe or a baseball bat to shatter the windows. Three days later one of the Bethel schoolteachers had the same thing happen to her, only it was at eight in the morning and she didn't have $4300 in her purse. As Mary told me the story, I wondered what the money was used for. Then I wondered if Mary had experienced feelings similar to those that Grandpa Johnson had back in Sweden when he was swindled.

Like any mother, I was terribly proud of my children and the contributions they were making, but when I thought of how physically separated we were, I ached. It wasn't difficult to develop a putrid case of self-pity in my longing and loneliness for each of my beloved children. Then I'd be put to shame at the remembrance of our togetherness in the spirit. And prayer, as it drew us to God's throne of grace, brought us together.

Yes, the beat goes on. My life goes on. I have a certain chair in my living room that is my prayer corner. Here, daily, I draw aside with the Lord and reaffirm our relationship; I get my marching orders for the day. It is a precious spot, for many battles of the soul have been fought here.

Clarence is still with me in spirit. When I am swimming in our pool here in the apartment building, I can see him at the end of the pool with that teasing twinkle in his eyes, questioning my accuracy at counting the lengths. Even as I write this, I sense him grinning over my shoulder.

When I am grocery shopping, he is more effective in spirit than he was in the flesh in discouraging some extravagance like strawberries out of season or a melon too highly priced. When he was there to vocalize his objection, I'd sometimes deliberately defy it. Now I'll have second thoughts and return the strawberries or the melon before I go through the checkout. I wouldn't think of buying a dime's worth of candy—that's how alive he is in what I do!

It's not just a negative influence though. He is still my encourager as I consider my response to invitations to speak. I can hear his voice within me, almost as clearly as when he was here, saying, "If God has given you this gift, you should use it." Though I miss that welcome sight of him at the airport and his admonition to slow down as I make my way along those long ramps, it seems that he still tells me to stop and take a nitroglycerine and not to move too fast. He used to even carry my handbag for me because sometimes the weight of that was too much for my wildly pumping heart. Yes, he is still very much with me.

It's been a struggle though, a daily fight to face the morning light and find meaningful things to do. My beloved church, with its dedicated leadership, has been of great help. Sometimes when I'm calling at the Augustana Home one of the guests will say, "You remind me of your husband." What a compliment. Not long ago I was sitting on a stool next to an 85-year-old in a wheelchair, and she patted my knee and said, "That's where he used to sit, and you sound just like him."

My difficulty isn't in not being busy; rather it's in deciding which of all the needs there are to attend to first and which are most important.

Even these last years God has given me opportunities to speak in one section of this great country after another. I am consumed with the need to pour out my heart about our distorted sense of values. How can we claim to be followers of Jesus Christ when we continue to spend billions for bombs to annihilate and give only token contributions to the millions who are starving to death? How can we in our comfort and affluence turn a deaf ear to the countless throngs who suffer from injustice and a subtle slavery?

It need not be too late if we will seek the will of our loving Lord
—and live it.

And so I move about as I have these last weeks from Washington, D.C., to Seattle, Washington, from Grand Rapids, Michigan,
to Savannah, Georgia, and on to Boca Raton, Florida, asking the
Lord to use my voice to stir people to *be* in today's world what
he wants them to be: channels of his redemptive love.

There was a time when I wondered if I would have to cancel
out on all the engagements I had made months before. In a family
volleyball game at Koja, I fell and broke my pelvic bone. Much
to my amazement, the X-ray showed 90 percent of the hip disin-
tegrated from arthritis. No wonder I fell. All along I thought the
aching in my hips was simply age creeping up on me. However,
after the metamorphosis from hospital to wheelchair to walker
to cane, I could make my way without any visible support only
three months after the fall. Surely that is a miracle of God's heal-

A walker helped me
get around after
breaking my pelvic bone

ing power. To him be the glory, from him is the power, and with him is the joy. May I steward whatever days on this earth he gives me.

And then—I have great anticipations! This was most clearly brought home to me last December when I was returning from a speaking appointment in Elgin, Illinois. At O'Hare airport I boarded a huge 747 for Minneapolis. We left at 7 P.M. and were due to arrive in Minneapolis at 8:05 P.M. It was a smooth flight. The lady next to me was sleeping and I was reading a book. The hum of passengers' conversations sounded from one end of the plane to the other. At 7:45 the public address system clicked on and the pilot announced, "Now there's nothing to be alarmed about, but we're not sure of the landing gear, so we are going to fly around awhile to try it out."

That "awhile" was an hour. Then the click again, "We think everything is all right, but we're going to fly over the tower and have them take a look at it." Down we went. For a minute we could see the airport, then swoosh—up into the clouds again.

Some moments elapsed before the next click and the pilot's voice saying, "Now really, friends, there's nothing to be anxious about, but prepare for a crash landing."

There was no conversation now, only a deadly silence as the attendants handed us pillows and blankets. They showed us how to put the pillows on our knees, remove any sharp objects, and then clasp our hands under our knees as we rested our heads on the pillows. What wouldn't I have given to know what was going on in the minds of the other passengers. What a confrontation of one's values. As I said to a pastor later, "What a time to sign a pledge card!"

Will you understand when I say that for me it was a time of joy, of anticipation of a reunion with my loved ones? There wasn't an ounce of fear! The one who had conquered death was my Redeemer and I had claimed his promises.

One silly little thought went through my mind. I had a $100 traveler's check in my purse as a reserve for an unexpected contingency. "Shucks," I thought. "That'll be lost in the crash, and the kids could surely use it in their work." But that was only momentary. There came to my mind Clarence's opening sentence of the last sermon we preached together the Sunday before the Lord took him. "Some of you may think," he said, "this is the last hurrah of a dying old man. But it isn't. It's the practicing up for the alleluias!" That's what I was doing too, practicing up for the alleluias.

Then we landed! A clapping of hands and a great shout went up from the passengers. As I made my way alone through the terminal to my car and headed for home, I thought of what might have been, and of what some day would be.

Great anticipation!!